Gay Identity, New Storytelling and the Media

Gay Identity, New Storytelling and the Media

Christopher Pullen
Senior Lecturer in Media Theory, Bournemouth University, UK

First published in hardback in 2009
Published in paperback 2012 by
PALGRAVE MACMILLAN

Palgrave Macmillan in the UK is an imprint of Macmillan Publishers
Limited, registered in England, company number 785998, of Houndmills,
Basingstoke, Hampshire RG21 6XS.

Palgrave Macmillan in the US is a division of St Martin's Press LLC,
175 Fifth Avenue, New York, NY 10010.

Palgrave Macmillan is the global academic imprint of the above companies
and has companies and representatives throughout the world.

Palgrave® and Macmillan® are registered trademarks in the United States,
the United Kingdom, Europe and other countries

ISBN: 978–0–230–55343–9   hardback
ISBN: 978–1–137–00924–1   paperback

This book is printed on paper suitable for recycling and made from fully
managed and sustained forest sources. Logging, pulping and manufacturing
processes are expected to conform to the environmental regulations of the
country of origin.

A catalogue record for this book is available from the British Library.

A catalog record for this book is available from the Library of Congress.

10 9 8 7 6 5 4 3 2 1
18 17 16 15 14 13 12 11 10 09

Printed and bound in Great Britain by
CPI Antony Rowe, Chippenham and Eastbourne

In memory of Peter Adair, David Kamens, Vito Russo and Pedro Zamora, who gave of themselves selflessly, in AIDS education.

Also in recognition of the inspirational political work of Tammy Aaberg, Mary Griffith and Judy Shepard, as devoted and caring mothers working to change the world, in memory of their lost sons.

Contents

List of Figures   x

Preface to the Paperback Edition   xii

Acknowledgements   xv

Introduction: Placing the Self within the Frame   1

Vulnerability, and intimate participation   4
Discourse, life story and identification   6
Mobility, becoming and thematic framework   9
Conclusion   10

1   New Storytelling: Transitions from the Past   12

Introduction   12
Outside the literary, and towards the vernacular frame   15
Transitions in new storytelling: rejecting the myth   17
Audience identification with iconic performers and the
   relay of narratives   20
BBC radio and *Male Homosexual*   22
Gore Vidal: the performance and the partnership   26
k.d. lang and Waymon Hudson: role models, vernacular
   voices and political forces   31
k.d. lang: establishing the arena   33
Waymon Hudson: the personal self and the political frame   36
Conclusion   40

2   Gay Identity and Self-Reflexivity   42

Introduction   42
Christopher Isherwood, storytelling and self-reflexivity   44
Stereotypes, archetypes and *The Green Bay Tree*   47
Social construction, Oscar Wilde and 'queer'   51
Quentin Crisp and *The Naked Civil Servant*   54
Trial by media: Peter Wildeblood and testimony   58
Ellen DeGeneres and George Michael: therapy and
   subversion   62
Conclusion   71

3   Community, History and Transformation   73

Introduction   73
The discursive gay community   75
History, the unified subject and postmodernity   80
Transformation   82
Victim and Dirk Bogarde: intended identification   83
Armistead Maupin and Sarah Waters: popular frames   89
Tony Kushner and *Angels in America*: community and
    transformation   100
Conclusion   104

**4   Factual Media Space: Intimacy, Participation
      and Therapy**   107

Introduction   107
Factual media space: Joshua Gamson, the talk show
    and vulnerability   108
Oppositional public sphere, intimacy and emotion   111
Russell Harty and Dirk Bogarde: signposting, domesticity
    and humanity   113
Peter Adair and Pedro Zamora: whole person learning
    and AIDS   119
The Ultimate Brokeback Forum: therapy and agency   130
Conclusion   135

5   Commodity and Family   137

Introduction   137
Family values and Debra Chasnoff   139
Commodity: use and exchange   141
Economy of narratives, shared experience and the real   144
Debra Chasnoff: school, narratives and humanist education   146
Derek Jarman and Russell T Davies: domesticity, exchange
    and transformation   149
Derek Jarman: domesticity under construction   151
Russell T Davies: commodity identity   157
Conclusion   163

6   Teenage Identity and Ritual   166

Introduction   166
Gay teen identity: similar experiences and expectations   168

Ritual and performance: liminality, participation
and antistructure 171
Jonathan Harvey, *Beautiful Thing* and reflective realism 174
Todd Haynes and Alan Bennett: gay youth narratives in film 178
Coming Out to Class and LGB Teens 185
The Gay Youth Corner: affirmation, disclosure and agency 190
Conclusion 194

7 **Other Storytelling and the New Frontier** 197

Introduction 197
New identifications within the queer diaspora 200
Dangerous Living: other storytelling, colonialism and
the new frontier 203
Nature and instinct in *Before Night Falls* 207
Uruguay, *Two to Tango* and *Gay on the Cape* 212
Out in Iran and *Jihad for Love*: civil rights, family and belief 219
Conclusion 226

Conclusion: Cohesion, Fragmentation and 'Becoming' 229

Notes 233

References 241
Works cited 241
Internet sources 251

Select Filmography 254

Index 258

List of Figures

0.1	*Beautiful Thing*	2
0.2	Dilcia Molina	3
0.3	Tammy Aaberg and Justin Aaberg	5
1.1	Gore Vidal	13
1.2	k.d. lang	34
1.3	Waymon Hudson	37
2.1	Quentin Crisp	43
2.2	Christopher Isherwood	45
2.3	Quentin Crisp	56
2.4	Ellen DeGeneres	62
2.5	George Michael	68
3.1	Tony Kushner	74
3.2	Poster for *Victim*	84
3.3	Dirk Bogarde and Tony Forwood	85
3.4	Armistead Maupin	90
3.5	Sarah Waters	91
3.6	*Tipping the Velvet*	96
4.1	Russell Harty	114
4.2	Russell Harty and Dirk Bogarde	116
4.3	Peter Adair	119
4.4	Pedro Zamora	125
4.5	Pedro Zamora	128
4.6	Members of the Ultimate Brokeback Forum	131
5.1	Derek Jarman	138
5.2	Debra Chasnoff	140
5.3	Derek Jarman	154
5.4	Russell T Davies	157
6.1	Marcos Brito	167
6.2	Jonathan Harvey	175
6.3	*Beautiful Thing*	176
6.4	*The History Boys*	182
6.5	*The History Boys*	183

7.1   Ashraf Zanati   198
7.2   Dilcia Molina   204
7.3   Mark and Cengay from *Gay on the Cape*   214
7.4   Esteban Hubner and Leonardo Gorosito   215
7.5   Arsham Parsi   220
7.6   Parvez Sharma   224

Preface to the Paperback Edition

When Palgrave MacMillan published the original edition of *Gay Identity, New Storytelling and the Media* in 2009, I was enthused by the opportunity to develop discussions that I had commenced in my first book *Documenting Gay Men* (2007) with regard to self-reflexivity within documentary forms. In *Gay Identity, New Storytelling and the Media* I extended these debates to include diverse media cultural significances, such as literature, radio, film and TV drama, online media, and celebrity status. I was thrilled to hear positive reviews such as in *Communication, Culture and Critique* (Christian, 2011), which praised the book for its ability to bring diverse contexts and forms together in connection to gay and lesbian identity, relative to the notion of 'new storytelling'. At the same time I was aware of *some* criticism, relating to the cohesive potential of new storytelling. Therefore in considering a 'revised' version of this book, I thought it pertinent, to accommodate wider developments in my own research evident in *LGBT Storytelling and Online New Media* (2010, edited with Margaret Cooper) and *LGBT Transnational Identity and the Media* (2012, edited by myself), which more directly focus on the opportunity for mobility, as much as the imagined drive to cohesion. Therefore this revised edition includes reworked text (particularly in the Introduction, and the Conclusion), which I feel offers more philosophical insight, revealing the shift from 'being' a subjective outsider identity, towards the opportunity of 'becoming', enabled by mobility within narrative.

Also within this revised edition, I wanted to offer a deeper focus on the vulnerability of gay youth, and significantly discuss responses to recent gay male youth suicides within the United States (see Introduction). This not only involves incidents of 'new storytelling' from those who might offer support to suicidal gay and lesbian teens (notably from Tammy Aaberg in discussing her son's valued life), but also this reveals the significance of media representation, relative to actual life chances. Hence this book acknowledges that although 'new storytelling' may increase opportunities for improved life chances though narrative identification, at the same time real world situations remain complex for lesbian, gay, bisexual, transgender and 'queer' individuals, of all ages. In this sense narrative potential should not consider the 'specificity' of gay and lesbian identity as 'responding to' or 'becoming whole' as *the* story to be told, but it should reveal the opportunity of gay and lesbian identity, as politicised, mobile, multivalent, and not fixed.

Hence this book offers a critical introduction to gay and lesbian identity within the media, focusing on the potential of 'new storytelling', foregrounding the potential of self-narrative, as fluid and enabling. The case studies are taken principally from television, film and 'on-line' new media, placing a central focus on the narrative potential of individual storytellers who as producers, writers, performers and (active) audiences generate new discourses. In exploring the potential of self-reflexive storytelling, gay men and lesbians challenge identity concerns, and offer new expressions of liberty. However, these expressions do not reveal fixity in new narrative expression, rather they offer mobility, and enablement of self-narrative potential.

Its important to note that unlike many previous volumes which have approached the subject of gay and lesbian identity within the media, this book does not rely on a film studies approach which might centralise the subjectivity of identity, and issues of spectatorship (see Aaron, 2004; Benshoff and Griffin, 2004; Farmer, 2000; Hanson, 1999), nor does it attempt to construct a history of non-heterosexual representation within the media (Bourne, 1996; Capsuto, 2000; Gross, 2001, Russo, 1987 [originally, 1981]). Furthermore, although 'queer theory' is contextualised, the book does not explore the binary of homosexuality in opposition or in challenge to heterosexuality (Butler, 1999 [originally, 1990]; Doty, 1993; Seidman, 1996; Warner, 1993). As David V. Ruffolo (2009) suggests in discussing 'post queer politics', the notion of 'queer' informs and reifies the non-queer, and subjectivity in these terms prioritizes a dyadic relationship, which reframes identity norms, and those in opposition. Hence opposition, per se is problematic, as it reinforces power relationships, and queer identity remains peripheral.

This book considers the opportunity of narrative to create new space, not its ability to overturn or challenge the ownership of space. I consider 'new storytelling' in this way offering a performative oriented approach, foregrounding narrative, social constructionist and political perspectives (relating the work of theorists such as Dyer, 2000 [originally, 1993], Gamson; 1993; Giddens, 1992, 1995 [originally, 1992]; Plummer 1997 [originally, 1995]; Weeks, 1990, 2000). This involves the contextualisation of advances in (Western) civil liberty, such as the advent of legalised same-sex civil partnerships in some countries; the accommodation of new technologies which offer enhanced opportunities for social networking, such as online new media; the consideration of new prospects and challenges within the developing world, such as the agency of transnational and non-Western performers; and the significance of gay youth as a central focus of political attention, in considering issues of vulnerability, and oppression from dominant worlds. Whilst this approach offers a degree of cohesion, in the ability to bring diverse narratives together, it also explores the shifting political axis of sexual diversity, as mobile and 'becoming' (Deleuze 1994 [originally 1968]), rather than static, and existing in some ideal form.

Gay Identity, New Storytelling and the Media is not an exposure of different experience; rather it is the celebration of diverse yet confluent and mobilised narratives. This offers deeper resonance to gay and lesbian voices, revealing the critical advance of new storytelling as the constant state of 'becoming', not necessarily arriving.

Acknowledgements

I would like to thank my partner Ian Davies, not only for his excellent editing skills, but also for his inspirational support in the development of this book. Also I would like to express thanks to a number of staff at Palgrave: Jill Lake, for the original commissioning of this book, plus Christabel Scaife and Catherine Mitchell as editors, respectively, of the original and revised editions.

I am particularly indebted to numerous writers, performers and producers within the media, and would particularly like to note the contribution of Alan Bennett, Jeanne Blake, Marcos Brito, Debra Chasnoff, John Coldstream, Janet Cole, Russell T Davies, Nick Grey, Farid Haerinejad, Jonathan Harvey, Waymon Hudson, Tony Kushner, Arsham Parsi, Hamish Priest, John Scagliotti, Lydia Sedge Wells, Veronica Selver, Parvez Sharma and Sarah Waters.

I would also like to express deep gratitude to the ABC, *The Advocate*, the BBC, Clifford Bestall, Steven Capsuto, the CBC, Keith Collins, Rob Epstein, The Estate of Dirk Bogarde, Film 4, John Frame, Michelle Garcia, Leonardo Gorosito, Michael Hanish, Esteban Hubner, ITV, Little, Brown Book Group, Kevin Loader, Minnesota Public Radio, PETA, *POZ* Magazine, Sneezing Tree Films, Nikki Tundel, Phillip Ward and Mandy Wragg, for the provision of valuable source material.

Furthermore, I would like to thank various friends and colleagues (including many at Bournemouth University) who have inspired and supported my work: Craig Batty, Richard Berger, Peri Bradley, the editors of *Continuum: Journal of Media and Cultural Studies*, Hugh Chignell, Margaret Cooper, Fiona Cownie, Dimple Godiwala, Francesca Guala, Robin Griffiths, Graeme Harper, Angela Healey, Trevor Hearing, Jo Hickey, Su Holmes, Alex Hunt, Andrew Ireland, Deborah Jermyn, Alexandra Juhasz, Stephen Jukes, James R. Keller, Shaun Kimber, Richard McGuickian, the editors of *Media, Culture and Society*, Richard Pride, Barry Richards, Katherine Sender, Leslie Strayner, Sean Street, Cate Sweeney, Jeffrey Weeks, Steve Wilson (of McFarland) and Brian Winston.

Introduction: Placing the Self within the Frame

In the closing sequence of the romantic drama *Beautiful Thing* (Hettie MacDonald, 1996, UK) (see Figure 0.1, also discussed in Chapter 6), playwright Jonathan Harvey leaves us with the image of two young gay men dancing in close embrace within the public space of a housing estate, accompanied by the intimate ballad 'Dream a Little Dream of Me'.[1] In a pivotal moment of John Scagilotti's documentary film *Coming Out in the Developing World* (John Scagliotti, 2003, US) (see Figure 0.2, also discussed in Chapter 7), we hear the story of Dilcia Molina who participated in the first gay and lesbian pride march in Honduras, and was the only person not to conceal her identity (her family was tortured because of this – discussed in Chapter 7). The representation of fictional characters in Jonathan Harvey's play, and the public appearance of Dilcia Molina, although set in entirely different textual media forms, I argue both progress identity ideals in new storytelling, enabled by diverse writers and performers.

This book defines a pathway of new storytelling for gay and lesbian identity tracing emergences within factual and fictional forms, where the iconic 'self' identity of the writer and performer is 'placed within the frame'. Jonathan Harvey discusses first romance between teenage gay men in *Beautiful Thing*, presenting a discursive framework for new stories of same sex desire. Dilcia Molina's brave public appearance in Honduras, offers a political and performative public vision of the lesbian self. It is the balance between personal agency and public participation, present within diverse media texts, which forms the theme of this book, and the idea of new storytelling. This connects writers, producers, performers and (active) audiences, offering political identity coalescence and mobility, in service of rendering change.

Foregrounding case studies from radio, film, television and online new media, and largely focusing on the personal agency of individuals within popular culture and literature, I explore a time frame from the mid 20th century to the present day (2012). I offer textual analysis of various factual and fictional forms, examining events, iconography, narrative potentials and political context. This is relative to the imagined personal and community aspirations of gay men and lesbians, also engaging with wider perspectives of sexual diversity including LGBT (lesbian, gay, bisexual and transgender) and 'queer' identity. However, I do not offer a purely historical framework, advocating a discrete canon of ideal performers and texts; rather I place a focus on the context of self-reflexive storytelling, and its relationship to gay and lesbian identity within discourse. This relates as much to the potential of narrative and issues of performance, as to the establishment of a historical arena with archetypal texts. Hence although this book presents an account of gay identity and self-reflexive storytelling, as emerging with writers such as Gore Vidal (discussed in Chapter 1) and Christopher Isherwood (discussed in Chapter 2), public figures such as Dirk Bogarde (discussed in Chapters 3

Figure 0.1   The characters of Jamie (left, played by Glen Berry) and Ste (right, played by Scott Neal) dance in public, in close embrace, in the final scene of Jonathan Harvey's *Beautiful Thing* (Hettie MacDonald, 1996, UK). Image courtesy of Channel 4 and Film 4

Figure 0.2 Dilcia Molina at the first gay and lesbian pride march in Honduras, 2001, appearing as the only person not to conceal her identity. Image courtesy of Michael Hanish and John Scagliotti

and 4) and performative audiences such as the partcipants within *Male Homosexual* (BBC Radio, 1965, UK) (discussed in Chapter 1), these are selected as representational and influential models, rather than as concrete beginnings or discrete pathways. To this end, whilst I argue that new storytelling offers a postmodern democratisation in narrative (discussed in Chapter 3) which allows diverse media participants the opportunity for subversion and transgression, this potential may be seen in various texts (and contexts), not accounted for here. Not only could many other performers, celebrities, documentaries, films, online content etc. be discussed in relation to the idea of 'new storytelling', but also the gay and lesbian political activists movement (see Clendinen and Nagourney, 1999) and the gay and lesbian press (see Streitmatter, 1995), could offer similar resonance. Hence, I do not attempt to define '*the*' history of gay and lesbian identity and new storytelling; rather I am offering contexts of engagement, relating defining moments and inspirational performers, and this may be a mobile theoretical model.

My central point is that contemporary media and performativity offer new scope for gay, lesbian and 'queer' identity, and this may be various and not necessarily fixed. Following David V. Ruffolo's (2009) ideas on 'post queer politics' related to Gilles Deleuze's work within *Difference and Repetition* (1994 [originally 1968]), this might involve a shift from 'being' towards 'becoming'. In this sense, not necessarily following a subjective identity, but working towards the potential of identity, which might be fluid and various. Furthermore, I contend that this largely involves the philosophy of the public sphere (Habermas, 1962; Negt and Kluge, 1993 [originally 1972]; Livingstone and Lunt 1994) and the general idea of a public space. This is pertinent in the example and juxtaposition of *Beautiful Thing* with Dilcia Molina (discussed above), which not only provides an introduction to this book in the expression of the diversity of textual, generic and personal storytelling ideas, but also foregrounds the iconography of public environments as a discursive arena for gay and lesbian identity. Consequently, the representation and the reality of public place, forms an axis of engagement, resonating with issues of political expression. This involves the establishment of gay men and lesbians as intimate icons of discursive power. Also it concerns issues of vulnerability, which for 'queer' youth may be particularly impacting.[2]

Vulnerability, and intimate participation

The advent of a number of gay male youth suicides occurring in 2010 and 2011 in the United States, offers vivid evidence of such vulnerability. Including the deaths of Justin Aaberg, aged 15 (see Figure 0.3), Asher Brown and Seth Walsh both aged 13, Billy Lucas aged 15, Cody J. Barker aged 17, Tyler Clementi aged 18, Raymond Chase aged 19, and Jamie Rodemeyer aged 14, these were all reported as the subjects of obsessive bullying by school or university peers for being gay (or imagined to be gay).[3] While limited mainstream media attention was focused on these events, online new media contributions on YouTube, offered progressive discursive agency (see Pullen, 2010). This involved the contribution of some of the parents whose sons had committed suicide, evident in formal video extracts posted on YouTube, including sequences from CNN on Larry King's and Anderson Cooper's shows, featuring the parents of Justin Aaberg, and Asher Brown. Also it involved the contribution of regular web users as 'citizen journalists', alongside high profile politicians, and celebrities submitting material on the YouTube channel: 'It Get's Better Project' (see YouTube, 2011), offering discourse which might be seen as contextual to the impact of the Ultimate Brokeback Forum (see Chapter 4) in the potential to offer new narratives for gay identity.

Tammy Aaberg's contribution as the mother of Jason (see Figure 0.3) advocating changes in the law with regards to school bulling, may be seen a paradigm of new storytelling. Similar to the work of Judy Shepard in response to the hate crime murder of her son Matthew in

Figure 0.3 Tammy Aaberg holds up a picture of her son Justin, that was just taken before the prom in spring 2010. Image courtesy of Minnesota Public Radio, photograph taken by Nikki Tundel

1998 (see Pullen 2007a), and her political work that contributed to the establishment of new legislation addressed to punish hate crimes (see Huffington Post, 2011), this involves 'placing the self within the frame'.[4] Foregrounding the potential of 'intimate citizenship' (Plummer, 1997 [originally 1995]), through pressing for changing democratic worlds, Tammy Aaberg similarly exposes her vulnerable self in recalling her responses to Jason's death, including on *Larry King Live* (CNN, 1985–present) describing her feelings on discovering Jason's body in the presence of her other sons (CNN, 2011). In this sense Tammy reveals both the vulnerable position of her son, not afforded the protection by a wholly caring society, and her significance as a vulnerable mother who discusses her loss, in highly intimate terms. Such references to vulnerability and testament to self-engagement, expressed through intimate narrative worlds, foregrounds intense personal investment. Tammy Aaberg literally places her intimate and vulnerable self within the media frame, offering personal expressions in support of political change. Such politics I argue is enabled though the construction of discourse, fore-grounding the potential of life chances, and the opportunity of identity, and identification.

Discourse, life story and identification

The following chapters (see below) focus on the significance of discourse, employing textual analysis in the examination of sociological contexts within media forms. Issues such as vulnerability, myth, reflexivity, com-munity, intimacy, commodity, ritual and 'otherness', are central contexts within this inquiry relative to issues of identity and performance. For example, the issue of mythic representation and the context of 'other-ness' reveals aspects of engagement and concern for gay men and lesbians established within dominant histories, while the opportunity of commu-nity, the potential of reflexivity and the foregrounding of intimacy offer passageways of progress in strengthening identity. At the same time, gay and lesbian engagements with the powerbases of commodity and ritual reveal substantial challenges to established ideals. Also vulnerability is central, in considering the lack of support for gay and lesbian youth within school environments (see Pullen, 2010b), at the same time gay men and lesbians are vulnerable, in exposing their intimate lives. These issues are relevant in the examination of new narrative strategies, and directly relate to the concept of 'new storytelling. This might extend Ken Plummer's (1997 [originally, 1995] and 2003) ideas of 'intimate cit-izenship' and 'telling sexual stories' (see Chapter 2), relative to Anthony Giddens' concept of 'the reflexive project of the self' (1992), where self reflection stimulates progressive narrative, and this can inspire social agency.

This largely extends from the potential of producers' and writers' per-sonal 'life stories' (Plummer, 2001) within the media, and relates the concept of 'new storytelling' to the idea of discourse as 'non-narrated stories'. As Seymour Chatman (1978) tells us with regard to discourse 'every narrative ... is a structure with a content plane (called "story") and an expression plane (called "discourse")' (p. 146). Chatman's idea of the 'expression plane' reveals the performative potential of narrative statements, which extends beyond the content of a particular story. Ultimately, narrative expressions offer landscapes of possibility, where multifarious personal stories may connect, and this enables rhetoric and the power of address. As Dick Leith and George Myerson (1989) suggest in exploring the power of utterances within language. '[T]he meaning of an utterance will always go beyond the conscious control of the speaker or writer, and there will thus be a "looseness" or play of meaning' (p. xii). Leith and Myerson illuminate the discursive nature of language, which not only involves an audience or a subject to be addressed, but also the ability to extend beyond the moment of the utterance, and that there is a fluid potential. Michel Foucault's concepts of discourse (1989 [originally, 1972]) and power (1998 [originally, 1976]) (see Chapter 2) are helpful here in considering the potential of storytelling with regard to the progression of public debates. As Danaher, Schirato and Webb (2000) suggest: 'a discourse can be understood as a series of events. Discursive practices occur at a particular time, they create effects within a discursive field' (p. 34).

Such ability to create 'effects within a discursive field', I believe integrates with concepts of Foucaultian 'modern power' as free flowing, energised by many components in society. This is in contrast to the Marxist concepts of base and superstructure (Marx, 1977 [originally, 1859]), which support fixed structures of power mainly held by organisations, authorities, institutions and governments. As Nancy Fraser (1989) tells us, modern power 'is more penetrating than earlier forms of power. It gets hold of its objects at the deepest level – in their gestures, habits, bodies and desires, [and it may be considered in Foucault's terms as] "self amplifying" (p. 24). The ability of 'modern power' to flow though varying contexts of social life, touching also on identity formations and narrative engagement, reveals discourse as central in potential challenges to established ideals.

Hence this book does not focus on a traditional narrative theory approach which might examine character function, story development and issues such as the role of the hero, the restoration of equilibrium, the significance of fables, or the traditional passage of narrative from one generation to another (see Campbell, 1988; Propp, 1968 [originally, 1927]; Todorov, 1981). Instead, it explores the production of a potentially 'cohesive' discourse enabled through foregrounding the power of life stories, which (on varying levels of engagement) offer narratives of change.

The context of the life story is the central component of new storytelling; which disseminating from various points, offers connectivity. Ken Plummer (2001) tells us that:

Life stories come through many blurred sources: biographies, autobiographies, letters, journals, interviews, obituaries. They can be written by a person as their own life story (autobiography) or as fiction by themselves; they can be the story coaxed out of them by another. Or indeed their own story told by someone else (as in biography). They can exist in many forms: long and short, past and future, specific and general, fuzzy and focused, surface and deep, realist and romantic, ordinary and extraordinary, modernist and postmodernist. (p. 19)

Although I am focusing on specific cases and on the agency of various media producers, Ken Plummer's ideas are useful in expressing the fragmented dispersal of life stories, which may be collated in the formation of personal identity narrative, and its larger discursive potential, within notions of identity, and identification.

Although inevitably identification is central in the construction of identity, and it may be understood 'as the play of difference and similitude in self and other relationships' (Fuss, 1995: 2), it is beyond the remit of this book to attempt to understand the psychological essence of gay and lesbian people, in terms of their sexual behaviour, or personal assessments of self. Rather, this book explores the discursive power of identity, which relates the potential of social construction in the formation of new ideas within sexual identity (see Chapter 2).

Nevertheless, this book acknowledges the complex relationship between a publicly displayed identity, and issues of personal identification. Whilst it is possible to argue that many of the writers and performers discussed in this book may exhibit their 'imagined' identification ideals, this is not necessarily a constant theme. As discussed in the case of the actor and author Dirk Bogarde who denied a homosexual identity, yet appeared to be homosexual (in assessment of his longstanding relationship with same-sex partner Tony Forwood and his contribution to homosexual discourse (see Chapters 2 and 3)), any certain knowledge of personal essential sexual identification cannot be possible. As Diana Fuss (1995) iterates:

> Identifications are the origin of some of our most powerful, enduring, and deeply felt pleasures. They are also the source of considerable emotional turmoil, capable of unsettling or unmooring the precarious groundings of our everyday identities. (p. 2)

Following Erving Goffman's (1989 [originally, 1959]) hypothesis of 'back stage and front stage performance', there is often a hidden inner self in the fabrication of the constructed outer appearance (or performance), and the tension between these two engenders engagement. In the light of Dirk Bogarde's contribution to homosexual discourse, his personal denial of a homosexual identity does not devalue his identity potential; rather it stimulates our interest in him. Therefore personal identifications may be powerful, and whilst they may not be congruous with an accessible exhibited daily appearance, they stimulate a need for answers, as much as they may offer solutions.

Mobility, becoming and thematic framework

New storytellers may work within diverse and conflicting genres; they may offer varying public authority, also they may not broadcast an immediately apparent gay and lesbian identity (as discussed above), yet despite this I argue that they are situated at a nexus of dissemination, expressing the potential of life stories. This might involve reiterating histories, oppressions, connections, sympathies, truces and disconnections. However, I argue that this does not involve sameness, in establishing some essential project of gay and lesbian identity, but it involves mobility in the manner of Gilles Deleuze's (1994) notion of 'transcendental empiricism'. As Claire Colebrook (2010) attests 'this frees thought of any metaphysical foundation by insisting that far from being some actual ground, life is a virtual multiplicity, not of things and agents but contemplations and contradictions, events and responses' (p. 87). Consequently mobility and becoming are central ideas within this book, revealing varying ideological and political themes offering a matrix of becoming and productivity. The themes are:

- The agency of writers, producers and performers within the media, and the relevance of 'factual media space' where myths may be challenged.
- The potential of self-reflexivity and intimacy within contemporary narratives, and the opportunity of therapeutic identification.
- The context of life stories and role models, and the relationship to narrative.
- The issue of education and the public sphere, and the dynamic of literature, documentary and drama.
- The coalescent opportunity of online new media within the world wide web.
- The vulnerability of gay 'queer' youth, yet the opportunity of youth narratives.
- The dominance of a Western-centred concept of gay and lesbian community, and its democratic and citizenship ideals.

Whilst these themes traverse varying identity, performative and community based potentials, these are frames of action, offering constant mobility. This may be related to the impact of life stories, which are enabled in a similar way to Anthony Giddens' (1995 [originally 1992]) concept of the 'transformation of intimacy' (see Chapter 4), and Ulrich Beck's notion of 'risk society' (1992 [originally 1986]). In essence, these potentials are situated within a progressing contemporary social world, where personal disclosure and intimacy form the narrative conduits of expression and development.

However it is important to note that this progressing narrative world is largely mediated through concepts of Western identity, evident in the significance of Anglo-centric worlds, and the opportunity of LGBT transnational potential (see Pullen, 2012). Therefore whilst this book relates issues of non-Western identity (see Chapter 7), these are situated in relation to the English language, and Western concepts of citizenship and democracy. Consequently a central point of concern is the dominance of Anglo-Western ideals, and how these inform yet potentially impinge upon non-western potentials.

Inevitably issues of 'colonisation' constitute an underlying theme throughout this book, not only with regard to the pioneering nature of the storytellers, whose emerging stories might be foregrounded, but also with regard to 'subsidiary' identities (such as non-Western identity) within concepts of gay and lesbian community. As Diana Fuss (1995) tells us:

> Identification is not only how we accede to power, it is also how we learn submission. In colonial relations, identification can operate, at once, as an ontological privilege of the coloniser and the subjugated position of the colonised. (p. 14)

This book does not intend to impose particular modes of gay and lesbian identity within 'new storytelling'. Rather it reveals the diverse, yet coalescent and mobile nature of individual storytellers, who through various media forms, crossing textual and generic boundaries, offer scope to the diversity of identity. This is largely focused on the self, and the potential for intimate disclosure, which through public display challenges established ideas.

Conclusion

In essence this book concerns 'placing the self within the frame', and the opportunity for mobility. This is particularly evident within the contribution of Jonathan Harvey and Dilcia Molina as openly gay and lesbian social agents, respectively within fictional and factual forms. Also Tammy Aaberg's contribution as the politicised mother of an openly gay son, who expresses her intimate narrative of Jason's valued life, involves placing the vulnerable self within the frame. Similar to the wider discussions within this book, writers, producers, performers and (active) audiences situate themselves within diverse media texts, challenging identity ideals.

Nevertheless, regressive constituents maintain their power, and although we are living in an era of increased visibility for gay and lesbian identity, at the same time we continue to experience dissention, and punishment. As evidenced in the case studies from the developing world, it often remains dangerous to announce one's homosexual identity. Also within Western society, as evidenced in the recent advent of gay youth suicides (see above), despite recent representational advances offering wider perspectives for gay identity, psychological (and physical) oppression from dominant worlds is often too hard to bear, especially within school environments (see Pullen, 2010b). Despite this, through dedication, commitment, courage and imagination, new storytellers offer mobility through personal expression. This may not permanently change the landscape, yet it reveals important journeys to take.

However, such progression, advancement and mobility should not involve a 'single subjectivity' as evident in the re-framing of identity ideals, it should move forward in the strategy of becoming. As David V. Ruffolo (2009) suggests this should involve 'challenges to how we traditionally think about politics where desire is based on production rather than lack' (p. 41). Such potential should not be defined by subjects and subject capacities, which in Freudian terms connects desire to repression, but by 'productive flows of desire that are creatively and indefinitely becoming other' (p. 41). This is enabled through the multiplicity of connections made by those who support sexual diversity, and who are involved in new storytelling within varying and diverse forms. For gay and lesbian identity, this reveals a shift away from 'being' defined by a corporeal framework, towards a state of 'becoming' produced as constant mobility.

1

New Storytelling: Transitions from the Past

Introduction

Celebrated American writer Gore Vidal's early work included the publication of the novel *The City and the Pillar* in 1948 (see Figure 1.1). This offered challenging representations of male homosexual desire as non-stereotypical and all-American (discussed below). In the documentary *The Education of Gore Vidal* (Deborah Dickson, 2003, US) he tells us of his subsequent rejection by literary critics at that time, revealing a shift in career potentials, and his development as a spokesman in support of homosexual liberty:

> TV became my medium, not only as a writer for television plays, but as a performer, as a voice.

> [Gore Vidal speaking in 1967 on CBS News]: It is as natural to be homosexual as it is to be heterosexual, and the difference between a homosexual and a heterosexual is about the difference between somebody who has brown eyes and somebody who has blue eyes.

> [Retort from the interviewer, off camera]: Who says so?

> [Gore Vidal]: I say so! It is a completely natural act from the beginning of time.

Despite Gore Vidal's initial rejection in 1948 for the publication of an audacious book, which foregrounded same-sex desire as normative, his career developed within the medium of television. His support for the 'normality' of homosexual identity is indicative of his active pursuit of confidence in self, repressing myths which contain same-sex desire. While later in his career Gore Vidal would become an icon in American

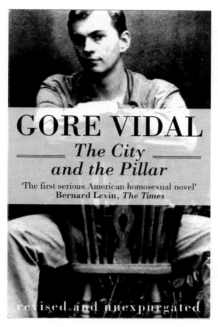

Figure 1.1   Gore Vidal depicted on the cover of the revised edition of his ground-breaking book *The City and the Pillar*. Reproduced by kind permission of Abacus, an imprint of Little, Brown Book Group

literature, and *The City and the Pillar* would be resituated as a defining rather than as a problematic text, he is discussed here for his potential to challenge oppressive traditions in storytelling which deny homosexual desire. Gore Vidal's brave and robust testament is indicative not only of his career and steadfast identity (discussed below), but also of the essence of new storytelling for gay and lesbian identity, which (I argue) rejects mythologies and histories of shame.

Consequently, this chapter explores a potential framework for new storytelling within the media, revealing instances of narrative progression where gay men and lesbians reject imposed mythic identities of the past and create new, optimistic and self-focused constructions. I argue that this involves transitions in storytelling, where new storytellers break free from the containment of stigma, shame and repressive myth, in service of narrative development and recreation. Whilst later in this book, I foreground the issue of self-reflexivity (Chapter 2), and how this is a central tenet in new narrative constructions involving the centring of the self within the frame, my purpose here is to explore the wider concept of storytelling, and the rejection of the oppressive, or ignorant, narrative past.

In this chapter, I present four case studies which reveal key themes in new storytelling for gay and lesbian identity. I discuss the literary and cultural work of Gore Vidal, who as a novelist, historian and essayist, not only offers challenging insights into American history and its political ideology, but also is considered an icon of homosexual identity. I explore the context of his novels *The City and the Pillar* (1997 [originally 1948]), *Myra Breckinridge* (1986 [originally 1968]) and *Myron* (1975), where he offers groundbreaking visions of sexual storytelling. Also in connection with Gore Vidal's iconic significance, I explore his enduring domestic life with partner Howard Auster[1] of over 50 years, as exhibited in his memoir *Point to Point Navigation* (2006), and how through celebrity and performative identity this produced new narratives of engagement. Furthermore, I discuss the vernacular narrative potential of gay storytelling, providing evidence of shifts in identity confidence towards gay citizenship. I examine the contributions of various men within the radio show *Male Homosexual* (BBC, 1965, UK), who whilst their identities are concealed and apparently disconnected from power, provide new voices of empowerment. In addition I examine the iconic identity of the popular singer and musician k.d. lang, who within celebrity culture provided the first shame-free lesbian public identity. This is largely evident in her early iconic performances where she experimented with gender identities, and in the album *Ingénue* (1992) where the intensity of same sex-desire is represented. Finally, I explore the new media work of Waymon Hudson, which offers a contemporary, personal and political challenge to the established order, which I suggest is the essence of new storytelling. I examine Waymon Hudson's video web log in response to the hate crime murder of Lawrence King (aged 15); in conjunction with his websites 'Fight OUT Loud' (2008a) and 'The Homo Politico' (2008a). Within these case studies, I argue that new storytelling for gay identity provides narratives of transition, confidence and authority, involving the rejection of oppressive mythologies, and the construction of new enlightened frames.

However, before examining the context of new storytelling in terms of a shift away from oppressive narratives relevant to the construction of myths, and the potential of audience identification in the stimulation of progressive narrative, it is first necessary to explain the general context of gay identity within literature.

Outside the literary, and towards the vernacular frame

Whilst many would consider the context of storytelling to be intimately connected with literature (and I have commenced this chapter by discussing the significance of Gore Vidal's literary work *The City and the Pillar*), I argue that new gay storytelling concerns gay identity in contemporary narratives generally outside, or beyond, the classical literary frame.[2] Although later in this book I express the significance of the literary work of Christopher Isherwood (in Chapter 2) in its connection with the idea of emerging reflexive storytelling, and the work of Armistead Maupin, Sarah Waters and Tony Kushner respectively (in Chapter 3) with relation to its adaptation within contemporary media, I argue that new storytelling is grounded in the performative opportunity of radio, television, film and new media,[3] and generally does not extend from literary traditions which might involve the canon, the primacy of language and the aura of authority.

This is not to say that new storytelling for gay and lesbian identity does not occur in traditional literature, as evidenced in works such as *Gay and Lesbian Literary Heritage* (2002) by Claude Summers, *A History of Gay Literature: the Male Tradition* by Gregory Woods (1998) and *The Gay Canon: Great Books that Every Gay Man should Read* by Robert Drake (1998); clearly gay and lesbian life potentials are prominently discussed. However, what (in my opinion) makes new storytelling distinct within contemporary media is that gay identity is presented as a 'positive' central narrative drive, rather than as a subsidiary to heterosexuality, or as something to be excavated which is not immediately present. Whilst it is clear that contemporary literature after *The City and the Pillar* has increasingly foregrounded gay and lesbian lives and that this is enabling (see Drake, 1998; Woods, 1998), many of the literary texts before, and during, this era explore gay, or 'queer', identity in ambivalent, subliminal or appropriated ways. This may be seen not only in the multifarious 'pulp fiction' works, mostly prominent in the 1950s, which discussed the inversion and the problem of gay and lesbian life (see Dyer, 2000 [originally 1993]), but also in the general subordination of sexual diversity in traditional literature.

My intention is not to criticise early literature as lacking in substance, as incidences within the Roman and Greek classics, the works of Shakespeare (Drake, 1998; Woods, 1998), the Enlightenment novels (Drake, 1998) and many others offer groundbreaking depth in imagining the historical identification of sexual nonconformity. However, the context of new storytelling involves not so much the narrative potential of reading between the lines and finding a place for oneself within the dominant (heterosexual) fictional or factual literary frame, but the intimate potential of immediate narratives of self. Furthermore, as my focus is contemporary, it is inevitable that contexts of modern gay identity and its storytelling potential relate to the emergence of social constructionist possibilities for gay men and lesbians (see Chapter 2). In these terms, my discussion commences at a point when definitions of non-heterosexual identity began to be authored by non-heterosexual people themselves, which I argue occurred in more recent times, when early restrictive literary and production constraints (which had denied the open discussion of diverse sexuality) had been broken down (see Chapter 2). At the same time, although early textual emergences in new storytelling (such the work of Gore Vidal (discussed below) and Christopher Isherwood (discussed in Chapter 2)) took place before the advent of coalescent and dynamic gay and lesbian politics (such as Stonewall, briefly discussed in Chapter 2), in many ways these texts stimulated the construction of later gay-identified opportunities in narrative. Consequently, these new narrative possibilities connect to and predict a 'post gay' world (Sinfield, 1998), where open discussion takes place, and identities are established within citizenship ideals (which are also open to debate).

Therefore, rather than taking early literature as being the inspiration for new storytelling within contemporary media, I would argue that it is the personal and ethnographical lives of gay and lesbian citizens, outside the literary frame. This may be found in the vernacular and citizenship narratives of gay men and lesbians. Texts such as *Between the Acts: Lives of Homosexual Men 1885–1967* (1998 [originally 1991]) edited by Jeffrey Weeks and Kevin Porter; *Coming Out under Fire: the History of Gay Men and Women in World War Two* (1990) by Allan Berube; *Farm Boys: Lives of Gay Men from the Rural Midwest* (1998) collected and edited by Will Fellows; *Love Makes a Family: Portraits of Lesbian, Gay, Bisexual, and Transgender Parents and their Families* edited by Peggy Gillespie with photographs by Gigi Kaeser (1999); and *Improper Bostonians: Lesbian and Gay History from the Puritans to the Playground* (1998) compiled by the History Project, I would argue bear more resonance with the idea of new storytelling than traditional literary works. These relate the everyday lives of gay men and lesbians, situated in historical, rural, domestic and popular worlds, thereby contextualising the citizenship narrative potential of homosexual life.

However, despite this positive agency, all storytelling involves the placement, or displacement, of myths, and potentially the context of stereotypical representation. Often gay and lesbian life chances are ignored in dominant storytelling, in favour of reinforcing wider social concerns, which ultimately results in the repression of same-sex desire.

Transitions in new storytelling: rejecting the myth

Various myths have surrounded homosexual identity, largely distancing same-sex desire from normative, or 'everyday', life.[4] However, at the time of writing, there have been advances in civil liberties for gay men and lesbians. This is particularly evident within countries that have removed legislation which had punished homosexuals. Also some countries have progressively adopted same-sex marriage, and/or the civil equivalents of this. Nevertheless, these changes are only beginning to emerge, and histories of homosexual equality are non-existent. Consequently, myths largely founded on social and legal prejudice have formed the essence of dominant storytelling addressed at containing and distancing homosexual identity. Evidence of this may be seen in the generation of repressive discourse by the institutions of religion, science and government. These engender discontent and abjection for homosexual lives, perpetuating the labelling of deviancy in the support of harmful myths.

The myth may be considered as repressive storytelling for gay and lesbian identity. Roland Barthes (1993 [originally 1957]) considers the authority of narrative, relating the power of the myth. He tells us:

> As a total of linguistic signs, the meaning of the myth has its own value, it belongs to a history, that of the [imperial power] or that of the [dispossessed]: in the meaning a signification is already built, and could very well be self sufficient if myth did not take hold of it and did not turn it suddenly into an empty, parasitical form. The meaning is *already* complete, it postulates a kind of knowledge, a past a memory, a comparative order of facts, ideas, decisions. (p. 117)[5]

Barthes informs us of the problematic nature of myths: they produce a kind of knowledge not necessarily connected to the indexical or original source. At the same time they are substantial, highly influential and enduring. As Claude Lévi-Strauss (1972 [originally 1963]) affirms, they offer explanations of 'the present and the past as well as [predicting] the future' (p. 209). Ultimately, they define pathways in storytelling through repetition, further channelling narratives and archetypal form, re-establishing tone. This may ignore the representation of social reality, distancing gay identity from authority in narrative.

Hayden White (1990 [originally 1987]), exploring the potential of narrative discourse and the issue of historical representation and reality, tells us:

> [W]e cannot but be struck by the frequency with which narrativity, whether of the fictional or factual sort, presupposes the existence of a legal system against which or on behalf of which the typical agents of a narrative account militate. And this raises the suspicion that narrative in general, from the folktale to the novel, from the annals to the fully realized 'history', has to do with the topics of law, legitimacy, or, more generally, authority. (p. 13)

Such authority is lacking in homosexual identity, as it is located as a peripheral 'other' to dominant ideas within storytelling, and the construction of history. Specifically with relation to law (as discussed briefly above) it is only recently that, in any form, legislative discourses have supported homosexual identity.

Furthermore, the recent support of same-sex desire, evident in the advent of gay marriage, is mostly framed within normative discourses of coupling and property inheritance between partners, rather than expressions of sexual liberty. Ultimately this leads to the issue of morality, as an inherent problem in dominant narratives which may support homosexual desire. As Hayden White (1990) further explains:

> [N]arrativity, certainly in factual storytelling and probably in fictional storytelling as well, is intimately related to, if not the function of, the impulse to moralize reality, that is, to identify it with the social system that is the source of any morality that we can imagine. (p. 14)

Whilst contemporary narratives for gay and lesbian identity concerning domesticity, coupling and social reproduction (involving child raising) might be connected to dominant narratives of ethics and morality (see Pullen, 2007a), historical narratives of same-sex desire largely evoke myths of 'otherness', and deviancy.

The problem of homosexual identification within narrative is the spectre of mythic representation, which might be charged with themes of otherness and deviancy. Roland Barthes (1993) elucidates the problematic relationship between reality and the myth:

> [T]he form [of the myth] must constantly be able to be rooted again in the meaning and to get what nature it needs for its nutriment, above

all, it must be able to hide there. It is this constant game of hide-and-seek between the meaning and the form which defines myth. (p. 118)

Myths which surround homosexual identity need to be 'rooted' in the likely narratives and representations evident within dominant society. For example, expectations of sexual promiscuity as normative homosexual behaviour are consequently embedded or implied in mainstream storytelling, defining the myth and thereby making vivid the archetypal identity.

This is evident within a wide diversity of texts, where even if challenges to myths are presented, the mythic concerns need to be evident to frame the discussions. As discussed later (in Chapter 5) with regard to Russell T Davies' television drama *Queer as Folk* (Channel 4, 1999, UK), whilst there is a challenge to stereotypes which surround gay identity which reveals the coalescence of gay friendship networks and the freedom of sexual acceptance, at the same time myths are resonant in the exploration of isolation and promiscuity within the text, the corollary being that: to address issues you have to name them, even if you provide solutions (by naming you redefine the problem). Myths inevitably offer tension, as they are powerful components of narrative construction, yet they do not necessarily reflect every expression of social reality.

As Claude Lévi-Strauss (1972) affirms, relating the diachronic potential of narrative to continue through and build a particular story over time: '[T]he true constituents of a myth are not the isolated relations but *bundles of such relations*, and it is only as such bundles that these relations can be put to use and combined so as to produce meaning' (p. 211). Lévi-Strauss reveals that the production of myth involves the coalescence of particular moments with persistence. In this way, the resurfacing of the myth within particular narratives builds a larger mythic story. For gay and lesbian identity a need to address and respond to problem narratives re-energises the problem myth. As discussed later (Chapter 2) with regard to Michel Foucault's (1998 [originally 1976]) concept of power and how resistance offers potential to reinscribe identity, at the same time it potentially reaffirms discursive and mythic concerns.

Consequently there is ambivalence in new storytelling. If this involves a need to respond to older stories, which may require the dispelling of myths, it is likely that problem narratives will resurface, and myths will continue to be established. I argue that new storytelling not so much ignores the past and problematic myths, but moves forward independently, creating new associations. Confidence in the storytelling self is established, over a need to connect to or draw through pre-existing

narratives. This relates to personal experience eclipsing institutional concern, and is endemic of self-reflexivity (discussed in Chapter 2). I argue
that this does not destroy the idea of myth, but allows for a transformation in history, and storytelling. As Claude Lévi-Strauss (1978 [originally
1973] affirms:

> [A] myth which is transformed . . . finally exhausts itself – without dis-
> appearing. [However] two parts still remain open: that of fictional
> elaboration, and that of reactivation with a view to legitimizing his-
> tory. The history in its turn, may be of two types: retrospective, to
> found a traditional order on a distant past; or prospective to make this
> past the beginning of a future which is starting to take shape. (p. 268)

New storytellers for gay and lesbian identity reinvent the discursive
myth. This occurs in the production of new narratives, and the establishment of pathways towards legitimization. Such agency moves beyond a
retrospective 'distant past' where repressive narrative shifted life chances,
towards a prospective new order of mythic construction. For gay and
lesbian identity, new associations, such as independence, domesticity,
political agency and caring community, offer stimulating narratives of
change. This, I argue, is enabled by identification processes, encouraging the audience, and potential new writers, to connect to the text or to
an iconic performer, and to produce a relay of narratives though active
engagement.

Audience identification with iconic performers and the relay of narratives

Richard Dyer's (1986) ideas on people who have achieved stardom
are relevant with regard to an audience's potential engagement with
iconic performers, and the opportunity for narrative stimulation in new
storytelling:

> Stars articulate what it is to be a human being in contemporary soci-
> ety; that is, they express the particular notion we hold of the person,
> of the 'individual'. They do so complexly, variously – they are not
> straightforward affirmations of individualism. On the contrary, they
> articulate both the promise and the difficulty that the notion of
> individuality presents for all of us who live by it. (p. 8)

In this way, public figures provide a means for the individual to negotiate
and explore their own personal identity, including the stimulation of

political and personal ideologies. This may be complex, revealing both promise and difficulty, evident in the stimulation of the iconic figure which might evoke idealism disconnected from the life chances of the audience. However, I suggest that this offers a point of reference for the creation of new stories, extending from the self.

The individual creates a relationship with the persona and discourse of the star, and through this audiences are able to examine aspects of their own personal life, and relate these to diverse features from the projection of the public figure. Richard Dyer (2001 [originally 1998]), relating the work of Andrew Tudor (1974), identifies four categories that can emerge in the relationship between public figures and audiences:

> *emotional affinity....* 'The audience feels a loose attachment to a particular protagonist.... [Creating] a standard sense of involvement.
>
> *self-identification.* [The audience may] feel as if [they were] themselves on the screen experiencing what [the star does].
>
> *imitation.* The star acts as some sort of model for the audience.
>
> *projection.* Imitation merges into projection at the point at which the process becomes more than simple mimicking of clothing, hairstyle, kissing [etc.]. (Dyer, 2001: 18)

These categories indicate the subjective way in which audiences can engage with the celebrity or public identity: an interaction that can result in the transformation and adaptation of an individual's own personal preferences and identity. This may also result in the construction of new stories, which may be told by the individual relating their impressions of witness, building on emotional affinity, self-identification, imitation and projection, the corollary being that new storytellers may be stimulated to progress narratives commenced by other public figures, offering extensions to stories which may develop, passing from one storyteller to the other.

Audiences potentially engage with and progress narrative and discursive ideas disseminating from media writers, producers and performers, of varying commercial and popular success. As John Fiske (1994 [originally 1987]) tells us considering Louis Althusser's (1971) ideas on 'interpellation' for the ability of a text to connect to and address an audience:

> [A]ny discourse is necessarily part of a relationship between addresser and addressee, and that any such interpersonal relationship is, in turn,

necessarily part of wider social relations. Interpellation refers to the way that any discourse 'hails' the addressee. In responding to the call, in recognising that it is *us* being spoken to, we implicitly accept the discourse's definition of 'us', or, to put it another way, we adopt the subject position proposed for us by the discourse. (p. 53)

Consequently, through the interpellation of narrative, gay men and lesbians are addressed within discourse. They potentially find themselves within the text and are able to identify, interpret and reconstruct narrative ideas. Just as Stuart Hall (1980 [originally 1973]) describes the potential for the audience to encode and decode the text, new storytellers identify their life narratives and potentially progress these within new productions. This involves a relay of narratives, where diverse producers interpret and rewrite their stories in progression.

The case studies below present new storytellers developing narratives of self-invention. I argue that they move forward in this way, uninhibited by histories of shame, stigma or oppression, providing a relay of new narratives, focused on the personal self. New storytellers offer narratives of vernacular and intimate engagement, revealing personal and everyday democratic ideals unencumbered by historical oppression. The contribution of the anonymous individuals in the radio documentary *Male Homosexual* (BBC Radio, 1965, UK) provides evidence of this potential. Although they may not represent high-profile individuals in the manner of celebrities or stars, their substantial display encourages audiences to engage with their vernacular and intimate voices.

BBC radio and *Male Homosexual*

Male Homosexual was a specially commissioned BBC radio programme recorded in 1963, and broadcast in the United Kingdom two years later. After numerous attempts by producers to explore the subject of homosexuality on British radio, dating back as far as 1954 with successive rejections, a BBC trainee, Colin Thomas, revisited this possibility, producing a landmark media event. *Male Homosexual* was produced in conjunction with Michael Schofield, who had researched the lives of gay men and had published his findings in the book *A Minority: a Report on the Life of the Male Homosexual* (1960). Michael Schofield produced this under the pseudonym of Gordon Westwood. In *Male Homosexual*, he interviewed six gay men whose personal identities would also be concealed.

Whilst in *Male Homosexual* there is a focus on concealed identity, at the same time there is an evocation of openness, dedication and a call for change. In the penultimate narrative of the first part of the programme,[6] we are told by a gay man:

> My friend now, I mean we've been together for a long time. I love him and he loves me, and without him I would be nothing. . . . I think really we are just quite happy being the way we are, if people would only leave us alone, just accept us a little bit. Give and take that's what I say, but they won't. They say 'oh they are two queers', and they sort of sneer when they say 'queer', as if you are a freak. Well I don't think that I am a freak. I don't think that I am different from anybody else, I just happen to be in love with a man instead of a woman. . . . I think it's a great love. Something far deeper than anybody could ever realise.

Although the programme focuses its concern on the condition of homosexuality (in terms which might be related to the suffering of an illness) at a time when male homosexual behaviour was still illegal,[7] at the same time the candid interviews display strong evidence of transgression and revolution. This challenges not only the possible audience perceptions of male homosexuals, but also indicates the failing of a dominant majority to understand and accept social diversity.

A focus on the extent of homosexual lives is foregrounded, revealing the potential of same-sex intimacy and expectations of equality. Whilst issues of isolation and rejection are inevitably discussed, these are expressed in the context of a repressive society, more than a problematic condition, or a psychological concern. Consequently, a tension is played out between the imagined isolation, and the potential, of male homosexual lives, contained by institutions of oppression or denial. In addition, the quest at the BBC for the commissioning of the programme reveals sublayers of expectation and fulfilment, foregrounding narratives addressed at changing ideas, often interwoven in complex relationships and scenarios.

Producer Colin Thomas had become interested in the subject matter after reading Peter Wildeblood's book *Against the Law: the Classic Account of a Homosexual in 1950s Britain* (1955), which recorded a personal account of oppression under the law and the details of the Lord Montagu scandal (discussed in Chapter 2). Although not homosexual himself, Colin Thomas considered the subject worthy of exploration, especially in the light of government debate on the possibility of changing the law (in the Wolfenden Report – see Chapter 2), and concern for the liberty of individuals. Colin Thomas' participation offers a sense of a collaborative work, which reveals elements of resistance to oppression, often contained within the institution of the BBC itself.

The radio documentary *The BBC and the Closet* (BBC, 2008, UK) focuses specifically on the commissioning of *Male Homosexual* (1965), and traces early attempts to make a similar programme in the early 1950s, which was vetoed under the leadership of the then BBC director general Sir Ian Jacob. Jean Seaton, a professor in media history, tells us in *The BBC and the Closet* that at this time there was an imagined association between the homosexual, subversive life and treachery, evident the legendary story of Guy Burgess, once employed at the BBC, who later worked for the government and finally defected to Russia as a spy.[8] Also there was tension in the broadcasting authority itself, between the corporate leaders and the constitution and the interests of the employees: Jean Seaton affirms:

> I think, of anyone, that it is very interesting that it is Jacob, of all director generals [who rejected the initial proposal], Jacob knew all about this kind of issue. He is there because he is a kind of establishment figure. [However consistent attempts to keep the project alive are made at the BBC] because the BBC is also simultaneously, a): full of practising homosexuals, b): very comfortable with it, c) understanding that youth is changing, [and] that attitudes are changing. (Cited in *BBC and the Closet*, 2008)

Whilst it was under the leadership of Sir Ian Jacob that initial attempts to make an early radio programme were finally halted, it is significant that the potential politics of BBC employees who as homosexuals (in some cases) themselves, potentially had a vested interest in seeing the production made, or at least explored in more depth, enabled the continuance of dialogue and discourse supporting homosexual lives.

Later at the BBC under the leadership of a new director general Hugh Greene, who 'brought from his experience in Weimar Germany of cabaret a completely different attitude of advanced progressive sexual liberalism, basically the modern attitude towards sexuality' (Jean Seaton cited in *BBC and the Closet*, 2008), *Male Homosexual* would be commissioned. Despite this, continuing mechanisms were apparent within the BBC (and society in general), which stimulated a repressive order, and potentially negated homosexual voices. This is particularly evident if we consider the contribution of Michael Schofield, who was not only employed by the BBC at that time but also by the government in the Home Office and the Department of Health. He tells us that his employers were not aware of his sexuality, and potentially considered him unsuitable if he were homosexual. To this end, they asked him to see a psychiatrist alone, with regard to his work: 'We didn't talk for very long. He just said that [your employers at the Department of Health] have asked me to find out if you are a homosexual, and I think that you probably are, but I am not going to tell them.' Michael Schofield affirms that psychiatrist Peter Scott had deliberately resisted investigating the issue of homosexuality, in order to preserve the potential for Schofield to continue his work. Whilst male homosexuality remained illegal at that time in the United Kingdom, and it is likely that his employers were more concerned about employing a potential criminal than desiring to explore his personal sexual life, this incident illuminates the coalescent nature of those in minor positions of power working together in resistance to institutional oppression and 'inappropriate' authority.

The coalescence of the anonymous voices within *Male Homosexual* reveals stories of strength and determination, in conditions of oppression and denial. Their strength lies not only in considering their honesty and bravery, but also in their collective voice representing a hidden community. At the same time, issues of concealment and containment are foregrounded. An older gay man tells us in *Male Homosexual*:

Oh I live two lives; I live a private life and the public life. There is this pressure of make believe, all the time. It is completely artificial. Having to live a lie to one's colleagues, and simply act a part, all day. You have to do it day in, day out, year after year.

Male Homosexual reveals the imagined potential of gay identity as a collective vernacular voice outside orbits of authority and progression. Also it reveals the endurance and trial of the daily necessity to conceal one's identity, often involving artifice in public self-representation.

I argue that *Male Homosexual* is a landmark in vernacular storytelling, offering challenges to myths through the display of real personal lives and tribulations. This tension between concealment and announcement, in the context of private and public lives, is the essential strand in new storytelling. It extends not directly from historical narrative traditions in myth or literature, but instead grows out of personal desires to reveal the self, to greater and lesser extents. This may occur though relative anonymity, such as the disconnected voices within *Male Homosexual* or the veiled support of homosexuals, and supporters, at the BBC. Also it is present in the display of personal unashamed voices, supporting homosexual lives. This book foregrounds many voices like these, where direct rebellion to an established order is displayed by writers, producers and performers who project a new future for gay and lesbian lives. I argue that the work of Gore Vidal may be viewed as a precursor to this, offering inspiration and a continuing voice for gay and lesbian new storytellers, despite his apparent disconnection from an imagined gay community (discussed below, also see Chapter 3). His contribution encompasses his extensive and provocative written work, including his personal performative exhibited life.

Gore Vidal: the performance and the partnership

In Gore Vidal's *Myra Breckinridge* the lead character, a confident and provocative transsexual, tells us:

> I alone have the intuition as well as the profound grasp of philosophy and psychology to trace for man not only what he is but what he must become, once he has ceased to be confined to a single sexual role, to a single person . . . once he has become free to blend with others, to exchange personalities with both men and women, to play out the most elaborate of dreams in a world where soon there will be no limits to the human spirit's play. (Vidal, 1986: 180)

This evocation might be emblematic of Gore Vidal's own personal philosophy, in its deconstruction of sexual identity and the blurring of distinctions between heterosexuality and homosexuality. It foregrounds not only his personal vision, but also the context of media, culture and personal identity, which, I argue, are significant elements in the construction and deployment of Vidal's philosophy. This is evident in considering the narrative of *Myra Breckinridge* and the sequel *Myron* which explore a sexualised and fantastic world where a homosexual man transforms his body into a transsexual female. Through fate he experiences a metamorphosis into a heterosexual male, then through the apparatus of contemporary television, travels back in time to the era of classic Hollywood (1948), where his identity is split between heterosexual and transsexual.

An ambiguity and provocation in Gore Vidal's work locates homosexual desire with equality at the centre of personal sexual orientation, however, despite this he provides no political arena which supports a gay community as distinct and separate. Consequently, Gore Vidal has not generally been associated with ideas of gay identity and the politics of gay community, and some have even berated him for his apparently isolationist position, preferring to talk of sexual liberty, rather than sexual identity. In an interview with gay activist and celebrated author Larry Kramer, entitled 'The Sadness of Gore Vidal' (1999 [originally 1992]), pressure is exerted on Vidal to support the politics of the gay community and the separateness of homosexual identity. To this he responds '[W]hat I am preaching is: don't be ghettoised, don't be categorised. Every state tries to categorise its citizens in order to assert control over them' (Vidal cited in Kramer, 1999: 254). Gore Vidal regards homosexual identity not as a subordinate other, needing substantiation, but rather as a constitution of everyday life, not necessarily connected to a minority group. Despite his apparent disconnection from a seemingly separatist political agenda, I believe that his focus on personal sexual identity as liberating conversely does offer a very strong political substance for gay identity and non-heterosexual community.

Gore Vidal is a pluralist, and not an assimilationist (see Chapter 3), as might be argued by those who would consider him to be too aligned with the dominant heterosexual ideology. Furthermore, I would argue that he offers the potential for transformation (see also Chapter 3) in his ability to connect to audiences through his writing and his personal iconic life. As a pluralist who offers transformation he challenges the status quo, foregrounding diverse philosophies of sexual identity which surround and stimulate contexts of gay identity, extending and challenging concepts of community. This potential might be traced from his early work, and is evident in his later essay and memoir-based writing, relating not only to his fictional storytelling but also to his personal narrative life.

Prior to *Myra Breckinridge* and *Myron* (briefly discussed above) Gore Vidal released *The City and the Pillar* in 1948, establishing at its centre a 'normative' homosexual desire, exhibited by an 'all American' male, evident in the romantic attachment of Jim Willard for peer Bob Ford. Although this potential relationship is ultimately unfulfilled, and concludes with a graphic and violent realisation involving the punishment of (heterosexual) Ford by (homosexual) Willard, who humiliates and rapes him,[9] the narrative places an enabled and morally untroubled homosexual character as the lead storyteller. Significantly, this represented a shift in homosexual narrative potential within fiction, where generally central characters exhibiting same-sex desire had been cast as extraordinary, troubled, despised and/or morally bankrupt (discussed above).

Despite the commercial success of the book (as discussed above) due to the provocative nature of *The City and the Pillar*, Gore Vidal (1997) tells us that the '*New York Times* would not advertise it and no major American newspaper or magazine would review it or any other book of mine for the next six years' (p. 5). Because of this, Gore Vidal became involved in television, not only writing screenplays, but also appearing as a performer (briefly discussed above). Consequently, he became a progressive constituent in an evolving contemporary medium, locating himself as a performer, as much as a writer. As Vidal tells us in *Myra Breckinridge* in the voice of the lead character, relating the move to the visual over the written word:

> Of course visual narrative will always be filmed if not in theatres, on television. Yet the *nature* of those narratives is bound to change as television creates a new kind of person who will then create a new kind of art, a circle of creation that is only now just beginning. It is a thrilling moment to be alive. (Vidal, 1986: 98)

I believe that this represents Gore Vidal's self-reflexive vision, as an enabler of new narratives largely played out within the medium of television. His persona as a novelist, essayist and playwright is complemented with his life outside the fictional and philosophical text, evident within contemporary media. I also believe that as part of this, his enduring relationship with Howard Auster (of over 50 years) becomes a central strand of his performative identity.

In the documentary *The Education of Gore Vidal* (Deborah Dickson, 2003, US) (discussed below), Howard Auster reveals details of their life together in Italy:

> We've grown up now with three generations of Ravellese, and they couldn't have been nicer to us. From the very beginning [when we arrived in Ravello, Italy], I mean two eccentric crazy Americans driving into town in a silver Jaguar with a little Australian terrier yapping, oh. [and] wearing cowboy hats. They thought we were,...I mean they kind of loved it you see. And Gore has besides the gift of writing, the gift of verbally communicating. He is an educator, which is really what's behind his art.

Howard Auster's praise for his partner and the celebration of their domestic life, foregrounded in a high-profile documentary, reveals diverse contexts of new storytelling where the discussion of domestic lives stimulates progressive narratives of change. In a similar manner to the partnership between Dirk Bogarde and Tony Forwood (discussed in Chapters 3 and 4), an iconic same-sex relationship is presented as representing levels of devotion and connectivity. Although Bogarde and Forwood's partnership was never openly discussed in the context of homosexual romance (although many commentators, and relatives, have read it this way), whilst Gore Vidal has proposed that his enduring partnership with Howard Auster did not involve a sexual relationship later in life (Vidal, 2006: 241), it is the devotion between same-sex partners which offers scope. With regard to Vidal and Auster, I would argue that this reveals a capacity of new storytelling, potentially more powerful than narratives which openly announce and/or confirm same-sex activity between partners. Gore Vidal's recollection of Howard's death in the memoir *Point to Point Navigation* (2006) reveals the emotional depth of same-sex pairing.

Gore Vidal's proposed original title for *The City and the Pillar* had been 'The Romantic Agony' (Vidal, 2006: 102), a title which (I would argue) situates the impossibility of a sexualised romance, yet also reveals a yearning for this. Whilst we are aware that the narrative of *The City and the Pillar* does involve agony or a lack of fulfilment (discussed above), Vidal's own relationship with Auster provides a direct contrast, revealing the fulfilment of a profound relationship between two men, which lasted for over half a century until death. Within *Point to Point Navigation*, Gore Vidal recalls details of Howard's illness which led to his death. However, rather than delivering this in purely emotive or expressly personal terms, Vidal frames this within the philosophy of Michel de Montaigne (1533–92). Gore Vidal (2006) opens the chapter by discussing Howard's death: 'I now must surrender to Montaigne's request. How do the living die and what do they say and how do they look in the end? Howard has now quietly entered this narrative, as he remains permanently present in my memory' (p. 77). The foregrounding of Montaigne in a chapter which discusses Howard's last days with Gore is significant, not only in relation to how the narrative should be conveyed, but also with regard to the philosophy of same-sex relationships. In an earlier essay on Montaigne (Vidal, 2000 [originally 1992]) Vidal tells us that 'It was Montaigne's view that true love, sexual or not, meant the congruence of two men as equals. This was the highest form of human relationship' (Vidal, 2000: 899). Gore Vidal's recollection of Howard's life is framed not only in the philosophical expectations of Montaigne, but also in the depth of human connectivity as evoked by Montaigne.

Gore Vidal (2000) foregrounds the depth of a relationship between two males, discussing Michel de Montaigne's relationship with Etienne de la Boëtie, affirming and citing Montaigne:

> Each was to become the other's self. [Montaigne tells us] 'If you press me to say why I loved him, I feel that it can only be expressed by replying "Because it was him: because it was me." ... We were seeking each other before we set eyes on each other.' (Vidal, 2000: 895)

The inevitability and depth of Montaigne's friendship are represented in the terms of finding a 'soul mate'. Vidal foregrounds the context of male bonding to illuminate the potential intensity of relationships between men. Furthermore, Vidal uses the stimulus of Montaigne and la Boëtie's relationship as a mirror to his own life with Howard. The death of la Boëtie stimulated Montaigne to commence his great work as a writer in 'free association', placing himself as his subject, and thereby moving away from a classical tradition in literature which restricted this form of expression. Howard's death, occurring in the later part of Vidal's life, may be related to la Boëtie's death during Montaigne's early career, and the significance of their same-sex relationships.

The contrast between Montaigne's relationship which stimulated his career as the first great essayist (see Montaigne, 1991 [originally 1580]), and Vidal's which similarly inspired and supported his great career, is profound. Vidal uses Montaigne to relate the meaning of Howard's life: his life was the inspiration, and his death a closing of a chapter. On suspecting that Howard has passed away, Gore tells us:

> I sat in the chair opposite and did all the things that we have learned from the movies to determine death. I passed a hand in front of his nose and mouth. Nothing stirred. Montaigne requires that I describe more how he looked – rather than how I felt. The eyes were open and very clear. I'd forgotten what a beautiful gray they were – illness and medicine had regularly glazed them over; now they were bright and attentive and he was watching me, consciously, through long lashes. Lungs and heart may have stopped but the optic nerves are still sending messages to the brain which, those who should know tell us, does not immediately shut down. So we stared at each other at the end. (Vidal, 2006: 87)

Gore Vidal contextualises Montaigne at the demise of his lifelong partnership with Howard, resonating inspiration, meaning and loss. Using

Montaigne's advice for descriptive rather than purely emotive language, Vidal places the audience within the frame, suggesting objectivity but foregrounding a subjective sense of partnership and eternity. Vidal presents an enduring and inspirational relationship in his witness and co-presence at Howard's demise. Through the gateway of Howard's eyes, the audience connect with aspects of new storytelling, valuing same-sex partnerships, as central, meaningful and profound.

Whilst Gore Vidal remains an evocative and often enigmatic force, and his contribution to new storytelling for gay identity is significant on many varying levels, his contribution to contemporary media is of particular note. Vidal's evocation within *Myra Breckinridge* that 'television creates a new kind of person who will then create a new kind of art, a circle of creation' (1986: 98) (discussed above), I argue, can be related to the context of popular culture, celebrity and the opportunity of vernacular media. Consequently my discussion continues by examining both the iconic influence of k.d. lang as a popular musician, who as a positive lesbian-identified celebrity challenged mythic representations in the early 1990s, and the impact of new media within the World Wide Web, as a discursive tool for gay identity, examining a contemporary case study on Waymon Hudson.

k.d. lang and Waymon Hudson: role models, vernacular voices and political forces

k.d. lang is a Canadian popular musician, singer and songwriter, who has achieved international success. Although her early career was devoted to country music, with lang offering youth-orientated interpretations of standard country songs, performed in a manner which might be considered as alternative in style, her groundbreaking success came with the release of a popular music album entitled *Ingénue* (1992). Significant in her career is her identity as an openly gay singer. Although many consider that she had never hidden her sexuality, shortly after the release of *Ingénue* she discussed her sexuality openly within the *Advocate* in 1992 (see Collis, 1999; Martinac, 1997; Robertson, 1993 [originally 1992]; Starr, 1994), and the popular press. As the first openly gay popular celebrity not to conceal a homosexual identity, I believe that she represents a watershed in transitions of homosexual identity within popular culture. Her shame-free identity emerges after many years of celebrities concealing homosexual identity, for fear of association with deviancy and 'otherness'. Celebrities such as the Hollywood film star Rock Hudson (1925–85) and the rock musician Freddie Mercury

(1946–91) concealed their homosexual lives and only announced their sexual identity when pressures from the media forced them to do so, in both cases after contracting AIDS and feeling a need to tell their audiences. In the early 1970s Electra Records (in the United States) signed the openly gay pop star Jobriath (1946–83), and marketed him in an unashamed way that capitalized on his sexual identity as part of the burgeoning glam rock movement. However mainstream and gay audiences rejected his effeminate identity, in an era when masculine identity was seen as a normative goal, in the desires and disseminations of the gay male political and social community.[10] Despite this a little later in the era, Sylvester (1947–88) an Afro American gender ambiguous pop star, achieved mainstream success as a gay icon, connecting with both the gay community and the wider audience (see Gamson, 2005). Meanwhile British pop stars from the 1970s such as David Bowie and Elton John had been associated with bisexuality; however in both instances, at that time, the idea of a purely homosexual identity was denied. Whilst Bowie would appear later to be heterosexual, and Elton John would celebrate his homosexual identity with partner David Furnish (including a civil partnership in 2006), it would be figures such as Tom Robinson and Boy George who would offer more apparent homosexual identities, in the late 1970s and early 1980s. Tom Robinson released his song titled 'Glad to be Gay' in 1978 and became an emerging celebrity advocating the honesty of his homosexual life, and Boy George achieved worldwide popular musical success whilst expressing a bisexual and androgynous identity. Despite this, it would not be until the early 1990s, when k.d. lang emerged, representing a fully realised homosexual identity, that such evolved and engaging role models would appear in the popular music industry.[11] k.d. lang represents an icon for lesbian identity, and as reported in several biographical books (Collis, 1999; Martinac, 1997; Robertson, 1993; Starr, 1994) her central narrative identity is that of a groundbreaking popular star. Her impact (I argue) possibly influenced Ellen DeGeneres to come out as a lesbian in the late 1990s (discussed in Chapter 2), encouraging her to believe that her honesty would be received with reasonable favour.

Waymon Hudson is a producer of new media on the World Wide Web. Although many possible contributors for gay and lesbian identity could be selected with regards to contributions within online new media (and later case studies develop this further, in Chapters 4, 6 and 7), I have focused on his work here for its direct political awareness, which for me represents a contemporary paradigm in new storytelling. Notably Waymon Hudson produced a weblog in response to the murder of 15-year-old Lawrence King, who had identified himself as gay. King had been murdered at school by a fellow male pupil aged 14, who used a hand gun at close range in the manner of an execution. Waymon's weblog questions why the mainstream media had devoted little space to the story, and petitions for a call to action. Also he produced the websites 'Fight OUT Loud' (2008a) and 'The Homo Politico' (2008a). In these sites we find strong evidence of a commitment to express personal stories, foregrounding a desire for change. Waymon's contribution in new media represents a self-reflexive voice, offering new stories of resistance. Within new media, a collective burgeoning generation of gay and lesbian storytellers are writing about themselves, and through the potential of social networking and weblogs, are revealing new visions of gay community which are highly politicised.

I am discussing k.d. lang and Waymon Hudson together, not so much for their mutual time frame or their textual congruence, but to reveal the vernacular and emotive potential of new storytellers, whether they are celebrities, or members of the public. Both k.d. lang and Waymon Hudson employ narratives of themselves in their performances, and that this offers an everyday vision of gay and lesbian lives for the public to explore. As discussed above with relation to the potential of stars, public personas and discursive production, audiences are potentially hailed by the text, and may identify with the identities or ideas expressed. This offers not only the potential for a connection in audience identification to be made, but also an opportunity for narratives to emerge, and for the progression of ideas. This is particularly evident with regard to the impact of k.d. lang and the potential of Waymon Hudson, working within diverse popular cultural forms. I will first discuss k.d. lang, as establishing an iconic arena where lesbian identity is positively represented, enabling confident audience identification. I will subsequently explore in more depth the work of Waymon Hudson, and the significance of new media and self-reflexivity.

k.d. lang: establishing the arena

k.d. lang's seminal album *Ingénue* (1992) may be seen as a landmark, not only in the progression of her musical career, but also with regard to the dissemination of her lesbian identity. Whilst her earlier work indicated a blurring of distinctions between gender identities, in presenting a masculinised vision of female country and western stardom, *Ingénue* would establish a narrative iconography which engaged directly with her personal identity. Her focus prior to *Ingénue* had been to support an image which was ambiguous. She tells us (at that time) that: 'I'm a very androgynous looking woman, and my goals are not to be a wife or necessarily a

Figure 1.2   k.d. lang depicted early in her career, in a PETA advertising campaign. The controversy of her vegetarianism would prove to be as significant as her lesbian identity. Image courtesy of PETA

mother. Androgyny is important in my life because I can deal with people on a human and not a sexual level' (cited in Robertson, 1993: 86).

Despite an acceptance of her nonconformist sexual identity, this became problematic when lang experienced a negative reaction from the public in Canada over her support for vegetarianism, and her contribution to an advertising campaign for PETA (People for the Ethical Treatment of Animals) (see Figure 1.2). In a backlash against lang for deterring people from eating meat (a staple produce in Canada, which also provides employment) one incident recorded the vandalising of a sign at the city limits in her own town, with the words 'eat beef, dyke' aerosol sprayed over 'Home of k.d. lang – Consort, Alberta'. Although this was an isolated incident, it reflected a sense of mainstream audience discontent with her ambiguous identity. Also at this time, she moved towards a more open sexual identity, reflecting her personal life. Consequently, lang's *Ingénue* represents a new coming of age where she has moved away from hybrid country music, and an androgynous identity which might reflect mainstream taste (and her support of dominant social traditions), and reveals a confidence in self which is direct, personal and confrontational.

Ingénue represents a personal reflection in the same manner in which new storytellers for gay and lesbian identity reveal details of their intimate lives. The album cover depicts lang looking down, away from the camera lens, and it is slightly out of focus suggesting contemplation and emotion. This is further borne out in the textual value of songs, produced with co-writer Ben Mink. In exploring issues of unrequited love, or love that could not be fulfilled, lang presents an introspective album, foregrounding the sensitivity and intensity of same-sex desire. Songs such as 'The Mind of Love' and 'Miss Chatelaine' directly locate female identities in relation to same-sex desire, with the latter providing a provocative upbeat tempo which would become a standard representing lang's coyness, and her confidence as an 'agent provocateur'. Furthermore, 'Save Me' and 'Constant Craving' offer insightful and melancholic themes, foregrounding disappointment within love, yet at the same time evoking romance and progression to fulfilment. This extends to identification with the audience, where a connection provides a collective sense of community. As Paul Martinac (1997) reports:

> Having recently wrapped up her *Ingénue* tour, lang commented on the positive effect [that] coming out had on her concerts. 'The really, really, big thing I experienced this year was the intimacy between me and the audience', she noted, 'not just because the [of] number of women, although that's part of it. It's that I felt comfortable knowing that they came there knowing [who I really was].' (Martinac, 1997: 124)

Through revealing a fully apparent sexual identity, k.d. lang offered new visions of a confident gay and lesbian life. This extends both to the textual value of her music, and to the collective nature of audience identification. In many ways she offered a personal, yet public, representation of a citizen within an 'imagined gay community' (see Chapter 3). This established not only a (celebrated) public representative of a hidden community, but also her positive and approachable identity challenged stereotypical ideas of sexual 'otherness' and deviancy, through her confidence in self and her 'everyday' personality. In this sense, while she was a public figure, she did not present herself as anything other than a typical citizen who just happened to be gay.

k.d. lang opened a gateway in popular culture, expressing the context of a fully realised, shame-free lesbian identity, supporting gay and lesbian citizenship within 'mass media'. Her impact within popular music might also be seen in the work of Melissa Etheridge and Rufus Wainwright, both of which have contributed to 'new storytelling' prioritising gay and lesbian narratives. Significantly, Rufus Wainwright has dedicated his entire recording career to a shame-free gay identity, foregrounding romantic songs such as 'Danny Boy' and 'The Consort', alongside confrontational texts such as 'The Gay Messiah', which became a celebrated anthem in his closing stage performances of 2008. However, in assessing the significance of 'public' and 'celebrated' media figures, issues of commodity inevitably may engender a potential reading of privilege and distance from 'everyday' citizenship. Waymon Hudson's contribution may be regarded as a progression of this potential and as part of a developing vernacular frame. This reveals the audience as 'citizen authors', using new media to record and broadcast their own stories.

Waymon Hudson: the personal self and the political frame

Waymon Hudson is a 'political consultant [who] deals with communications through modern media and youth outreach, [focusing on] social networking sites and YouTube' (Hudson, 2008) (see Figure 1.3). He founded the website 'Fight OUT Loud' (2008a) with his partner Anthony Niedweiki, a law professor and lawyer. 'Fight OUT Loud' is a 'national non-profit organisation dedicated to empowering the [LGBT] community to fight discrimination and hate' (Fight OUT Loud, 2008a). 'The Homo Politico' (2008a) is Waymon Hudson's weblog site, linked to 'Fight OUT Loud', which foregrounds his personal reports on homophobia. This includes a diverse range of subjects, of international and local concern. Hudson's responses to the Lawrence King murder are posted within 'The Homo Politico' (with links to the popular video site YouTube), and are discussed below. I will begin by examining Hudson's website 'Fight OUT Loud', the context of his partnership and his 'call to action'.

'Fight OUT Loud' opens with a page title: 'Our Mission', with a political statement of intent:

> The mission of Fight OUT Loud is to provide immediate resources, support, education, and assistance for gay, lesbian, bisexual, and transgender individuals who are faced with discrimination and hate. We do this by empowering everyday people to stand up for themselves in the fight for their rights, because no situation of discrimination should slip through the cracks and go unchallenged. (Fight OUT Loud, 2008a)

Evoking Waymon Hudson and his partner's political ideology, to provide a discursive arena for issues and concerns, this statement sets the tone of the website. It suggests that LGBT people need to work together against discrimination and oppression, and that new media discursive space may offer a beneficial place to share stories and reveal opportunities. This

Figure 1.3 Waymon Hudson depicted in demonstration against Proposition 8, which In California overturned gay marriage (see page 325, note 1). Image courtesy of Waymon Hudson

involves a focus on spreading awareness of crime against LGBT people and a need to respond.

Foregrounded on the 'Our Mission' page is a video collage entitled 'Hate in 2008 = a Call for Action: Violent Crimes are on the Rise against LGBT People in 2008', which offers a succession of images of LGBT individuals who had been murdered earlier in the year. Using a contemporary music background with the song 'Fearless' by Cyndi Lauper (1996), suggesting a call to action, the images are punctuated by text recounting the essential details of the crimes. For example:

> Sanesha Stewart was stabbed to death by an ex con, who told cops [that] he flew into a rage when he found out [that] his date was transgender. – February 2008.
>
> Alexio Bello, a 68-year-old gay man, was found stabbed to death, at his home Miami, Florida. – January 2008.
>
> Simmie 'Beyonce' Williams Jr., 17, was killed [on] the streets of Fort Lauderdale. – February 2008. (The Homo Politico, 2008b; YouTube, 2008a).

Also included within this list is information on Lawrence King (discussed below). A political tone is set, which melds emotive contemporary pop music with optimistic images of LGBT people, contextualised with descriptive and statistical details. This presents a collage of ideas, showcasing a call to action. In the manner of a postmodern narrative construction (as discussed in Chapter 3), democratising juxtapositions are made, blending narratives of sexual liberty, criminal action, popular emotion and political awareness. These disseminations extend from Waymon Hudson's personal call for action, which is foregrounded within the page 'Our Story'.

The 'Our Story' page subtitled 'The Story that Started a Movement' (Fight OUT Loud, 2008b) reveals the catalyst for Waymon, and his partner, to commence their political work within new media. I believe that this reveals a personal narrative thread which offers self-reflexive visions in his motivation, and largely represents a contemporary paradigm of new storytelling. Waymon recalls an oppressive incident when returning to Fort Lauderdale airport late one night in May 2007. He and his partner heard a threatening announcement over the public address system: 'A man that lies with a man as a woman should be put to death.' This event stimulated the couple to complain to the airport authorities, who only became interested and eventually punished the responsible party after receiving media coverage of the incident. An airport employee had used his mobile phone to broadcast a web-sourced dialogue over the public address system, at a time when Hudson and his partner could be targeted. Ultimately the media attention to the event, which was diverse and contentious, stimulated Waymon Hudson's call to action, and the foundation of 'Fight OUT Loud'. This involved oppressive responses from religious fundamentalists against the couple, and abuse in public. As Hudson reports:

> The media coverage made us public enemy #1 for the extreme religious movement. A few days after they identified [the culpable airport employee], a woman stopped me in our neighborhood grocery store and said, 'Didn't I see you on the news?' I said yes, and she looked me in the eye and replied, 'You faggots deserve exactly what that man said.' The next day, my car windshield had 'FAG!' scrawled across it. (Fight OUT Loud, 2008b)

Waymon Hudson uses the narrative of his personal life, revealing oppression to his liberty, as a catalyst for a call to action. He identifies himself within the frame, not only offering a 'transformation in intimacy' (Giddens, 1995) (see Chapter 4) where contemporary society is stimulated though personal display, but also he politicises his ideology, revealing unacceptable behaviour and persecution. This is particularly apparent in his later work, and is notably evident in his discussion on Lawrence King.

Lawrence King, a 15-year-old school student, was murdered by Brandon McInerney, a 14-year-old peer. This occurred some time after King expressed an attraction for McInerney (Broverman, 2008), implying that potential homosexual identification could be a motive for murder. Waymon Hudson describes Lawrence King and the surrounding events in his 'video blog', telling us:

> He was gay. He liked to wear make-up and jewellery and heels to school, and was bullied [and] teased a lot because of it. What has really been shocking to me is the lack of outrage and anger, and the lack of media coverage of it, within the mainstream media. The gay blogs and LGBT media has really been buzzing about it, but it doesn't seem to be picking up much traction in mainstream media, which is really bothersome to me. Because I can't remember when there was a violent school shooting like this, that didn't get 24/7 news coverage. But it seems because this happened to a young gay man, and that makes a lot of people uncomfortable, they don't want to talk about it. They want to brush it under the rug. . . . When you look at the picture of Lawrence and you read his story, I know I personally see myself in it. He was just like me. In school I was teased because I was too girly. I was called gay I was beat up a lot. And luckily I made it out OK, but Lawrence didn't. (The Homo Politico, 2008c; YouTube, 2008b)

Through using his own personal language, setting his image in a confessional manner direct to video camera, Waymon offers a heartfelt interpretation of the event of Lawrence King's murder. Notably he not only offers insight into the context of media coverage, or its absence, but also he places himself within the frame both literally and metaphorically. We are presented with a political agency, which engages with the potential of intimate citizenship (see Chapter 2) offering democratic scope in personal storytelling. The juxtaposition of Lawrence King with Waymon Hudson parallels narratives of youth and imagined social development in coming of age, at the same time revealing contexts of injustice and persecution. Waymon uses Lawrence's story not only to express his discontent with mainstream media, but also to peel back the layers of potential within gay and lesbian youth, devalued in dominant narratives.

While later in this book I explore the context of youth as a progressive force in new storytelling (see Chapter 6), Waymon's contribution here uses the conduit of shared experience at school to personalise his political message. The context of self-reflexivity (discussed in more depth in Chapter 2), encourages personal experience to form the axis of political action. Waymon's connection with Lawrence's tragic story offers a vivification of his own identity, built upon a foundation of personal experience. Furthermore, his call to action, and the foundation of his

. work, extends from responses to oppression, stimulated and conveyed though personal narrative and experience.

Waymon Hudson's expressions of personal storytelling and the discursive opportunity of new media for political action display a contemporary vision for new storytelling. Building on positive identification narratives evident in popular culture such as the audience reception of k.d. lang and emerging opportunities for homosexual identity, a new confidence in self-reflexive narrative is revealed. This extends beyond the limits of celebrity identity, which might be contained by popular sensibilities, and progresses towards political action, in the advent of new citizens in media production. This offers both a positive sense of self-identity, and the political expression of hope.

Conclusion

New storytelling offers a relay of narratives. Oppressive myths are challenged and new stories emerge, through a succession of narrative producers in contemporary media. Whilst it is not possible to argue that this relay involves a distinct passage from one story to another, travelling though obvious connections between writers, producers and performers, through a collage of possibility and audience identification, gradually new stories emerge and progress. This is largely attributed to the potential for individuals to write stories centred on their personal lives, in a manner which is self-reflexive and involves intimate display.

Gore Vidal's presence in contemporary media, and in the literary world, offers an iconic vision of a new storyteller. Although apparently disconnected from a realised gay community, he constructs narratives of engagement which not only foreground the energy and invention of his sexual storytelling, but also the dynamic of his personal life. With regard to his relationship with life partner Howard Auster, this offers an iconic representation of same-sex endurance and devotion. In these terms, Gore Vidal's continuing contribution is that he offers a philosophy of sexual identity extending between his written work and his public life which is performative and transgressive. From his groundbreaking work in the novels *The City and the Pillar* (1997), *Myra Breckinridge* (1986) and *Myron* (1975), to his memoir *Point to Point Navigation* (2006) (and numerous other works), and his personal life, he is seen to commence a dialogue in new storytelling, and may be considered as a prime protagonist.

The anonymous contributors to *Male Homosexual* (BBC Radio, 1965), whose voices seem disconnected from authority and social standing, offer vernacular emergences of homosexual citizenship. The coalescent nature of various individuals involved in attempts to commission and produce a series examining homosexual identity at this time, reveals the complexity of narrative production, and a political move for change. The example of *Male Homosexual* reveals the potential of hidden or discredited voices, and is a landmark towards new emergences in factual programming discussed later in this book. Although disparity may be apparent between the high-profile work of Gore Vidal and the disconnected voices in *Male Homosexual*, I argue that they are contiguous in their property of intimate release. Audiences hailed by these discussions inevitably recognise themselves within the frame, and potentially move forwards in narrative identification.

The identity of k.d. lang as an openly gay celebrity within the popular music world offered an emerging point of reference for gay audiences. Her standing as a populist icon may be seen as a new threshold in contemporary media and new storytelling for gay and lesbian identity. Marking a shift within popular celebrity, away from the concealment of homosexual identity and towards the celebration of same-sex desire, this offers transgressive potential. Her iconic status challenges myths of denial, lack of fulfilment, and isolation, offering audiences new opportunities for narrative invention.

Waymon Hudson's contribution reveals new scope in media production, where intimate dialogue foregrounds political ideology. Through the advent of new media within the World Wide Web, Hudson presents a personal narrative life, enmeshed within political narratives advocating change. Marking a paradigm of new storytelling, the personal self is increasingly evident in narrative progressions. Waymon Hudson's work represents a contemporary vision of the citizenship expectations displayed by the anonymous contributors to the radio documentary *Male Homosexual*, marking an advance towards change. At the same time it reflects the narrative precursors evident in the work of Gore Vidal including his iconic life, and that of k.d. lang (and many others who follow in this book).

It is the personal narrative which forms the foundation of new storytelling for gay and lesbian identity, extending and interweaving between written, and various media-based, fictional, factual and largely discursive worlds. Also it extends to the iconic narrative potential of individual lives, offering new identification potentials for audiences and producers alike.

The focus on the self and the issue of self-reflexivity are the essence of new storytelling. The next chapter further explores this idea, revealing a narrative progression involving testaments of personal identity and incidents of popular engagement.

2
Gay Identity and Self-Reflexivity

Introduction

In the closing sequences of the autobiographical drama *The Naked Civil Servant* (1975, Thames Television, UK) actor John Hurt playing the role of Quentin Crisp (1908–99) tells an aggressive gang of youths who are threatening blackmail: 'You cannot touch me now, I am one of the stately *homos* of England.' Here on mainstream British television, we are presented with a defining moment which would stimulate a shift in the representation of non-heterosexuals in the media. Quentin Crisp's words iterated a new confidence in gay representation and personal storytelling. I argue that he was a new storyteller of gay identity, tracing yet rewriting stories which surround non-heterosexuals (see Figure 2.1). Also as a character representing himself within *The Naked Civil Servant* as a book (Crisp, 2007 [originally 1968]) and a television adaptation, and also through his later public appearances (and anecdotal and philosophical publications, see Crisp, 1981, 1984, 1997, 2008), he is an 'intimate citizen' (Plummer, 1997) attempting to reform social worlds through personal agency within entertainment media.

Consequently this chapter examines the emergence of new storytellers who for gay identity present self-reflexive visions of themselves within both factual and fictional media forms. Furthermore, it contextualises gay identity in connection with stereotyping, archetypal forms and disavowals, presenting a textual analysis of Mordaunt Shairp's play *The Green Bay Tree* (1933). In examining the potential of self-reflexivity, this chapter initially explores the narrative potential of Christopher Isherwood, who as an openly gay man and a pioneer of semi-autobiographical fiction set a precedent and a theoretical model for the idea of self-storytelling and gay identity. Following this there is an examination

Figure 2.1   Quentin Crisp, pictured later in life when he lived in New York. Photograph © Phillip Ward. All rights reserved. Used by permission. Courtesy of the Quentin Crisp Archives (crisperanto.org)

of Quentin Crisp, who as an autobiographer and raconteur (briefly discussed above) engendered a landmark event through the impact of *The Naked Civil Servant*; Ellen DeGeneres, who as a leading situation comedy actor offered a media spectacle through coming out within her own popular television series, and George Michael, who as an international pop star following his arrest for lewd conduct in a public place, exhibited a shameless and empowering identity in media confessions. In building this progression, the significance of Oscar Wilde (1854–1900) is foregrounded in relation to emergence of queer identity, and its relationship to homosexual identity constructs. Also the impact of Peter Wildeblood (1923–99) is explored, revealing his significance as an openly gay man trapped in confessional and oppressive legislative domains.

Within these case studies, gay people speak about themselves, relating their personal identity issues and desires. This may be seen as part of a larger political connectivity: the progression of gay and lesbian identity within diverse media forms, broadcasting, and stimulating change. These personal actions may be related to a desire to achieve citizenship enfranchisement for gay identity within dominant communities. Specifically, I argue that there are connections with Ken Plummer's (1997) discussions concerning 'telling sexual stories', and how this can be enabling. Consequently this chapter examines Plummer's ideas, and contextualises issues concerning discursive power, as this forms the conduit through which (I believe) new stories are formed. However, it is first important to set out the context of 'new storytelling', and how this may be connected to gay and lesbian social actors working within the confines of the media. It is notable that there is a complex relationship between personal socio-agency exhibiting self-identity and desires, and the potential to progress discourse within entertainment forms aimed at meeting dominant identity expectations. I argue that potential may be offered through the exhibition of self-reflexivity in storytelling; however, it involves situating or challenging identity within the confines of mainstream media.

Christopher Isherwood, storytelling and self-reflexivity

Just as Renaissance philosopher Michel de Montaigne (1991 [originally 1580]) posited 'I am myself the subject of my book', thereby breaking a tradition which encouraged personal ideas to be disconnected from classical thought, the performers discussed in this book speak about themselves through their texts, contradicting a history of dominant heterosexuality in popular narrative forms. This occurs not only within personal testaments, but also it is evident within fictional forms. I argue that Christopher Isherwood (see Figure 2.2) may be considered as the 'founder of a new documentary fiction' (Bucknell, 2000: 17) in this way. His personal identity is traced through autobiographical and fictional forms, foregrounding the non-heterosexual as a self-reflexive agent in storytelling. This is particularly evident in the case of Isherwood, who not only produced personal diaries (between the 1920s and the early 1980s), but also deliberately represented himself within his fictional forms. In *Goodbye to Berlin* (1978 [originally 1939], based on his diaries) whilst representing himself as the character of Christopher Isherwood, he produces a personal reflexive story which foregrounds a homosexual character within the historical context of Berlin in the 1930s (contextualising the rise of the Nazi Party).

Later *Goodbye to Berlin* would be adapted into the play *I Am a Camera* (Van Druten, 1958 [originally, 1951]) which was subsequently adapted into a film of the same name (Henry Cornelius, 1955, UK), and finally

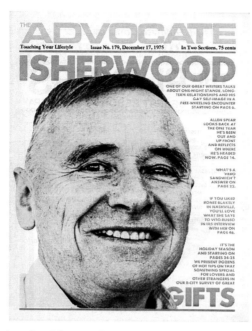

Figure 2.2   Christopher Isherwood on the cover of *The Advocate* (17 December 1975), presented as an iconic leader of the gay and lesbian community. Image courtesy of *The Advocate* and LPI Media Inc.

transformed into the musical film *Cabaret* (Bob Fosse, 1972, US) (with Isherwood now rewritten as the character of Brian Roberts, played by Michael York). These instances provided further discursive moments, which whilst they would not fully explore Isherwood's homosexuality, did foreground his personal identity within the narrative frame. This is particularly evident in *Goodbye to Berlin* (and *I am a Camera*) where he tells us:

> I am a camera with its shutter open, quite passive, recording, not thinking. Recording the man shaving at the window opposite and the woman in the kimono washing her hair. Someday all this will have to be developed, carefully printed, fixed. (Isherwood, 1978: 11)

Whilst Isherwood 'came to rue this metaphor of the camera as misleading' (Bucknell, 2000: 14), I would argue that this represents evidence of his emerging status as an interpretive and reflective personal character. This relates not only to his recording of the everyday lives of those caught within Nazi Germany at that time, but also to his situation within the text. As semiautobiographical fiction (Buckhill, 2000: 14), the personality of Isherwood becomes enmeshed within history through personal storytelling. Isherwood's situation of observing and waiting for the metaphorical 'fixing of a film' reveals evidence of his self-reflexivity and complicity, inscribing homosexual identity within media.

I argue that Christopher Isherwood represents evidence of the emerging 'self-reflexive' homosexual in storytelling. Whilst later Isherwood would write more directly in autobiographical terms in *Lions and Shadows* (1947 [originally 1938]) and *Christopher and his Kind* (1977), I am focusing here on his potential to incorporate his personal self within the fictional form.[1] Isherwood's focus on the self may be related to Anthony Giddens' (1992) idea of the 'reflexive project of the self' where the individual in contemporary society identifies with personal visions of fulfilment, not necessarily informed by dominant structures or motifs. Isherwood wrote about himself, expressing and prioritising the homosexual as an integral part of the narrative. This may be related to the process of 'autobiographical thinking', which Giddens (1995 [originally 1992]) describes not only as a central element of self-therapy (which is discussed further in Chapter 4), but also it should be considered as a process which may engender change. As Giddens (1992) tells us:

> For developing a coherent sense of one's life history is a prime means of escaping the thrall of the past and opening oneself out to the future. The author of the autobiography is enjoined to go back as far as possible into early childhood and set up lines of potential development to encompass the future. (p. 72)

Isherwood through autobiographical thinking within his fictional work played out issues concerning his reflexive identity, and at the same time he laid a pathway towards future progress.

In terms of homosexual identity, this relates to Isherwood constructing a modified future through personal narrative inventions. In terms of self-reflexive potential, Giddens (1992) would argue that through this process: 'in [the] conditions of modernity ... the media does not mirror realities [in a passive sense] but in some part forms them' (p. 27). Isherwood integrated his personal identity within a diary, novel, play and film, and these produced discursive moments which reflected and reproduced Isherwood as the integral personal narrator. This challenge involves not only what constitutes appropriate textual form by questioning whether authors should integrate their personal identity, but also who should capture and frame the narrative by placing the homosexual as the dominant storyteller. Through challenging dominant form and heterosexual authority, Isherwood may be considered as working towards change through intimate self-reflexive storytelling.

Ken Plummer's (1997 [originally 1995], 2003) term 'intimate citizenship' might be applicable to Christopher Isherwood's narrative potential within his self-reflexive storytelling. Connecting Anthony Giddens' ideas of 'life politic' (1992) and 'intimacy as democracy' (1995), Plummer (1997) tells us: 'The ideas of life politics and intimate citizenship are not the ideas of a relative moral vacuum. They lead to new sexual stories and new communities of support, championing new ways of living together' (p. 161). Through revealing details of the intimate self as a social (sexual) identity, this can be related to the idea of citizenship. Further discussed in David Bell and Jon Binnie's (2000) idea of the 'sexual citizen', this is both imbued with the transgression of queer politics and the cohesive potential of arguing for democratic social ideals, framed within the narrative of intimacy.

Consequently, Isherwood expresses the potential of his intimate self as citizen, and this connects to the larger potential of homosexual lives, challenging and reinventing ideas. Jeffrey Weeks, Brian Heaphy and Catherine Donovan (2001) suggest that: 'The moment of transgression is characterized by the constant invention and re-invention of the self, and new challenges to the inherited institutions and traditions that hitherto had excluded these new subjects' (p. 196). The performance of 'intimate citizenship' within Isherwood's work not only connects to his personal reflexive self through introspection, it is mobile and transgressive: it focuses on the narrative potential of homosexual identity through reaching out. This I would argue forms the context of new storytelling, where individuals author new visions of themselves through personal narrative engagement and reinvention.

However, the issue of self-reflexivity, homosexual identity and new storytelling provides only part of the context for the case studies which follow. An issue of equal importance undoubtedly must be the identities which are connected to the gay man or the lesbian. These may be connected to stereotypes and archetypes which are related to the imagined traits of the homosexual.

Stereotypes, archetypes and *The Green Bay Tree*

John M. Clum (2000 [originally 1992]) focuses on the issue of stereotypical traits connected to homosexual identity within drama. He points out that due to restrictions in British theatre from the Lord Chamberlain's Office between 1737 and 1968, there was a prohibition of the representation of the homosexual on stage.[2] During this time, in order to replicate homosexual identity, a repertoire of male homosexual stereotypes could be used. These included:

Effeminacy (mincing, limp wrists, lisping, flamboyant dress)

Sensitivity (moodiness, a devotion to his mother, a tendency to show emotions in an un-manly way)

Artistic talent or sensibility

Misogyny

Pederasty (... this became the stereotypical formula for homosexual relationships, with its connotations of arrested development and pernicious influence)

Foppishness

Isolation (the homosexual's fate, if he or she remained alive at the final curtain). (Clum, 2000: 77)

Through engagement with these traits or devices, playwrights would be able to produce a 'recognizable' homosexual identity. This would also occur with relation to lesbian identity; however, the performative traits would more squarely focus on masculinisation, introspection, isolation and aggression. Vito Russo (1987 [originally 1981]) explores this with regard to Hollywood cinema, exposing the stereotyping of lesbian and gay male identities. This reveals the (male) sissy and the (female) dyke, as hyperfeminised or masculinised identities, offering simplistic visions of the diversity of sexuality. Although Russo notes that gay men and lesbians were often cast as outsiders, or perpetrators and victims of murder, a central concern is not so much the typical role offered, but issues of difference and commodity in producing recognisable forms for audiences to engage with.

Such ability to 'recognise' homosexual identity undoubtedly connects to audience expectations within archetypal forms. Whilst I have argued elsewhere that a primary archetype is that of the 'sad young man' (Pullen, 2007a, inspired by Dyer, 2000), where the vision of the youthful male homosexual form is connected to unattainable beauty and melancholy, I would like to briefly examine the archetype of the homosexual as a predator in relation to the findings of John M. Clum within theatre.

This is particularly relevant as it connects to the issue of 'queer' identity, not only as a point of homosexual identification in a positive social constructionist sense, but also as a sensational conduit for representation as an entertainment form which is disavowed.

John M. Clum cites Mordaunt Shairp's play *The Green Bay Tree* (1933) as a defining moment in the covert depiction of the male homosexual on stage.[3] Although the homosexuality of the lead character Mr Dulcimer is not overtly discussed in the play, through the plot scenario and stereotypical connotations the audience is able to understand that the character has a sexual proclivity towards young men. Through the interest displayed by the Dulcimer character for a 'poor Welsh boy' called David Owen (Dulcimer is impressed with his singing ability and becomes his unofficial guardian for 15 years), *The Green Bay Tree* 'vitiates the myth of the vitalizing sexual force of the working-class man [and] declines to celebrate relationships that cross class lines that had been an integral component of early gay literature ... by linking them to pederasty' (Clum, 2000: 80).[4] The presentation of an upper-middle-class man obsessed with a working-class boy becomes the central 'problem' of the play. Although it was 'common for upper-middle-class homosexuals in this period to seek lower-class sexual partners' (Clum 2000: 79), the issue of age-based moral corruption is not openly addressed or discussed.

Shairp's creation of a potentially corrupting elder homosexual is created through allusion and association. Dulcimer's interest in floral arrangement is used to suggest that he has feminine interests and therefore possibly homosexual tendencies, and the location of the hothouse (as an environment where young plants are tended, nurtured and are grown under supervision) is used as a metaphor for containment and corruption. Consequently, we may consider the youthful David as a tender seedling that has been taken from a cold and static environment (the youth's original unsophisticated location), and planted in the warmth and nurturing of the hothouse (Dulcimer's opulent household). Consequently, as the hothouse bears the connotation of interference, untrammelled growth and exotic colourful display, by inferring that David has been metaphorically placed in this environment, the text suggests interference and corruption.

John M. Clum tells us that *The Green Bay Tree* may be considered highly influential in establishing

the stereotypical picture of the homosexual as wealthy, effete and British. He would be played in Hollywood by Charles Laughton or George Sanders. Slightly Americanised in Alfred Hitchcock's films, he would be one of the effete psychopathic killers of *Rope* (1948) and *Strangers on a Train* (1951). (Clum, 2000: 84)

In this way Mordaunt Shairp's characterisation of Mr Dulcimer would not only easily transfer from stage to screen, it would at the same time perpetuate and elevate an uneasy and pernicious homosexual archetype.

Whilst inevitably playwrights (at this time) were under the constraints of the Lord Chamberlain's Office, as were the screenwriters within Hollywood in the 1930s concerning the Hays code (see Russo, 1987), these representations became embedded as archetypes of intense engagement. I would argue that such interest in homosexual identity may be indicative of disavowal, which in Stuart Hall's (1997) terms 'is where what has been tabooed nevertheless manages to find a displaced form of representation' (p. 267). In this way homosexual identity represented as dangerous, engaging, seductive, illegal and ultimately entertaining, is eagerly consumed by audiences for use, rejecting it as the norm (or as acceptable in everyday behaviour). As Hall tells us, 'it is displaced', occurring as an object of consumption, rather than subject of understanding.

Offering further vision of this, elsewhere (Pullen, 2007a) I have discussed the issue of disavowal and displaced identity with regards to the popularity and influence of the contemporary reality television series *Queer Eye for the Straight Guy* (Bravo, 2003–present, US). This provides a prime example of the process, as the performers/presenters are represented as experts within their fields – as authorities on decor, fashion, culture, cuisine, personal grooming and partnership making, yet with an exclusively homosexual cast of presenters this is addressed in support of heterosexual clients. In other words homosexual lives are denied in service of the entertainment and pleasure of heterosexuals. In these circumstances queer identity is subordinate, and consumed by the masses.

Whilst many queer theorists (Doty, 1993; Seidman, 1996; Warner, 1993) would challenge such subordination, arguing that 'queer' identity is transgressive and revolutionary in its rejection of hierarchy suggesting identity should be fluid, my purpose here to explore the context of gay and lesbian identity with regards to coalescence and formation. In these terms queer identity is less about philosophy and idealism than structure and potential. Such opportunities, however, do not necessarily appear in the subculture and new queer cinema (Aaron, 2004; Benshoff and Griffin, 2004; Hanson, 1999), but within mainstream media contexts. In order to examine this further it is necessary to consider the emergence of queer in the context of self-reflexive storytelling, and the issue of social construction in connection with non-heterosexual identity.

Social construction, Oscar Wilde and 'queer'

Since the emergence of the homosexual as a socially constructed identity, mainly as a result of scientific enquiry in the late nineteenth century, when the causes of same-sex desire were investigated (see Katz, 1995; Plummer, 1997; Weeks, 1996, 2000), stories have abundantly circulated around non-heterosexual desire.[5] However, these stories have predominantly involved those which focus on the difference of the homosexual from the heterosexual, and the disconnection of homosexual life from the family and respectable society. The earliest stories which were told about homosexuals were those authored by medical scientists, religious authorities and the government: how same-sex desire was against normal procreation and the continuance of the family: it was rejected in theological belief and everyday worship, and as a sexual practice it was often legally punishable. This book examines the emergence of gays and lesbians as new storytellers; however before the late nineteenth century, non-heterosexuals lacked a personal social identity outside of those connected to sexual transgression or inappropriate sensibility (such as the Sodomite, or the Molly – see Sinfield, 1994). Through examination, inspection and rejection this would change: the homosexual was provided with a vivid social identity.

As Michel Foucault (1998 [originally 1976]) tells us in the groundbreaking *History of Sexuality*, Vol. 1, through responses to oppression, identification as different, and under scientific examination:

> The nineteenth-century homosexual became a personage, a past, a case history, and a childhood, in addition to a type of life, a life form, and a morphology, with an indiscreet anatomy and possibly a mysterious physiology. . . . The sodomite had been a temporary aberration; the homosexual was now a species. (p. 43)

In a shift away from the sodomite (which was connected exclusively to a sexual act and not necessarily involving same-sex desire) the homosexual now had a social form (see also Mary McIntosh, 1996 [originally 1968]).[6] Ironically those who wanted to suppress homosexual activity, through examining its existence outside procreation and normative coupling, engendered a transformation which created an identity. As David Gauntlett (2002) tells us:

> It was precisely the discourses about sexuality, in Victorian times and the early twentieth century, which sought to *suppress* certain kinds

of behaviour, which simultaneously gave an *identity* to them, and so (ironically) launched them into the public eye. (p. 121)

Through such actions the social identity of the homosexual was formed. Also new interest was placed upon stories which surrounded individuals who might be homosexual, and this was particularly evident in the public interest in Oscar Wilde (1854–1900) and the media attention given to him whilst he was on trial for sodomy and gross indecency.

Alan Sinfield (1994) in the provocatively titled *The Wilde Century* explores Wilde's connection to queer/homosexual identity, and his performative potential. Whilst Sinfield notes that 'there is no reason to suppose that Wilde either envisaged, or would have wanted, a distinctively queer identity' (p. 18), he is discussed here as an iconic presence, framed through an intense media interest at the time of his trials and later conviction.[7] This attention occurs not only with reference to Wilde's presence as a raconteur, socialite and celebrity, but also as a homosexual with a personal, if somewhat indulgent, identity. As Alan Sinfield (1994) (discussing the impact of Wilde's trials) tells us:

The trials helped to produce a major shift in perceptions of the scope of same sex passion. At that point, the entire, vaguely disconcerting nexus of effeminacy, leisure, idleness, immorality, luxury, insouciance, decadence and aestheticism, which Wilde perceived, variously, as instantiating, was transformed into a brilliantly precise image. . . . The principal twentieth-century stereotype entered our cultures: not just the homosexual, as the lawyers and medics would have it, but the queer. (p. 3)

Here Sinfield notes that Wilde's heritage is that he is attributed with engendering the emergence and personification of the homosexual as the 'queer'.[8] This marks a progression beyond the homosexual in scientific discourse (discussed above) as a newly formed but indecipherable subjective identity, and represents an objective new vision and strengthening of form, evident with 'queerness'. As Sinfield attests, this was a 'precise image' which offered agency in the ability of queer identity to capture the attention of audiences.

Furthermore, as Jeffrey Weeks (1990 [originally 1977]) attests, 'The Wilde trials were not only the most dramatic, but [they provided] a terrifying moral tale of the dangers that trailed closely behind deviant behaviour' (p. 21). In this way the trials of Oscar Wilde not only established a 'recognisable' personal identity connected to the homosexual as the 'queer', but also provided an intense point of audience interest and engagement which was imbued with the warning of deviancy, for queerness. This occurred also for lesbian identity, in the establishment of a single character within Radclyffe Hall's *Well of Loneliness* (1928) (see Sinfield, 1994 and Weeks, 1990). This vision offered press and audiences a precise stereotypical vision of discontent and difference. Oscar Wilde's and Radclyffe Hall's queer identities provided vivid moments for audience connectivity and engagement, at the same time reinforcing the difference and otherness of homosexual lives.

It is this relationship between homosexual identity and difference (or queerness), which has been the context of engagement for the self-reflexive storytellers discussed in this book. The difference of the homosexual encourages a mainstream audience's likely interest and stimulation. However, at the same time through connecting to difference it is embroiled with the physiognomy of the 'other' (see Hall, 1997), and the process of labelling deviancy. As Jeffrey Weeks (2000) tells us, the labelling of homosexuality as deviant operates in essentially two ways:

1. It helps to provide a clear-cut threshold between permissible and forbidden behaviour, preventing drift into deviant behaviour by creating the likelihood that a small step will lead to a total fall into the deviant role.
2. It serves to segregate the deviants from others, thus containing deviant practices within a relatively narrow group. (p. 56)

Subsequently, the promulgation of these labelling methods effectively operates as a mode of social control, which distances homosexuals from mainstream society and contains them within manageable groups, encouraged to be disconnected from the norm.

The analysis which follows navigates a difficult path between the homosexual as producer of their own identity, and as exhibiting a social identity for audience reception. It locates queerness as a productive new identity for the homosexual, but also this represents a sign of difference, otherness and deviancy. Therefore it is necessary to consider the performative potential of new stories of reflexive engagement in imagining how you would like to change your world, on your terms by inventing new narratives. At the same time we must recognise that homosexual identity is imagined as other, deviant and consumable, and it is often necessary to frame these voices within the constraints of dominant perspectives which sometimes re-energise old narratives.

This balance between the potential to make new space and the recognition of situation could be related to Marvin Carlson's (1996) ideas concerning the context of performance:

> Unable to move outside the operations of performance (or representation), and thus inevitably involved in its codes and reception assumptions, the contemporary performer seeking to resist, challenge, or even subvert these codes and assumptions must find some way of doing this 'from within'. (p. 172)

Herein lies the quandary of those attempting to involve themselves in 'new storytelling' within dominant media: in order to influence or progress the narrative you have to engage yourself within the storytelling histories, which you may be attempting to critique or dismantle. For Quentin Crisp this involved identifying himself as a regular citizen, and framing himself in irony, parody and personal sensibility.

Quentin Crisp and *The Naked Civil Servant*

The Naked Civil Servant (Thames Television, 1975, UK) was based on the autobiography of Quentin Crisp (1908–99), a flamboyant, openly gay author and social commentator. It was broadcast by Thames Television through the national ITV network in the United Kingdom and reached large audiences. Responses from audiences at the time suggested that homosexual identity could form an acceptable part of television entertainment, and the telling of his story possibly engendered some understanding of homosexual life. As Keith Howes (1993) notes,

> according to a survey commissioned by the Independent Broadcasting Authority, only 18 out of the 475 viewers [who] switched off [did so] because of [unsuitable] content ... [a]nd 85 per cent said that the production was 'not shocking', [while] few felt that Crisp's story 'encouraged' homosexuality. (p. 535)

The drama focused on Crisp's life in London between the 1920s and the 1970s, foregrounding his personal identity as an effeminate homosexual who was strong in character and unashamed of his identity. Being broadcast only a few years after the legalisation of male homosexual acts,[9] it may be considered as the first television drama in the United Kingdom which revealed a contented and determined homosexual character.

In a pivotal sequence in *The Naked Civil Servant* not long after Quentin Crisp has been subject to physical aggression for going out in public with the appearance of an effeminate homosexual, he tells his best friend, in a gesture of defiance: 'The world is full of [primitive people] who don't even realise that homosexuals exist. I shall go about the routine of daily living making this fact abundantly clear to them.' This is followed with a series of scenes where Crisp dressed in a feminised male business suit, complete with dyed long red hair, make-up and painted fingernails, confidently parades the streets of 1930s London. He is met with hostility, including a man at a bus stop who deliberately treads on his feet (Crisp is wearing sandals), and a woman who he has accidentally blocked in the passage of a doorway slapping his face as if in disgust. Accompanied with 1930s-style comedic music suggesting irony, these sequences foreground the courage and determination of Crisp. This is further evidenced when he is later represented as being savagely beaten by a gang of male thugs and is denied escape from this by a taxi driver who is complicit with the aggressors. Despite this Crisp daringly and ironically asserts to his assailants in modest tones 'I seem to have annoyed you gentlemen in some way?...'

The bravery of Quentin Crisp is foregrounded in *The Naked Civil Servant*, however it is presented with a defiance and steadfast dedication more in common with a political cause than an entertaining docudrama. In this way whilst Crisp's identity is often connected to his anecdotes and his entertaining philosophy, as evidenced in *The Naked Civil Servant* (Crisp, 2007 [originally 1968]) and his later publications *The Wit and Wisdom of Quentin Crisp* (1984) and *Resident Alien: the New York Diaries* (1997), his commitment is towards homosexual visibility. As he attests in *The Naked Civil Servant*: 'it is my crusade'(see Figure 2.3, revealing Crisp's dedication with audience correspondence evoking personal ideology).

I would argue that Quentin Crisp's significance is more contiguous with the gay rights movement in the United States, and in particular the discursive resonance of the Stonewall riots, than with his more readily acknowledged status as a provider of 'aphoristic witticisms' (Kettelhack, 2007). Just as the events in the Stonewall riots were headed by 'drag queens and effeminate men [who were] never in the closet' (Riviera, 1995: 66), Quentin Crisp represented a political force unashamed of his sexuality, or of his effeminate identity. This politicisation is played out in *The Naked Civil Servant* in many sequences where he is represented as defiantly resisting compliance to dominant forces. As Alan Sinfield (1994) notes, this centres on the performance of effeminacy as part of Crisp's

Figure 2.3   Quentin Crisp, depicted at his office. Photograph © Jean Harvey. All rights reserved. Used by permission. Courtesy of The Quentin Crisp Archives (crisperanto.org)

own perceptions of 'authentic' homosexual identity. In this way through Quentin Crisp performing his 'true' self, he is represented as defiant not only to heterosexual oppressors, but also to homosexual dissenters.

This is particularly evident in a sequence in *The Naked Civil Servant* where during the Second World War, after clampdowns on homosexual behaviour, Crisp is rejected by his group of friends. This occurs in a gentlemen's club frequented by homosexuals. Quentin Crisp enters the club. He is dressed in an effeminate manner with long dyed hair. All those around him appear in 'respectable' masculine formal wear. Two men are dancing together (in close embrace). One observes Quentin and remarks that they had not seen him in a while. The other responds: 'Well you don't want to be seen with her, she is a dead giveaway.' As Quentin approaches the bar and is in the process of ordering a drink, the manager of the club confronts him asking for his club membership card, and then tears it up in front of him, adding 'you are spoiling it for the others'. Crisp retorts rhetorically, 'You don't want to be a martyr to the cause?'

It is this focus on 'the cause' and 'the crusade' which signals the discursive resonance of *The Naked Civil Servant* as political. Embedded within this is also the issue of citizenship and benevolence: Quentin Crisp is represented as a worthy citizen. This occurs in the many sequences where it appears that he is selflessly helping people (or continuing relationships which would seem to favour the other party), and is particularly evident where he maintains a supporting friendship with an older Polish man who is institutionalised for many years. This may be related to Michel Foucault's (2000 [originally 1984]) idea of 'the ethic of care of the self', where he suggested that working on the 'project of the self' for the benefit of others connects not only to citizenship ideals, but also the improvement of the self in service of society. Crisp's relationship with society and his status as a good citizen is notably played out in a sequence where he is in court on trial for alleged importuning. Here not only does he defend himself, citing the authorities (the police) as untrustworthy (he had been subject to entrapment by the police), but also he presents numerous character witnesses who support him. This includes testaments from supporters (presumed heterosexual, and apparently wealthy or well educated) who in response to the court's enquiry 'do you know he is a homosexual?' describe him on separate occasions as a 'friend', 'respectable' and a 'good man'. This sets an agenda where the judge is not only impressed with these affidavits, but also believes that Crisp is telling the truth and is thereby an upstanding citizen.

The foregrounding of political dedication and valued citizen identity is the embedded theme of Crisp's performed identity within *The Naked Civil Servant*. This I would argue represents an iconic pastiche on the idea of Stonewall, reportedly heralded by drag queens and effeminate men. However in this instance it is represented by foregrounding a single vulnerable character working in isolation. Through his vulnerability, audiences read Crisp as non-confrontational. This is evident in the soliloquy at the close of his court case. He tells the court: 'The golden rule: in public places I do not speak to anyone unless they speak to me, I do not look at anyone unless they demand that I look at them. It is the only way I know of getting safely to my destination.' Consequently on the one hand Crisp is a 'queer' political agent standing up for homosexual visibility (and by implication, for gay rights), and on the other he is a non-confrontational, subjected person who (to a degree) accepts his subordinate role.

Whilst he seems not concerned with physical resistance, I would argue that Crisp maintains his identity, and his political cause, precisely through this process: the process of not physically resisting, which deflects oppressive power rather than stimulates it. As Michel Foucault (1998) suggests, in power relations there is a

> ... plurality of resistances, each of them a special case: resistances that are possible, necessary, improbable; others that are spontaneous, savage, solitary, concerted, rampant, or violent; still others that are quick to compromise, interested, or sacrificial; by definition, they can only exist in the strategic field of power relation. (p. 96)

Power relations flow in and out of arenas, spreading discursive potentials, which perpetuate certain themes and strands of authority. In the very act of directly resisting the forces of authority these are authenticated. As Alan Sinfield (1994) notes:

> Even attempts to challenge the system help to maintain it: in fact, those attempts are distinctively complicit, in so far as they help the dominant to assert and police the boundaries of the deviant and the permissible. ... Dissidence plays into the hands of containment. (p. 15)

Through Crisp not responding to challenge (failing to engage), essentially he is not dissident to social authority. However, through maintaining his aesthetic identity he subverts from within. In this way though playing the subjective homosexual, whilst appearing as the evocative 'queer', he challenges those power frames which surround him. He is subversive rather than dissident. Through subversion, playing the role of the compliant and productive citizen, which for Crisp includes volunteering to join the army (though he is denied entry because of his 'sexual perversion'), he represents himself as a willing contributor to society. His denial comes not from himself but from those who do not understand, revealing his willing spirit and potential value as a citizen.

Trial by media: Peter Wildeblood and testimony

Quentin Crisp's appearance in *The Naked Civil Servant* involved not only the representation of a trial where he is foregrounded as a worthy citizen, but also the context of the television drama (and responses to it) reiterated the idea of trial by media. As we have seen in the case of Oscar Wilde, trial within the media is a discursive framework 'resonant' with homosexual identity. Because of the illegal status (in the United Kingdom) of male homosexuality, it was inevitable that challenges to the law would be played out in legislative scenarios. Consequently I would now like to consider the issue of framing homosexual discourse within the media, and how there are strands of potential within personal storytelling which might challenge oppressive contexts. This connects not only to actual legal situations where homosexual identity is on trial within the courtroom, with the media reporting on this, but also the idea of trial within the arena of media entertainment. A discussion follows which examines Ellen DeGeneres and George Michael (discussed below) as 'tried' by the media. However, it is first important to consider the context of the legislative trial. This is particularly evident in the Montagu trials (in 1953 and 1954), relating most notably to the impact of Peter Wildeblood (1923–99), a high-profile journalist working for the *Daily Mail* at the time of his arrest, within the second Montagu trial (1954).

The Montagu trials had a significant impact on public opinion concerning the illegality of homosexual activity. These events informed the government-commissioned Wolfenden Report (HMSO, 1957) which explored the 'problems' of homosexual offences and prostitution, with a prime concern as to the possible legalisation of homosexuality, and led to the eventual change in the law in the United Kingdom. Earlier, in the United States of America, Alfred Kinsey et al.'s *Sexual Behaviour in the Human Male* (published in 1948) had revealed the existence of widespread homosexual activity.[10] Whilst this undoubtedly informed the Wolfenden Report, it was largely through the media event of the 1954 Montagu trial, and the impact of Peter Wildeblood who admitted his homosexual identity, that public attention was drawn to this, and it ultimately stimulated change.[11]

Peter Wildeblood, along with Lord Montagu and Michael Pitt-Rivers, appeared in court charged with homosexual offences, including charges of gross indecency and buggery. Their court appearance was concerned principally with producing a high-profile court case which might deter widespread homosexual activity, rather than with the specifics of their lawbreaking. As Peter Wildeblood (1955) reports in his groundbreaking book *Against the Law: the Classic Account of a Homosexual in 1950s Britain*, whilst in the United Kingdom there was evidence of a clampdown on homosexual behaviour, this was more openly reported in the foreign press. The *Sydney Morning Telegraph* published a cable (25 October 1953) from its London correspondent David Horne advising of:

A Scotland Yard plan to smash homosexuality in London .... [which originated] . . . under strong United States advice to Britain to weed out homosexuals as hopeless security risks – from government jobs. . . . The Special Branch began compiling a 'Black Book' of known perverts in influential Government jobs after the disappearance of Donald Maclean and Guy Burgess [to communist Russia], who were known to have 'pervert' [my characterisation] associates. (Cited in Wildeblood, 1955: 46)

Peter Wildeblood, arrested for homosexual offences whilst employed as a high-profile journalist about to ascend to the role of diplomatic correspondent at the *Daily Mail*, would have been considered as such a 'security risk'. However despite this, court attention would focus not on Wildeblood and his promising journalistic career as 'risk', but on his social connection to Lord Montagu and issues of sexual morality within the upper classes.

Montagu had been subject to police attention after contacting them to report that an expensive camera had been stolen from his stately home. When reporting that visiting boy scouts may have executed the crime, Montagu was questioned with regards to his possible sexual relationship with the scouts. The police 'instead of investigating the theft . . . counter-charged him with interfering with the boys' (Jivani, 1997: 111). Whilst this case was well reported, and as Peter Wildeblood alleges, Montagu's 'passport had been altered [by the police to discredit an alibi and] prove that he was a liar' (Wildeblood: 1955: 50), it would be the second case (involving Wildeblood) which was conclusive. In this case Montagu, Wildeblood and Michael Pitt-Rivers were all found guilty. Montagu was sentenced to one year, with Wildeblood and Pitt-Rivers receiving 18 months each.

Whilst the allegations commenced with air force officials discovering love letters written by Peter Wildeblood to an airman called Edward McNally which were found in the serviceman's possession, it was a connection to Lord Montagu which stimulated the investigation. Wildeblood and McNally along with John Reynolds (who was a friend of McNally from the air force) and Michael Pitt-Rivers (who was a cousin of Lord Montagu) had attended a weekend vacation as the guests of Lord Montagu. Details in the love letters (including those written by Montagu to Airman Reynolds) suggested to the police that illegal sexual activity may have taken place at the weekend vacation. This provided the ideal opportunity for an example case to deter homosexual behaviour (as discussed above). However, it would be the interest in the exploits of the men which would engage those in the courtroom and the press, suggesting a calculated performance involving subjugation and disavowal. As Jeffrey Weeks (1990) tells us:

> The prosecution offered an amazing display of prejudice and malice – and a careful loading of dice. A small party attended by all three was turned, in the prosecution's vivid imaginings, into a wild orgy; a meal of simple food and cider was turned into luxury food and champagne. . . . What emerged in this, as in other trials in the period, was the attempt to sustain a stereotype of male homosexuals as decadent, corrupt, effete and effeminate. And this endeavour was aided by the popular press. (pp. 161–2)

In this way, the courts and the popular press expressed a sensationalist interest in the case, promulgating known stereotypes. This I would argue was aided by the likely knowledge that the men were homosexuals from suspicions in the first Montagu case, and in some way the audience enjoyed the tension being played out. However in the early stages of the trial, possibly to avoid punishment, humiliation and incarceration, all those charged denied a homosexual identity.

Nevertheless as the trial developed there was a change in focus, drawing attention to more meaningful social contexts of homosexual identity. This largely occurred in the eventual admission of Peter Wildeblood that he was indeed a homosexual. In this way Wildeblood, as evidenced in his book, rejected his imposed identification with shame, and argued for the acceptance of homosexuals, and the changing of the law. As Wildeblood (1955) argues, making connections with mainstream society, those who object to homosexual identity 'will argue that [we] are by nature vicious and depraved, because they cannot know that [our community], branded by them as "immoral", has an austere and strict morality of its own' (p. 5). Through drawing attention to homosexual identity with regard to strength and morality, Wildeblood set an agenda which would attempt to distance the homosexual from stereotypical connotations such as indulgence and ephemera. He reframed the context of homosexual lives, laying a pathway towards not only arguing for acceptance, but also more importantly expecting equality.[12]

Whilst inevitably Peter Wildeblood's impact could be argued to have influenced a wide range of further homosexual identity performances rejecting shame and leading to contemporary attitudes, the discussion continues, foregrounding an expectation of equality over acceptance and

Figure 2.4   A confident Ellen DeGeneres foregrounded on the cover of *The Advocate* (25 September 2001). Image courtesy *The Advocate* and LPI Media Inc.

the context of trial by media. Consequently, the following case studies on Ellen DeGeneres and George Michael follow this strand, providing contemporary resonances to Wildeblood's confessional legacy.

Ellen DeGeneres and George Michael: therapy and subversion

Ellen DeGeneres was a highly successful television actor, whose sitcom *Ellen* (ABC, 1994–98, US) was a primetime hit in the United States of America.[13] On 30 April 1997, a special episode of *Ellen* was broadcast in the United States of America to a massive audience of over 36 million people (Nielsen Media Research, cited in Kiska, 1997), also reaching large audiences in the United Kingdom (when it was broadcast in the following year).[14] Within this not only did the fictional character of Ellen come out as lesbian in the sitcom narrative, but also audiences identified with the personal story of Ellen DeGeneres herself who was also revealing her sexuality (see Figure 2.4).

George Michael was an international popular singer when on 7 April 1998 he was arrested for an alleged incident that had occurred in a public toilet in the Will Rogers Park in Los Angeles, 'after an undercover officer on a crime suppression detail allegedly saw him engaging in a lewd act' (Webb, 1998).[15] As news gradually unfolded, the media in the United States and the United Kingdom speculated as to the potential damage to his career.

These two seemingly disparate events are discussed here for their connection to iconic gay identity performance, and the significance they had in reforming the media's interest in the representation of homosexuals. Whilst many would cite the advent of *Queer as Folk* (the original UK version and its US adaptation) as a defining moment which would stimulate change in the media (and particularly in dramatic representations),[16] the different performative events of Ellen DeGeneres and George Michael not only predated this, but also they were played out to far larger audiences as media spectacle. I argue that these stimulated the creation of new space for gay and lesbian identity within media representations. As discussed above, these events echoed the idea of 'trial by media' as exhibited with reference to Peter Wildeblood (discussed above); however, rather than centred on issues of legislation they were discursive trials of homosexual identity played out within the media.[17]

Such a media spectacle involved for the producers of *Ellen* the planning and staging of the event almost a year prior to its broadcast. This was partly due to rumours spreading within the industry as to whether Ellen DeGeneres was actually gay and if so, would she come out in real life or just as her character within the series. Also careful negotiation and planning were no doubt necessary, both concerning the form of the script written for the 'Puppy Episode' (a covert name for the coming-out episode),[18] and discussions with ABC's parent company Disney as to whether the coming-out episode could actually be made. Attention and conflict circulated around the promotion given to the series, which was of particular concern to Christian evangelists petitioning the production company ABC and the parent company Disney. Many shareholders and religious authorities wanted to prohibit Ellen's coming out, for not reflecting the family ethos of the Disney corporation and failing to reflect dominant Christian values. This was evident in condemnations of ABC, Ellen DeGeneres and the 'Puppy Episode': 'First Assembly of God pastor Van Venter declared that homosexuality was "demonic" [suggesting that] the show [was] "part of a diabolical plan to drag down society"' (Tracy, 1999: 207). Also Reverend Jerry Falwell simply branded her 'Ellen Degenerate'. Such attention formed a media circus, engendering a trial of

DeGeneres and of homosexual identity. However, such attention stimulated public interest in the event, forming resistant discursive space where DeGeneres could respond to her critics.

Similarly, attention drawn towards George Michael's arrest involved subjugation. This took the form of a media trial by the press in the United States, discussing reasons why he would have engaged in such irresponsible behaviour. The popular press imagined that his actions would impact on his status. In the United Kingdom the tabloid newspaper *The Sun* 'playfully' parodied one of George's most famous hits *Wake Me Up Before You Go Go* (1984) on its front page (9 April 1998). The page carried a seemingly dejected image of George as if he was being pursued, accompanied with a banner headline 'Zip Me Up Before You Go Go', implying that his career was over.

Such attention drawn towards both Ellen DeGeneres and George Michael between 1997 and 1998 (in entirely different circumstances), offered opportunities for subversion and dissidence. DeGeneres had challenged mainstream sensibilities as to what was appropriate content for primetime audiences, placing lesbian identity within the frame; Michael had transgressed what may have been considered as normative (homo) sexual behaviour. These situations, DeGeneres' involving a highly organised strategy, and Michael's reflecting a passing moment of personal indulgence, I argue, highly impacted on the discursive possibilities for lesbians and gay men. In order to explore this further I will first examine Ellen DeGeneres' strategic coming out, then look at George Michael's inadvertent exposure.

Two weeks prior to the broadcast of Ellen DeGeneres' coming-out episode of *Ellen*, she had appeared on the front cover of *Time Magazine* represented in a casual stance affirming in the headline 'Yep, I'm Gay!'[19] Here she capitalised on the media attention, expressing her personal self in an intimate performance. Similarly in the 'Puppy Episode' itself, at the point where DeGeneres affirms her sexuality, it appears that this is therapeutic for her. As Laura Dern (co-star with Ellen in the coming-out scene) reports in the *Real Ellen Story* (Channel 4, 1998, UK) (a documentary made about the event): 'I was looking into her eyes and I was trying to hold on to her, and she was starting to shake. I could feel in her body the need to just let something go that been in her for years.'

Clearly DeGeneres' participation in the project, including the media attention and performing in the episode itself, offered a glimpse of her personal life which she openly expressed. This I would argue was not only self-therapeutic for DeGeneres, but also audiences' engagement with this was enabling. Similar to Mimi White's (1992) discussion on 'therapeutic discourse', this may be considered as 'a particular strategy of discourse; [which generates] narrative by setting [into] place a sequence of symbolic interpersonal exchanges' (White, 1992: 12). Within the media, we may view the framing of emotion between the 'therapist' and the 'patient' as a transaction which offers the audience, through witness, opportunities for personal reflection and empowerment.

The idea of therapeutic discourse is literally played in the 'Puppy Episode' of *Ellen*, in a sequence where DeGeneres consults a therapist. Here the identity of the therapist played by Oprah Winfrey (celebrated talk show host) is foregrounded. This allows not only for the audience to consider the support of DeGeneres by a high-profile celebrity, and the likelihood that the engagement between them is more of a public inter-view than a fictional staging, but also the identity of Winfrey as one of the most powerful black women in America offers a resonance which connects black and gay civil rights. This discursive thread is evident in the dialogue of the therapy session:

Ellen   Society has a pretty big problem with [gay identity]. . . . Do you think I want to be discriminated against? Do you think I want people to call me names to my face? To have people commit hate-crimes against you just because you're not like them?

Oprah   (cutting in) To have separate bathrooms and separate water-fountains, sit at the back of the bus.

Ellen   Oh Man. Do we have to use separate water-fountains?

(Ellen and Oprah look at each other knowingly.)

Through DeGeneres making a humorous aside about separate bath-rooms and sitting on the back of the bus, she makes an allusion to oppression seen in the emergence of the black civil rights cause. This could also be read as specifically relating the significance of DeGeneres to that of Rosa Parks, who was attributed with sparking momentum in the black civil rights movement when she refused to give up her seat on a bus (in 1955). Here it is suggested that DeGeneres is a catalyst for change, using humour and subliminal associations in the narrative construction.

This is most notable in the sequence where Ellen recalls a dream to the therapist, presented purely through visual representation. This scene fea-tures Ellen on a shopping trip at a supermarket, with the camera statically fixed upon her uneasy expression and awkward movements, suggesting a focus on her 'otherness'. Whilst she is there, members of staff and customers make open references to Ellen's sexuality:

Ellen   How much are those melons?

Salesman   We're running a special for lesbians this week you might want to stock up.

Announcement   Attention shoppers. Red tag special in aisle 2, gay woman in aisle 5. (Ellen looks up and sees herself in aisle 5.)

Saleswoman   (presenting new chocolate bars for sale) For the woman on the go, or in the closet.

Sign at sales checkout   10 lesbians or less. (Allusion to 10 items or less.)

Cashier   That will be lesbian 29.

Ellen   Pardon.

Cashier   (repeating) $11.29.

Salesman   (to Ellen) Do you want some help loading that into your gay car?

Ellen   (now awake in the presence of the therapist) Do you think that dream means anything?

Here parodying the idea of 'dream work', where a therapist in discussion with the patient explores the possible meanings of a dream and renders this less disturbing, DeGeneres subverts the therapist's role, by expressing self-knowledge. Such self-confidence presented through humour extends not only to reading subliminal signs, but also to the direct expression of political needs and challenging ideas.

Through irony, parody and political association, Ellen DeGeneres with her supporting 'star-studded' cast subverted normative everyday televisual situation comedy forms, thereby projecting subaltern discourse as a central focus within the mainstream. Such challenge to authority also occurs reaching out to higher levels of authoritative engagement, and is notably evidenced in the association made between Ellen DeGeneres and American president Bill Clinton. Four days before the broadcast of the 'Puppy Episode' at the White House Correspondents' Dinner (26 April 1997) she was officially pictured in the company of Clinton with her (then) girlfriend Anne Heche. This powerful image of a lesbian couple socialising with the American president challenges normative iconic ideas surrounding homosexuality as disempowered, and supports the citizen enfranchisement of sexual outsiders. Whilst the popular press reported variously on the event (with some praising, and some demeaning, the connection), Clinton (at the event) advised her that he 'admired her' for her groundbreaking work.[20] DeGeneres placed herself within the frame of political possibility, questioning citizenship potentials.[21]

George Michael in response to his arrest and indictment in the press, also questioned the subjugated citizenship status of gay men and women in relation to authority. This is primarily evident in his composition of the song *Outside* (1998), and his performance within the accompanying promotional video where he employed irony, parody and subversion. The lyrics parody the event of his arrest in the public toilets, and the idea of coming out, suggesting that to go 'outside' is to offer freedom of sexual expression and strengthens personal identity. Also the video narrative expresses self-effacement and inversion. Here Michael is dressed as an American police officer, performing his song within the vicinity of a public toilet. In this scenario we are presented with a parody of his arrest, foregrounding a heterosexual scenario where an older man is arrested for attempting to make love to an attractive woman by an elderly female police officer (Michael's arresting officer was a young man). This is impacted with a swift transformation of the dingy public toilet into a makeshift glitter-ball disco, with the urinals themselves covered with glitter and mirrors, showcasing George Michael and various dancers performing there. Through parodying his arrest and blending aspects of his earlier 1980s career (circa *Wake Me Up Before You Go Go* – discussed above), he challenges the legislative authorities who had subjugated him. He constructs a vision which offers a kind of Brechtian distantiation (see Willett, 1964), where our relationship to the original event is framed and reinterpreted in a manner which, while it is distanced from realism, does contain political questions and suggests a move to action. Also he employs a carnivalesque inversion (Bakhtin, 1994), where those who are in power are displaced, and those who are subjugated represent authority. Through such iconic playfulness, George Michael reinterprets the events of his arrest, making it a commodity not only for his monetary reward in the sales he would gain, but also as a challenge to authority (see Figure 2.5, where on the front cover of *The Advocate* the iconography of 'the closet' is similarly parodied).

Ultimately through his willingness to expose and parody the intimate details of his arrest, he constructs an identity which rejects shame.

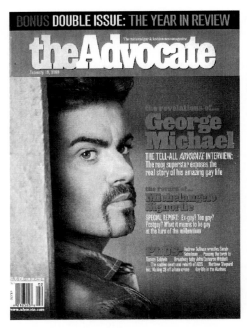

Figure 2.5   George Michael appearing on the cover of *The Advocate* (19 January, 1999), parodying his coming out (after a police arrest for 'lewd behavior'). Image courtesy of *The Advocate* and LPI Media Inc.

Marking a distance from the numerous male homosexuals who were arrested for illegal sexual encounters in the United Kingdom at the time of the Montagu trials (discussed above) (and those in the United States – see Clendinen and Nagourney, 1999), George Michael transforms the image of the shamed male homosexual. He presents a knowingness, not only drawing comparisons with the past which reveal progression and change, but also personally refocusing historical legislative connotations which parody the idea of arrest and culpability. George Michael used the opportunity of media attention for identity reconstruction, relating himself within the context of gay and lesbian lives. Such potential and ultimate self-confidence were played out in the song and the video of *Outside*, and showcased in the United Kingdom on a primetime television talk show dedicated to him.

George Michael's appearance on the *Parkinson* show (transmitted on BBC1 on 5 December 1998) was an unprecedented success, bolstering his threatened career, and propelling homosexual discourse within the mainstream. At the close of the interview, such confidence is framed with Michael humorously philosophising, 'Now, I never even think about masturbation before calling my lawyer.' Audience response to this event can be monitored not only through the fact that the following week the 'sales of his album *Ladies And Gentlemen* . . . soared by 70%, . . . according to [his] record label Sony',[22] but also that the rapturous studio response was echoed by the popular press. Whilst they had earlier condemned him (see the reference to *The Sun* above), he was now vaunted as an iconic popular hero:

> *The Mirror*: Rarely has a star of such stature opened his heart in such a candid way.
>
> *The Sun:* George Michael is more than a rock star; he is a spokesman for his generation. (Ellen, 1999)

Such transformation of media status is notable as at the time of his arrest he had spoken exclusively to CNN, hoping to pre-empt 'what he feared would be a slew of sensational and speculative tabloid reports in his native England' (CNN, 1998). Whilst this did happen initially, after the impact of the *Parkinson* interview, a transformation occurred. I argue that his metamorphosis from imagined sexual deviant to iconic leader was enabled not only through his strategies of parody, irony and subversion in *Outside* (discussed above), but also through his openness to audiences, playing out therapeutic scenarios in a similar manner to Ellen DeGeneres (see above).

George Michael employs this strategy in the *Parkinson* interview where he offers personal transparency. Recalling details of the event that led to his arrest, he tells us: 'I think it was the danger of the situation that must have compelled me to do it . . . I won't even say it was the first time it ever happened . . . I've put myself in that position before and I can only apologise.' Also at the time of the arrest rather than deny reports or hide away from the media, he carried on as normal, even going out for dinner (as he usually did) the next evening with his partner, despite the pursuit of the press. Michael presents himself as someone with nothing to hide, offering closeness to the audience. This is particularly evident in the choice of music used to introduce George Michael on *Parkinson* with the lyrics 'If you don't know me by now, you will never never know me at all.' The suggestion is that the audience have complicity with him, and are considered as confidants who support his position.

Such engagement with the audience may be considered as represent-ing therapeutic discourse (Mimi White, 1992 – discussed above), and is primarily evident where (in the manner of a therapy session) comparisons are made in terms of 'before' and 'after'. George Michael delivers his confession relating events that occurred in the Will Rogers Park to events that occurred before and after this. Michael uses these temporal contrasts to relate a process of change or evolution within his life. Mimi White (1992) considers this analytical process as 'that was then; this is now' (p. 145), and how through continually referencing change and contrast audiences empathise with your progress. Audiences witness Michael's discussion of his early career when he had concealed his sexuality, he then confides how lately he has come to terms with it. Also audiences potentially engaged with the details of his illegal sexual digression, and how since his arrest whilst being subject to contentious media exposure, this had actually offered him positive potential. Audiences potentially witness Michael's expressions of coming to terms, and his learning about the self.

Thus 'therapeutic discourse' is represented in confessional form, which possesses agency. As Michel Foucault (1998) argues, confession is

> a ritual that unfolds within a power relationship, for one does not confess without the presence (or virtual presence) of a partner who is not simply the interlocutor but the authority who requires the confession, prescribes and appreciates it, and intervenes in order to judge, punish, forgive, console and reconcile. (p. 61)

Through audiences witnessing confessional processes, they engage in a power dynamic. This involves not only a focus on George Michael as one who confesses and Michael Parkinson as interviewer, but also the potential for audience members to become part of this process as 'authorities' who require the confession. This engenders a matrix of power possibilities, which in Foucaultian terms allows all those involved to possess discursive agency. Such agency was primarily executed by George Michael, who connected with audiences through his 'intimate citizenship' (Plummer, 1997, 2003), thereby offering himself as both an equal citizen in terms of revealing his personal self, and as a leading citizen in prescribing ways forward for gay identity beyond shame.

The performances of Ellen DeGeneres and George Michael created impact, challenging archetypes and stereotypes connected to gay and lesbian life. This, I argue, stimulated changes in discursive possibilities, leading to the production of many new opportunities of representation in television, film and new media. This not only challenged representational histories, but also offered opportunities for social agency foregrounding new life chances. In these terms the audiences of George Michael and Ellen DeGeneres were stimulated with new, confident visions of gay and lesbian identity. This is particularly evident in the case of Ellen DeGeneres, where many people were inspired by her story and decided to 'come out' themselves,[23] and some were even dissuaded from suicide (Capsuto, 2000).

Ellen DeGeneres and George Michael follow an emerging tradition of self-reflexive storytelling, which (I argue in this book) offers a new dialogue for lesbians and gay men. This may be traced across diverse genres and media, representing new pathways not formed by specific engines of change, but by personal reflections on selfhood which coalesce and offer change.

Conclusion

This chapter has foregrounded gay identity in connection with the issues of intimacy, self-reflexivity and ultimately the potential of performativity within storytelling and discursive expression. This, I argue, offers a potential for 'new storytelling', where lesbians and gay men provide new narratives which extend from themselves, and these are directed to large audiences within the media. Rather than focusing on stories which are inspired by others, the narrative drive extends from the self and is concerned with issues of personal identity fulfilment. Furthermore, as new stories authored or performed by self-identified homosexuals, they are indicative of new confidences since the emergence of homosexual social identity.

Whilst I have not applied a strictly historical approach, I have defined key moments of engagement which are related to chronology and progression. In this way I have argued that Christopher Isherwood stimulated new expressions in self-reflexive storytelling, largely connected to his creative production in autobiographical fiction. Through placing himself within the fictional frame, this not only conflates factual and fictional forms, but also challenges dominant voices of authority. Isherwood as an openly gay man expressed his personal self, and thereby stimulated the emergence of the confident homosexual as observer and narrative performer.

Whilst the Wilde and the Montagu trials have offered a subjective view of queer and homosexual life as contained within legislative and oppressive scenarios, they also offer the potential for identity framing. In this way the later performances of Quentin Crisp, Ellen DeGeneres and George Michael are connected more for their exploration of trial by

. media and how this can offer a discursive focus and performative potential in the progression of new storytelling ideas, rather than negative and punishment attention for rule breaking.

From Peter Wildeblood admitting his homosexual identity within the Montagu trial, to George Michael expressing his identity without shame in his response to arrest and trial, media focus has been intensely interested in homosexual social performers. Here attention is drawn to the periphery of dominant identity where homosexual identity is usually placed, and new foci reflect new visions of change for lesbians and gay men. I have argued that such potential for change is not enabled through confrontational dissident engagement, but through subversion from within. This involves the projection of recognisability and the value of citizenship: Crisp, DeGeneres and Michael appear as outsiders, but in essence they are 'intimate citizens' (Plummer, 1997, 2003). Through the display of their intimate selves, making connections to their citizenship potential, they present themselves as powerful forces for change.

This is ultimately attributed to the audience's engagement with individuals who possess discursive agency, rather than the digestion of real social facts or quantitative data. As evidenced in the gradual shift in public perception leading to the legalisation of male homosexuality in the United Kingdom after the Montagu trials, this was largely stimulated by individuals who testified in court that they were homosexual (notably such as Peter Wildeblood – discussed above) rather than the presentation of calculable homosexual social evidence, as evidenced in the work of Kinsey (in 1948 – discussed above).

This focus on individual discursive potential is the primary drive in what I term as new storytelling. Storytellers in these terms inevitably involve themselves in writing history, and define themselves in relation to dominant historical forms. For gay identity, negotiating histories that have been subjugated or that have ignored real social lives becomes an axis of engagement and a tributary of potential, in attempting to confront or reform historical ideas. The next chapter considers the confrontation of issues such as historical denial and histories of oppression, which for the self-reflexive storyteller engenders scope for potential change. This becomes an opportunity for challenge to authority, at the same time questioning the fixity of gay and lesbian identity forms.

3
Community, History and Transformation

Introduction

Tony Kushner, award-winning playwright and political activist, tells us in the documentary *Wrestling with Angels* (Freida Lee Mock, 2006, US): 'As far as I am concerned it's an ethical obligation to look for hope, it's an ethical obligation not to despair. If you look there is always a possibility of finding where action can change the course of things.' Evoking the spirit of his groundbreaking play *Angels in America* (HBO, 2003, US) (discussed below), Kushner affirms his positive stance in suggesting the agency that ordinary people may possess to influence their social environments (see Figure 3.1). In *Angels* Kushner worked towards changing the course of life through exploring the significance of AIDS in relation to the connectedness of minority identities, negated within President Ronald Reagan's America. Such a focus on community ideals and historical settings renders *Angels in America* a central site of investigation, which evokes not only the agency of producers such as Kushner, but also stimulates audiences' engagement to political arenas. Whilst this book explores fictional and factual forms, a consistent point within this is the social agency of the producer, the performer and the audience. This foregrounds transgressive scenarios where dominant and oppressive identity is challenged. As Kushner affirms, these are opportunities for action and change, grounding the self in the political.

Consequently this chapter explores the political agency of those involved in production, examining issues concerning the definition of community and contexts of history. At the same time I foreground the possibility of transformation, and issues of postmodernity in narrative construction. This I argue occurs where self-reflexive storytellers progress narrative ideas, and extend boundary potentials. I explore the issue of

Figure 3.1   Tony Kushner, in a moment of introspection. Image courtesy of Tony Kushner

storytelling, relating the context of the audience and community as central in discursive reproduction. I argue that new storytellers not only produce self-reflexive narratives of personal desire, but also that they engage with selected textual forms and attempt to reinvent them. This is particularly relevant for gay men and lesbians in connection to normative community and dominant history: often they are situated at the periphery. However, through the potential of new storytelling, gay men and lesbians as producers, performers and audiences exhibit agency in the progression of community and historical ideals.

To explore these ideas this chapter presents various case studies which cross the producer/performer and audience/community divide, making connections within self-agency and reflexive storytelling. Subsequently within various performative and identification contexts, this chapter explores the discursive potential of community and historical ideals, relating the social agency of gay men and lesbians involved in media production and performance as new storytellers.

The film *Victim* (Basil Dearden, 1961, UK) is discussed, with relation to the agency of actor Dirk Bogarde (1921–99), who whilst he did not affirm that he was gay, personally identified with homosexual narratives, and attempted to reform ideas (furthermore his family willingly present him as a valued icon in the canon of gay men – discussed below). The significance of the television series *Tales of the City* (Channel 4 for PBS, 1993, UK and US) is related to the personal vision of community as expressed by journalist and author Armistead Maupin, making connections to the recent past. The impact of celebrated novelist Sarah Waters is examined, exploring *Tipping the Velvet* (BBC 2, 2002, UK) and *Fingersmith* (BBC 2, 2005, UK), which I argue are historical reformations foregrounding contemporary lesbian ideals. The groundbreaking work of Tony Kushner is discussed, particularly in relation to the play and television event of *Angels in America* (discussed briefly above). This I suggest offers a complex dynamic between conformity, rebellion and transgression. These case studies examine the work of a diverse range of people whose ideas coalesce, representing new community through contextualising historical expressions.

It is first necessary to examine the context of gay and lesbian community, with regard to the potential of discourse and storytelling. Furthermore, issues of history and postmodernity inform narrative potentials for transgressive and subversive storytellers. I argue that the media offer a discursive arena through which debates are played out (see Pullen, 2007a). At the same time ownership of community and its historical forms inevitably is a site of contention and political desire.

The discursive gay community

Jeffrey Weeks (2000) tells us that:

> The idea of a sexual community may be fiction, but it is a necessary fiction: an imagined community, an invented tradition which enables and empowers. It provides the context for the articulation of identity, the vocabulary of values through which ways of life can be developed. (p. 192)

The social constructionist possibilities of the 'imagined (gay) community' (see Anderson, 1983; Bauman, 1992; Pullen, 2007a) offers a context of engagement which is both recognisable to its self-appointed members and to those who are outside. The concept of the discursive gay community offers personal and social recognition yet may be disconnected from the real gay community.

Therefore whilst John D'Emilio (1983) tells us that during the early part of the twentieth century 'Gradually a subculture of gay men and women was evolving in American cities that would help to create a collective consciousness among its participants and strengthen their sense of identification with a group' (p. 13), this forms more of a discursive building block and the imagination of a homeland, rather than the representation of a solid state of existence. Although various historians and theorists such as Simon LeVay and Elisabeth Nonas (1995) and Brett Beemyn (1997), have further contextualised the historical and contemporary emergences of gay communities, the communities explored are more incidences of discursive potential than sustainable physical formations. This is not to say that real gay communities within San Francisco, New York, Toronto, Sydney or Manchester are not necessarily powerful locations of potential, but I argue that gay community is a context of engagement between diverse individuals whose lives are largely disconnected. However, such coalition between those who do not necessarily live in close proximity and are not necessarily connected, is problematic with relation to power potential and the dispersal of identity.

Although we may not consider gay men and lesbians strictly as a diaspora (because there is no real original terrain), in terms of identity subjection they may similarly have been dispersed from their psychological heartland (through parental, familial and societal rejection). Diasporic identification processes are highly relevant for gay men and lesbians. They may consider San Francisco, Toronto or Manchester, etc. as a metaphorical homeland, yet the majority are geographically separated from these areas. The evident dispersal of gay identity within dominant communities, suggesting wide encompassing spread yet minimal social force, is emblematic also of those who are distanced from larger groups and denied access to power. As Paul Gilroy (1997) affirms, 'Diaspora identification exists outside of, and sometimes in opposition to, the political forms and codes of modern citizenship' (p. 329), and in doing so fails to work within modern social (state-based) discourses of engagement. Whilst in some countries such as the United Kingdom, Spain, Canada and (parts of) the United States of America, gay men and lesbians are moving towards enfranchised citizenship (for example, with the advent of civil partnerships and same-sex marriage), there remains a lack of institutional engagement, and full citizenship potential is denied.[1] Although the discursive potential of the imagined gay community is enabling, it is distanced from real sites of power.

Michel Foucault's model of power suggests that a discursive disenfranchised community identity may possess agency. Foucault (1998 [originally 1976]) affirms that:

> Power is everywhere; not because it embraces everything, but because it comes from everywhere ... power is not an institution, and not a

structure; neither is it a certain strength we are endowed with; it is the name that one attributes to a complex strategical situation in a particular society. (p. 93)

Instead of dominant groups exclusively having access to power, there is a potential for subjugated groups and individuals to be involved in power relations. Furthermore, those who are subjugated or possess diasporic identification may be united though shared experience and discursive impetus.

However as I have discussed elsewhere (Pullen, 2007a), whilst Foucault's model of power is useful, it fails to fully recognise the over-arching power of dominant hierarchies, which contribute to identity formation and its potentials. As Nancy Fraser (1989) explains, while '[Foucault's] modern account of power is both politically engaged and normatively neutral [a]t the same time he is unclear as to whether he suspends normative notions or only the liberal norms of legitimacy and illegitimacy' (p. 19). Normative notions such as constraints and oppressions inevitably impinge on the progress of discursive power. Consequently rather than power having no structure, it inevitably involves strategies of engagement which take shape, stemming and accelerating the flow of power. This may involve a degree of organisation and influence within the power dynamic.

Anthony Giddens (1995 [originally 1992]) elucidates this further. He suggests that Foucault's model of power should be adapted and termed as 'institutional reflexivity'. This accommodates the potential for social action which may be coalescent, rather than purely free-flowing (p. 28), he tells us:

> Without denying its connectedness to power, we should see the phenomenon rather as one of *institutional reflexivity* and constantly in motion. It is institutional, because it is a basic structuring element of social activity in modern settings. It is reflexive in the sense that terms introduced to describe social life routinely enter and transform it – not as a mechanical process, not necessarily in a controlled way, but because they become part of the frames of action which individuals or groups adopt. (p. 28)

Giddens focuses on the possible limitations of Foucault's ideas, suggesting that his power model should be modified to accommodate the concept of 'frames of action', where power is mobilized in organisations and it is at times cohesive, and not necessarily totally free-flowing.

This hypothesis is useful in considering the opportunity of the imagined gay community, and the self-reflexive potential of new storytellers within this. Giddens' model accommodates the potential of the self and the contexts of identity production in coalescence. In this way the social actions of individuals working together may influence institutions through discursive performativity. The emergence of civil partnerships (United Kingdom) and same-sex marriage (Spain) would be a prime example of this, revealing discursive power which expresses the potential of the gay community to authenticate citizenship equality.

However, concepts of gay citizenship and community are various. There are many diverse racial and sexual identities, and polyvalent personal expectations and political desires. Whilst we may argue that discursive formations have produced change, those representing the community do not necessarily reflect the same ideas or mobilise similar strategies.

This is particularly evident in the various factions representing the gay community. In the broadest sense there are those who may be termed as assimilationists, who argue on a rights-based strategy for the equality of gay men and lesbians. These focus on the similarity of gay and lesbian life to everyday dominant heterosexual identity. There are also those who may be termed as pluralists, who argue that 'power is not concentrated in the hands of any one element in society; it is widely distributed among a host of competing groups' (Rimmerman, 2002: 4). In essence cultural commentators such as Andrew Sullivan (1995) and Bruce Bawer (1993) could be termed as assimilationists. Sullivan argues that gay and lesbian identities are already assimilated in their connection to straight families and friends, and are 'part of America' (Sullivan, cited in Vorlicky, 1998: 94). Alternatively, pluralists such as Michael Warner (1993) and Steven Seidman (1996) focus on the potential of queer identity, arguing that diversity is an important component of social structures, and this may enable change. Assimilationists and pluralists may have similar goals, such as working towards the liberty of sexual outsiders; however, they are conflicted in terms of situating identity.[2]

A central tenet of the pluralist and queer approach is that 'instead of viewing identity as something an individual learns or accomplishes or fashions as a positive basis for self-evaluation and politics' (Seidman, 1996: 19), potential for change may be enabled through various collaborations and structures of engagement. At the same time a pluralistic view of homosexual identity may be considered as a 'non-unitary, unstable ... and an ongoing site of social and political conflict' (Seidman, 1996: 19). This instability relates not only to the divided nature of homosexual identity in diverse political ideologies, but also to the knowledge that gay community does not consist of any specific identified social form. Whilst assimilationists may speak of an imagined connection to dominant ideas of heterosexual identity, this suggests a foregrounding of white mainstream middle-class sensibilities (of Western industrial societies) in the priorities expressed. Alternatively a pluralist approach might be more accommodating to the diversity of gay and lesbian ethnic and sexual identity, as these are often distanced from mainstream contexts of engagement.

The issue of ethnic diversity and its situation within concepts of gay community is contentious. Marlon Riggs (1957–94) highlighted the invisibility of black identity within dominant concepts of gay community. In the documentary *Tongues Untied* (see Pullen, 2007a) named after the poem of the same name, he tells us (concerning his early coming out, and his life in San Francisco):

> Pretended not to notice the absence of black images in this new gay life, in book stores, poster shops, film festivals, even in my own fantasies. . . . In this great gay Mecca, I was the invisible man, I had no shadow, no substance, no place, no history, no reflection. (Riggs, 1991: 202)

Riggs focuses on the disconnection felt by black men within the mainstream gay community, and its media images. He foregrounds a sense of worthlessness, attesting that histories written about the gay community fail to integrate the wide ethnic diversity of citizens within this. Such focus on the construction of histories connected to the gay community reveals the power dynamics involved in supporting certain identities or preferred stories.

As José Munoz (1999) tells us concerning the issue of 'performing disidentifications' and 'queers of colour', there are diverse queer identities who have been 'locked out of the halls of representation' (p. 1). In challenging their 'disidentified' status through public social performance they may engender change. This I would argue happens as much within the gay community itself in power struggles addressing the issue of visibility, as it does outside, revealing the coalescence of the community and evidence of working together. As Munoz states, 'the term *identities-in-difference* is a highly effective term for categorising' (p. 6) the multivalent identity struggles which circulate within and without the gay community. This reveals the gay community as both a contentious site of struggle which needs to resolve internal conflicts, and also a powerful

. axis of engagement which offers the provision of external power. This involves both fragmentation and cohesion.

Issues of connection and disconnection are also evident in examining the context of modern history and the storytelling of gay identity. In history we witness preferred stories of engagement, often rejecting subaltern identity forms.

History, the unified subject and postmodernity

Modern history involves preferred storytelling, revealing the problematic nature of the 'unified subject' within this. Histories offer a teleological view in the presentation of narratives as progressing in a linear fashion, with one (unified) subject focus leading to specific dominant outcomes and stories. For national identity this involves the evocation of authentic history, imagined citizenship ideals, the context of the homeland, dominant society and cultural iconography. In the United States this might involve a unified subject relating to the early years of colonisation, the trials and achievements of the pioneers who settled the land, and the dominant language of the American constitution. This might appear to be all-empowering to the American nation, but it often reflects the cultural domain of early white citizens and the heterosexual majority. Similarly for the gay community the unified subject may involve a historical trajectory representing white, middle-class male homosexuals who established the early gay rights movement, ignoring diverse gender and cultural potentials. Furthermore, dominant histories in Western culture can often ignore or malign subaltern histories, such as the citizenship potential and storytelling of minorities (including gay men and lesbians).

Michel Foucault's ideas are helpful here in exposing the problematic nature of progressing history through a unified subject. In his concept of 'archaeology and the history of ideas' (Foucault, 1989: 151), Foucault explores the writing of modern history and its 'instrumental role in the colonising process [which] is unable to provide a perspective that offers a useful critique of colonisation' (Danaher et al., 2000: 99) (colonialism is further discussed in Chapter 7 of this book). This reveals the determining nature of modern history writing which fails to be self-critical and potentially ignores certain facets or identities in expressing one unified subject. As discussed above, in terms of American history, white identity may possess the dominant voice framing 'normative' concerns, and minorities are distanced in this process.

In the unified subject of dominant heterosexual history, real gay and lesbian social lives are marginalised or rejected in favour of composing one heterocentric history. Teleological processes such as the unified subject within history offer no critique of the dominant stories it promotes. As Foucault (1989) attests:

> It is the analysis of permanences that persist beneath apparent changes, of slow formations that profit from innumerable blind complicities, of those total figures that gradually come together and suddenly condense into the fine point of the work. Genesis, continuity, totalization: these are the great themes of the history of ideas. (p. 154)

This relates to a singularity within modern history writing, which I argue denies gay community as part of modern history. Such negation may be evident in considering (for example) the contribution that gay men and lesbians had provided in the Second World War, many of whom, as Allan Berube (1990) reports, willingly joined the armed forces knowing that if their sexuality was discovered they may be dishonourably discharged.

Such failure to report these important historical efforts in the mainstream marginalises the contributions of a minority. As Danaher et al. (2000) advise making equations between authentic and unauthentic historical forms, there are many missing stories in the collation of modern history:

> For example, the oral histories of indigenous peoples, or the folk tales of European peasants find no place within the written historical records, but they come to 'haunt' this record through their silences, opening up gaps within the historiographic enterprise. (p. 101)

Such address to 'haunting' I argue is present in the attempts by gay men and lesbians to reform ideas of community, and rewrite missing histories which might include or foreground them.

This might relate to the issue of belonging, where gay men and lesbians want to place themselves within the frame of both community and history. As Vikki Bell (1999) affirms, 'one does not simply belong to the world or any group within it. Belonging is an achievement at several levels of abstraction' (p. 3). Such possibility, I would argue, is achieved through the performative potential of media producers engaged in new storytelling exhibiting belonging.

This drive towards connection foregrounding belonging is enabled through the shift from modern to postmodern in narrative dynamics. As Anthony Elliott (1996) tells us:

> The [modern] grand narratives that unified and structured Western science and philosophy, grounding truth and meaning in the

> presumption of a universal subject and a predetermined goal of
> emancipation, no longer appear convincing or even plausible....
> [Postmodern] [k]nowledge is constructed, not discovered; it is con-
> textual, not foundational. (p. 19)

Such contextual appropriation of knowledge in postmodernity enables
gay men and lesbians to perform their sense of belonging where there is
an erasure of 'distinctions of high and low culture, of appearance and
reality, [and] of past and present' (Elliott, 1996: 19). Postmodernity
offers a democratic frame, composed of segmented and collage-like
components which seem to be of equal worth.

Whilst postmodernity, compared to the unified subject, may be
'decentred and dispersed' (Elliott, 1996: 19), I argue that it enables the
audience to more easily consume diverse identities which might normally seem distant and disconnected. Through the postmodern ethic of
surface and collage (see Jameson, 1991; Woods, 1999), postmodern narrative juxtaposition offers the democratisation of multivalent identity
forms. Whilst inevitably there are hierarchies in the media environments
which might express interest in broadcasting the new storytelling of gay
and lesbian social agents such as audience expectations and normative
recognitions, it is the shift towards the consumption of micro-narratives
within the postmodern ethos, which offers horizontal scope for new
democratic recognitions of narrative, style and form.

Although this suggests that gay and lesbian identity is denied its
vertical political axis which might be confrontational and enabling,
I would argue that it is precisely through the horizontal shift of postmodernity, which proffers collage, surface and same unit value, that
identity politics seep through and boundaries dissolve. Gay and lesbian
ideals connect and progress through self-reflexive stories of engagement.
These bleed through the colours in a postmodern patchwork quilt of
storytelling, offering narrative juxtaposition, democratic potential and
transformation.

Transformation

Through offering democratic potential, gay men and lesbians involved
in new storytelling focus on the expression of community, challenging and transforming historical forms. This involves self-reflexive social
agents expressing their personal identity ideals, framed within the
power potential of institutional reflexivity. Political ideology is subtly expressed, focusing on personal identity and subversion occurring

through postmodern horizontal (discursive) flow, rather than social challenge and rebellion which might lead to modern vertical (ideological) confrontation. Whilst this involves lateral movement and integration which some queer theorists may argue is *assimilationist*, I would argue that this is not only *pluralist* in offering new scope which encompasses diverse levels of identity, but also that it is *transformative* in presenting new stories which offer hope and change.

Visions of transformation are offered by diverse members of the gay community, producing fresh formations of identity through new storytelling. Apparently fragmented components of an imagined gay community rewrite new narratives and challenge social ideas. This also includes an agency in non-Western and non-white identities who lead concepts of new civil life, new family and new community (see Chapter 7). Rather than the gay community seeming disconnected and ignorant of disparity, new storytellers from divergent racial and social extractions work together in forming ideas of community and history. This engenders a reading of new storytelling as offering not only cohesion, but also personal strength.

Such personal challenge, endurance and potential for transformation is evident in the contribution of Dirk Bogarde in the groundbreaking film *Victim* (1961), where issues of personal identity are foregrounded, and communities and histories reinscribed.

Victim and Dirk Bogarde: intended identification[3]

Victim (Basil Dearden, 1961, UK) was a significant landmark in the visibility of gay men within the media (see Figure 3.2). As a film release in 1961,[4] and later as a television broadcast in 1968, in the United Kingdom it reached large mainstream audiences who for the first time would see gay men represented in communities.[5] Whilst the story was essentially a crime drama and the representations focused on the social problem of blackmail, it was innovative in exploring what was known about the lives of gay men. Evoking the aims of the Wolfenden Report (1954) which eventually led to the legalisation of male homosexuality in the United Kingdom, *Victim* formed part of a new realism in British cinema in the late 1950s and early 1960s (Hill, 1986; Murphy, 1992). Directed by Basil Dearden and written by Janet Green and John McCormick, following Dearden and Green's earlier 'realist' collaboration *Sapphire* (Basil Dearden, 1959, UK) which similarly used the crime drama genre to expose racial prejudice and hatred, *Victim* may be seen as a collaborative project with a political cause.

Figure 3.2   The poster for the film *Victim* (Basil Dearden, 1961). Dirk Bogarde is depicted in a highly emotive state, contextualizing his political beliefs in supporting the film. Allied Film Makers/Rank. Image courtesy of ITV

Most significant in this collaboration was the casting of movie star Dirk Bogarde in the lead role, and the relationship between Bogarde and his life partner and manager Tony Forwood (of over 40 years) (see Figure 3.3). This coupling would represent an intimate and political union, evident in the questions that it raised and the potential that it offered. Whilst the extent of their intimate relationship was never personally disclosed, as an alliance they supported the representation of homosexual identity. As Phillip Hensher attests (shortly after Bogarde's death), 'What Bogarde did, and did with all bravery one can reasonably expect, was present gay men with versions of their lives and their desires' (cited in Coldstream, 2004: 543). *Victim* may be considered a landmark within this, expressing self-reflexive ideas of normative homosexuality.

In *Victim*, Dirk Bogarde plays a young successful married lawyer (Melville Farr) who becomes involved with a younger single working-class gay man (Jack Barrett, played by Peter McEnery). Whilst the suicide of the young man (stimulated by a need to protect the reputation of

Figure 3.3 A rare image of Dirk Bogarde (right) with partner Tony Forwood (left), depicted working at their home in France. Image courtesy of the Dirk Bogarde Estate 2007

Farr/Bogarde) is the central dramatic context, the representation of the homosexual community, and the contribution of Bogarde provide the most enduring dramatic scenes. This is primarily evident where Bogarde as the character of Melville Farr admits to his wife his attraction for the young man. Sylvia Syms, co-star in the film playing the role of Farr's wife (Laura), was deeply impacted by this dramatic moment. John Coldstream (2004) interviewing Syms and asking for her observations tells us:

> After watching the 'I wanted him' scene again recently, Sylvia Syms said that Dirk 'obviously felt about it very passionately. It was deeply moving'.... She recognised 'the pain behind his eyes'. She considered that in their big scene he revealed 'quite a lot about himself'. (p. 272)

In a similar manner that Ellen DeGeneres (discussed in Chapter 2) was represented as finding the coming-out sequence (in her sitcom *Ellen*) emotionally charged and therapeutic, I argue that although Dirk Bogarde did not openly admit that he was homosexual we may read observations of his performance in a similar manner. Sylvia Syms alludes to his likely homosexual identity, and considers the scene as a cathartic moment.

Also Dirk Bogarde in his autobiography *Snakes and Ladders* (1978) alludes to the normalcy of homosexual identity in his recollection of assessing the script for *Victim*. In the book he situates his father in a domestic scenario, with his partner Tony Forwood. Dirk recalls:

> My father was struggling at the top of the tree trying to fix the fairy on top. A little pink angel with wings and benevolent wand. [Bogarde:] 'Pa.... Would you mind if I made a rather, difficult film.... I mean in the moral sense: serious stuff?' [Father:] 'I don't think I quite follow you. Political do you mean?' [Bogarde:] 'Homosexual'. [Father] pulled out his handkerchief and mopped his brow gently; had a sip of beer.... [Tony] Forwood and Capucine [(Dirk's female best friend)] were laying cloths on the long tables in the hall ready for the evening party. (p. 200)

Bogarde presents us with a careful juxtaposition of his father in ironic representation (next to a fairy on a Christmas tree), with his enduring male partner and female best friend all in close domestic proximity. Whilst Bogarde does not reveal his sexuality, he implies the normalcy of homosexuality as within everyday family and friendship scenarios in the context of 'families of choice' (Weston, 1991).

Such evidence of normalcy was apparent not only in Dirk's performance and his connection to the film, but also it was apparent in the community representations within the text. Whilst the homosexual characters were mostly scripted as victims of blackmail or protagonists of extortion, an everyday homosexual community was represented in the manner which suggests a subjugated minority, rather than a criminal division. This impetus to understanding is vividly represented in a pivotal exchange between the two investigating police officers, following the announcement to Farr that Barrett has hanged himself. We see a brief shot of Farr (clearly distraught) in the shadows outside the police station, and immediately after this the two officers (Detective Inspector Harris and Sergeant Bridie) are in conversation:

> *Harris* This blackmailer has as good as murdered Barrett.... If only these unfortunate devils would have come to us in the first place.

Bridie   If only they led normal lives, they wouldn't need to come at all.

Harris   If the law punished every abnormality, we would be kept pretty busy sergeant.

Bridie   Even so, this law Sir was made for a very good reason; if it were changed other weaknesses would follow.

Harris   I can see you're a true puritan Bridie, eh!

Bridie   Nothing wrong with that Sir.

Harris   Of course there was a time when that was against the law.

Echoing a similar exchange between senior and junior policemen in Basil Dearden and Janet Green's earlier collaboration *Sapphire* (1959) (briefly discussed above), the progressive voice is given to the senior officer, and the status quo to the junior. Consequently, this scene (as does the whole film) actively contributes to ideas of democratic public debate concerning homosexuality and the law at that time. This not only provided a voice for the many 'victims' (in the audience) who may themselves have been subject to blackmail,[6] but also it sent a message of support to those who were homosexual and were unable to live openly as citizens in the community (see Chapter 1, and the discussions of participants from *Male Homosexual*).

As Stephen Bourne (1996) reports, *Victim* 'had an enormous impact on the lives of gay men, who for the first time saw credible representations of themselves and their situations in a commercial British film' (p. 155). Furthermore as John Hill (1986) reports concerning class divides, 'despite verbal addresses to the contrary, the gay community is to this extent "normalised". Far from being socially isolated it conforms exactly to the "normal" parameters of class and cultural division in British society' (p. 92) at that time. This impetus towards credibility and normality offered a sense of realism recognisable to homosexual audiences, and may be considered as offering affirmation. As Dirk Bogarde reports in *Snakes and Ladders*, illuminating his sense of personal connection to the film:

> The countless letters of gratitude which flooded in were proof enough [that the film was a success], . . . and I had achieved what I had longed to do for so long, to be in a film which disturbed, educated, and illuminated as well as merely giving entertainment. (p. 202)

Bogarde attests that the film was a turning point, not only in the potential that it offered to audiences, but also in his sense of personal achievement. Whilst his subsequent appearance in the films *The Servant* (1962), *Modesty Blaise* (1965) and *Death in Venice* (1970) also had associations with gay sexuality (and additionally his earlier film *The Spanish Gardener* (1956) offers a connotation of 'forbidden desire' (Medhurst, 1993)), Bogarde openly rejects his homosexual identification, yet in many ways willingly displays its evident traits.

The imagined identification of Dirk Bogarde as homosexual is an important context in exploring the significance of *Victim*, and his contribution as a self-reflexive storyteller. Clearly audiences read him as possibly homosexual, and more importantly close friends and peers considered him so. John Coldstream reports that the lifetime relationship between Tony Forwood and Dirk was considered as 'a marriage like few are' (Mary Dodd, cited in Coldstream, 2004: 586), and most significantly Glynis Johns (Tony Forwood's first partner and ex-wife) considered that 'they were happy together and they shared it with their friends' (cited in Coldstream, 2004: 586). Furthermore, actor John Fraser (2004) in his autobiography makes an account that Dirk and Tony were long-standing homosexual lovers, and that Dirk had confided in him that their relationship had been sexual but gradually became more fraternal (Fraser, 2004: 146).

Notably within the BBC *Arena* documentary *The Private Dirk Bogarde* (2001), the imagined identification of Dirk Bogarde and Tony Forwood as homosexual lovers becomes the central axis of engagement, continuing Bogarde's discursive power. The producers report that Bogarde in the late 1980s had destroyed many personal items which would have indicated the depth of his intimate relationship with Tony Forwood, and constructs a sympathetic representation of their personal lives together through recently discovered archive home movie footage. Whilst the documentary offers up many family members who attest that Dirk and Tony had the perfect (and likely homosexual) relationship, again clear evidence of his homosexuality is lacking.

Nevertheless, I would argue that Dirk Bogarde not only exhibited the traits of a self-reflexive homosexual-identified new storyteller, but also that he intended his 'educated' audience to interpret him in this way. In a verbal exchange within *The Private Dirk Bogarde* between Bogarde and homosexual-identified interviewer Russell Harty which had originally appeared in the documentary *Dirk Bogarde: Above the Title – a Conversation with Russell Harty* (Nick Gray for Yorkshire Television, 1986, UK) (discussed in more depth in Chapter 4), he willingly offers himself up for close examination. Bogarde challenges Harty to delve deeper in the questions he poses, conjuring a situation where he all but affirms a homosexual relationship with Tony Forwood. As the producers of *The Private Dirk Bogarde* propose concerning the seven autobiographies which avoid an explicit account of his sexuality, taking Dirk's dialogue from *Dirk Bogarde: Above the Title*, 'you need to read between the lines, it's all there'. Such representation of their openly displayed yet privately closed relationship, I would argue, engenders Dirk Bogarde as an architect of his own identity. He deliberately placed his devoted partner Tony within the marital family frame, but resisted a development and exposure of these scenes. I suggest he did this wishing not to obscure a particular view, but in order to fix an enigmatic yet lasting iconography.

Such permanence and resistance to exposure are less evident in our next case study which focuses on Armistead Maupin and Sarah Waters, who both (respectively) place themselves as icons within the fictional frame.

Armistead Maupin and Sarah Waters: popular frames

Armistead Maupin's *Tales of the City* originated as a newspaper serial. It initially appeared (in a different form) as *The Serial* in 1974 in the Marin County (California) newspaper *The Pacific Sun*, and then later it was fully developed as *Tales of the City* in 1976 gaining high-profile attention in *The San Francisco Chronicle* (Gale, 1999: 49). Achieving popularity, it was later transformed into a book (stimulating a number of sequels), and in 1993 it was adapted into a television miniseries (by Channel 4 (UK), and later Showtime (US)).[7] Set in 1970s San Francisco and telling the tale of a diverse group of people centred on a rooming house headed by a transgendered woman and featuring gay, lesbian and bisexual characters, *Tales of the City* may be considered as a nostalgic yet evocative exposé revealing the interconnectedness of sexual minorities within American (mainstream) culture. Maupin's vision reflected not only his political ideology in expressing gay and lesbian rights (see Capsuto, 2000; Clendinen and Nagourney, 1999; Deitcher, 1995), but also it employed an everyday popular tone in its contemporary audience connection within the newspaper, the book and the television event.

Sarah Waters' award-winning novels *Tipping the Velvet* (1998) and *Fingersmith* (2002) were adapted by the BBC for television production in 2002 and 2005 respectively. Featuring central lesbian characters, which would be situated within Victorian London, these texts offered progressive visions of sexual minorities placed within the centre of historical

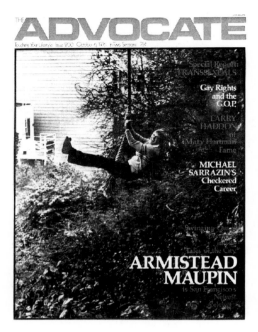

Figure 3.4   Armistead Maupin, depicted in playful mood, on the cover of *The Advocate* (6 October 1976). Image courtesy of *The Advocate* and LPI Media Inc.

fiction.[8] As BBC television costume dramas they evoked a certain aesthetic sensibility which connected to the romance of the past. However, through the foregrounding of the lesbian heroine, this not only challenged traditional narrative sensibilities, but also it placed the outsider within the popular frame.

The work of Armistead Maupin (see Figure 3.4) and Sarah Waters (see Figure 3.5) is discussed here for their creativity in popular history (and nostalgia) storytelling. Whilst both writers engage in very different traditions – contemporary nostalgic serial (Maupin) and progressive historical drama (Waters) – they are discussed here together for their creative use of popular narrative tone and strategic plot development, which presents challenging ideas. I argue that both writers present a certain popular tone in fiction which resonates with the success and narrative devices of Charles Dickens (1812–70) and Wilkie Collins (1824–89) in the nineteenth century. As Christopher Isherwood noted in reviewing Maupin's *Tales of the City* and comparing it to Dickens (Gale, 1999: 148), these writers develop a popular serial tone which is both intimate and

Figure 3.5 Sarah Waters, author of *Tipping the Velvet* and *Fingersmith*. Image © Charlie Hopkinson

contemporary. Where Dickens and Collins foregrounded stories of the poor, the disenfranchised and the social outcast in complex and engaging plotlines, Maupin and Waters represent sexual outsiders within the popular frame in a similar way, challenging dominant ideas of social exclusion.

Echoing Peter Thoms' (1992) ideas on Wilkie Collins in *Windings of the Labyrinth*, I argue that the narrative constructions of Maupin and Waters offer intense engagement. Though their plot invention and narrative complexity, this offers a 'quest for [identity] design' (Thoms, 1992: 9) which is enabling. Where Collins focused on female protagonists in the 'sensation novel' of the late nineteenth century (such as in *The Woman in White* (Collins, 1994b [originally 1860])) involving complex plots through which they struggle and triumph, Maupin and Waters similarly progress the identity potentials of gay men and lesbians. As Thoms (1992) considers of Wilkie Collins: 'Dominant in each novel is the struggle of one or more protagonists to impose meaningful shape on their lives – to tell their own stories and thus attain a sense of freedom and identity'

(Thoms, 1992: 9). Maupin and Waters in a similar manner stimulate progressive discursive contexts foregrounding identity possibilities, which are enabled by careful plot construction and inventive iconic juxtaposition. They expose interconnectedness between story, discourse and author.

As Seymour Chatman (1978) tells us with regard to story and discourse:

> Structuralist theory argues that each narrative has two parts: a story (*histoire*), the content or chains of events (actions, happenings), plus what may be called the existents (characters, items of setting); and a discourse (*discours*), that is, the expression, the means by which the content is communicated. (p. 19)

Narrative involves a complex relationship between the essence of the story as expressly indicated by the plot, and the discourse involving the mode of delivery and connotations. Such delivery inevitably involves the discursive connotations of the media through which it is delivered, the social and cultural institutions which surround this, and the author as part of the discursive and storytelling world.

For Maupin and Waters writing respectively as political activist, journalist and popular writer (Maupin) and novelist and historical dramatist (Waters), inevitably this presents discursive connotations which are embedded within the narrative frame. The institutions of politics, journalism, writing and history potentially contextualise the stories they present, echoing stylistic and formal expectations. Also as openly gay and lesbian writers, inevitably Maupin and Waters are implicated as co-present in the stories they tell, becoming self-reflexive storytellers of their (personal) identity ideals. Through connection to institutional style and form, Maupin and Waters create complex narrative and plot devices, which foreground progressive discursive contexts placing their 'political' selves within the narrative frame. In order to discuss this further I will first examine the work of Armistead Maupin, and then Sarah Waters.

Armistead Maupin directly places himself within the narrative frame. This occurs not only in his references that the lead gay male character of Michael Tolliver is in some way inspired by his life, but also he appears in *Tales of the City* in a Hitchcockian cameo. Through appearing within the series briefly depicted at a typewriter through a window of Mrs Madrigal's rooming house, a vision is produced which is not only self-reflexive, but also it is an allusion to the complexity of the Hitchcock-style narrative and its iconography. Further references to the influence of

Hitchcock are evident in *Tales of the City* where certain filming locations and stylistic traits are well-known references to Hitchcock (mostly relating to the film *Vertigo*). However, I would like to focus on the Hitchcock labyrinthine style of narrative within *Tales of the City* which allows for the interweaving of very complex and interconnected stories. The predominant narrative arcs concern: room-mate Norman and his attempts at blackmail, Mrs Madrigal and a romantic encounter, the bisexuality of Beauchamp Day, and Michael Tolliver's quest for love. These are presented within a multi-layered narrative plot offering suspense, not dissimilar to the pursuit of truth in a crime drama or thriller. This allows for interesting juxtapositions, alliances and associational readings.

In *Tales of the City* we are presented with a maze of identity possibility, with a central cast led by the character of Mrs Madrigal, a male to female transgendered woman who embarks on a covert romance with Edgar Halcyon a married businessman, which becomes the central love story. Whilst tragedy inevitably ensues with the death of Halcyon at the close of *Tales of the City*, it is the drive supporting nonconformist identity and its potential that bonds the disparate cast together. This occurs on many levels with the central gay character of Michael Tolliver stimulating proceedings. Whilst Mary Ann Singleton who has recently moved to San Francisco is framed as the lead storyteller at the outset, by the close of the first series Michael Tolliver is established as arbiter of moral guidance and narrative enabler. This switch in storytelling authority is primarily evident when after listening to Mary Ann Singleton's confession that blackmailer Norman had accidentally fallen to his death after she had confronted him, Tolliver makes light of the incident, advocating a need to suppress the truth and challenging and modifying her moral code.

Such display may be seen as a carnivalesque narrative device, which ignores the regular conventions of crime solving and locates the normally disenfranchised in sites of power. In this way female (Mary Ann) and homosexual (Michael) are represented as sites of authority, and the heterosexual male victim (Norman) is punished. Whilst a normative reading of this would allow for the punishment of the victim (Norman) as he was involved in blackmail and was a child pornographer, it is the resistance of normative authority which engenders this as a carnivalesque inversion. As Peter Stallybrass and Allon White (1995 [originally 1986]) affirm exploring carnival culture and iconography, this involves a

... reversible world and a world upside down (WUD) which encodes ways that carnival inverts the everyday hierarchies, structures, rules and customs of its social formation. . . . [There is a] linking up of inversion of hierarchy (kings become servants, officers serve the ranks, boys become bishops, men dress as women and so on). (p. 183)

Such narrative inversion is the coherent thread that weaves through the complex narrative of *Tales of the City*. In the manner of the carnivalesque 'world upside down', authority is challenged and dominant order is overturned.

However, narrative inversion and its potential are complicated in their relationship to hybridity. Stallybrass and White (1995) tell us that in carnival iconography, hybridisation 'produces new combinations and strange instabilities [often including] inversion and demonization [or subjugation] mixed up together' (p. 58). On the one hand *Tales of the City* offers a progressive vision of this, in the romance between a heterosexual male and a male-to-female transsexual, alluding to the potential of new hybrid forms of relationship, yet on the other it signals the problematic nature of the bisexual, in the character of Beauchamp, where punishment is exacted for traversing boundaries between free-spirited behaviour and conformity. Such prioritisation of transsexual, heterosexual and homosexual narrative over that of the bisexual, indicates the possibility of 'displaced abjection' (Stallybrass and White, 1995) in Maupin's identity struggles to prove (transsexual and homosexual) value by favourable juxtaposition. Indeed whilst the strongest characters are not necessarily sexually exclusive, they adhere to the performance of either heterosexuality or homosexuality. Evidence of the abjection to bisexuality is primarily apparent in comparing the deaths of Edgar Halcyon (in *Tales of the City*) and Beauchamp Day (in *More Tales of the City*). Whilst both had been unfaithful to their wives, Halcyon's death is represented as heroic and epic with the covert request on his deathbed that his daughter's unborn female child be named after his mistress (Anna, after Mrs Madrigal) and Mrs Madrigal looks at the night sky and sees Edgar's soul passing in a star, whilst Beauchamp dies in a tunnel en route after an attempt at sexual assignation, thoroughly buried underground.

Inevitably such identity juxtaposition involves a degree of suspense in the likely outcomes of punishment for behaviour. As Noel Carroll (1996) tells us concerning the dramatic device of suspense:

[It] arises when a well structured question – with neatly opposed alternatives – emerges from the narrative and calls forth an answering scene. . . . [It] is generated by combining elements of morality and probability in such a way that the questions that issue in the plot have logically opposed answers. (pp. 100–1)

Whilst Carroll (1996) goes on to hypothesise about the likely outcomes of 'moral and evil' behaviour in narrative development, and that 'suspense occurs when a moral outcome is improbable' (p. 111), I would argue that in *Tales of the City* this strategy is denied. Rather than constructing answering scenes as conclusions to moral failings which might resolve the suspense, there is no permanent conclusion leading to learning or understanding.

Whilst indeed Armistead Maupin does punish Beauchamp Day for bisexuality, and beatifies Edgar Halcyon for the union between the heterosexual and the transsexual (as discussed above), there is no lasting political evocation. In this way moral positioning is played out, but it is not resolved in the manner that a traditional suspense narrative achieves closure. This may be seen in further exploring our comparison between Day and Halcyon, revealing Halycon's death as impacting but made light. At the close of *Tales of the City* (in the book and television series) instead of Mrs Madrigal expressing undying love for her lost partner at his freshly closed grave (now desolate, after the family funeral service), she places a marijuana cigarette on the earth mound, and muses: 'have fun; its Colombian'.

Armistead Maupin plays out identity ideals, involving punishment, favourable juxtaposition and carnivalesque inversion, however he also focuses on the instability of his hybrid identity forms, and denies them affirmation. Therefore whilst Maupin indeed does foreground very progressive identity and community scenarios, these exist in a constant state of flux: they possess discursive power, but they do not offer literal conclusions. This I would argue reveals a pluralist and queer theory approach, which foregrounds 'identities as multiple, unstable, and regulatory [yet through discursive power presents] new and productive possibilities' (Seidman, 1996: 12). Through the multi-layered plot, Armistead Maupin presents new ideas concerning the constitution of a minority community and its relationship to the mainstream. He does this however without citing diverse sexuality as necessarily oppositional and worthy, but plays out scenarios which might offer scope. Essentially the power within Maupin's work is the constant flux of mystery and possibility. This engenders not only an audience's engagement, but also the quest to find some affirmation. The denial of affirmation is evident in the ongoing nature of his serial work in *Tales of the City*, offering a continuous narrative which has no real closure. His recent recommencement of

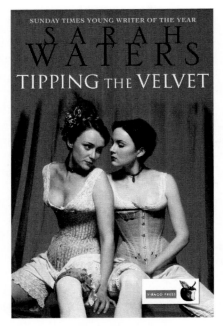

Figure 3.6   Sarah Waters' *Tipping the Velvet*, depicted on the cover of the novel with an image from the television series, featuring Kitty Butler (left, played by Keeley Hawes) and Nan Astley (right, played by Rachel Stirling). Reproduced by kind permission of the BBC, and Virago, an imprint of Little, Brown Book Group

the *Tales of the City* series after a break of 18 years with *Michael Tolliver Lives* (2007), offers contemporary evidence of this, in its continuing but inconclusive narrative. Armistead Maupin denies affirmation and resolution; instead he continuously opens doorways which offer vivid glimpses, and potential pathways, unending.

In contrast Sarah Waters offers romantic scenarios with closure. In *Tipping the Velvet* and *Fingersmith*, both texts resolve in fulfilling romantic lesbian union. *Tipping the Velvet* (see Figure 3.6) focuses on the story of Nan Astley, a young girl who falls in love with Kitty Butler, a music hall entertainer, but through rejection embarks on a destructive journey involving abuse and prostitution until she finds true romantic love with socialist Florence Banner. *Fingersmith* involves a complex plot of double-dealing and deception, which whilst it focuses on punishment within the madhouse (for a deceptive claim on a financial inheritance), results in the unlikely reunion of opponents Maud Lilly and Sue Trinder becoming romantic lovers. Through these inventive narrative exploits, Waters echoes the literary and iconic frames of reference connected to the Victorian novel and televisual period drama, here subverting the normally heterocentric. This is particularly evident not only with reference to the labyrinthine plots (similar to Armistead Maupin – discussed above), but also through the foregrounding of the female protagonist. This I argue may be connected to the stylistic implications of the nineteenth-century sensation novel, and its recognisable discursive power.

As Lisa Jardine tells us in the BBC documentary *Sarah Waters: Sex and the Victorian City* (2004, BBC, UK): 'There is a lovely way in which *Fingersmith* rolls Dickens and Wilkie Collins into a great bundle of sensational narrative, and teases out of it a new kind of intensity between women.' Here referring to the hybrid nature of Waters' efforts in foregrounding lesbian identity within the stylistic genre of the sensation novel, she evokes a progressive engagement. Furthermore, as Sarah Waters admits herself (in the same documentary): 'Sensation fiction is full of transgressive female characters. I only had to nudge them a little further in their deviance, and they would do wonderfully lesbian things.'

Sarah Waters' homage to sensation fiction provides a recognisable generic form set in a romanticised past, which audiences may easily engage with by recognising the quality signs of period drama (see Brandt, 1993; Brunsdon, 1997). Through this the female character progresses as heroine, unfettered by male desire. Whilst sensation novels focused on normative heterosexuality, it was the propensity for the female character to conceal identity issues which enables Waters to make a synthesis which foregrounds lesbian possibility. As Lyn Pykett (2005) tells us considering *The Times* review of Wilkie Collins' sensation novel *The Moonstone* (1994a [originally 1868]): '[T]he distinguishing characteristic of the sensation school was not its bestial women, nor its faulty morality, but its "habit of laying eggs and hiding them", a "propensity for secretiveness" which it is argued, Collins had in a complex form' (p. 109). Through the iconic reading of female sensation characters as secretive, this engenders a characterisation which offers potential for the concealment of sexual (lesbian) identity, yet foregrounds this in the social possibilities displayed.

In *Tipping the Velvet* and *Fingersmith* the leading female characters adhere to this 'sensation' trait by concealing their sexuality. Although heroines Nan Astley (in *Tipping the Velvet*) and Sue Trinder (in *Fingersmith*) act on their sexual desire, the display of affection is hidden from their peers. Whilst in the closing scene of *Tipping the Velvet* we are presented with a more overt contemporary depiction of lesbian desire with

Nan Astley taking her new partner (Florence Banner) to meet her parents, in *Fingersmith* there remains a concealed, yet intense romantic and sexual connection. Such concealment may be connected to the Victorian interest in psychology and madness.

In *Fingersmith* the madhouse forms a central theme in the narrative delivery. Sue Trinder is incarcerated there; within a scenario where she is double-crossed by Maud Lilley (her mistress, covert lover and intended victim) and Richard 'Gentleman' Rivers (Sue's criminal associate). Lyn Pykett (2005) tells us, referencing an essay entitled 'Madness in Novels' which appeared in the *Spectator* in 1866, that:

> The rise of madness in the novel in the 1860s as a fictional convention...allows for an author to dispense with probability or to transcend the limitations of a prosaic and materialistic modern age.... Madness was the device that sensation novelists used to 'intensify' such qualities or propensies as courage, hate, jealousy, or wickedness. (p. 181)

Sarah Waters used the dramatic scenario of the madhouse to offer up intense and emotional visions of strong female characters. Through connecting to the 'sensation' interest in psychological states, this presents an emotional connection with the leading female protagonist. In *Fingersmith* this allows for the rejection of male authority, by foregrounding and qualifying female emotive responses to betrayal by men.

Whilst Sue Trinder is betrayed by both her female lover (Maud Lilley) and her male criminal accomplice (Richard 'Gentleman' Rivers), a bias towards a purely female perspective is presented. This occurs in our knowledge that whilst both Trinder and Lilley had duped each other despite finding physical attraction between them, they are united in their abuse by men. This is evident where Maud Lilley had been made by her uncle to work as a scribe and reader of pornographic books, and that Sue Trinder had been forced into a life of crime by Richard 'Gentleman' Rivers. Such responses to male subjugation engender a female-centric world, where the women are united in their concealed yet emotive display.

The representations in *Tipping the Velvet* offer more contemporary visions of overt lesbian display within Victorian England. As discussed above, the closing sequence offers a kind of normative display. As Sarah Waters tell us (in *Sarah Waters: Sex and the Victorian City*): 'There is no reason why my characters shouldn't have happy endings. That has been

quite important for me, especially with *Tipping the Velvet* I was determined to give that an upbeat resolution.'

The shift towards an affirmative closure in Waters' work may be indicative of a transformative politics in her work. This is particularly evident
in her focus on romance between her central lesbian protagonists. As
Anthony Giddens (1995) tells us concerning romance, it is 'a potential
avenue for controlling the future, as well as a form of [expressing] psychological security' (p. 41), suggesting that the performance of romance
(in narrative) connects with deeper ideas in society, correlating with well-
being, self-knowledge and future development. However, as Giddens
further elucidates with regard to the eighteenth century, '[i]deas about
romantic love were plainly allied to women's subordination in the home,
and their relative separation from the outside world' (p. 43), revealing
patriarchal power within the domestic environment and the continuance of separating women from political and social authority. The
invention of Sarah Waters' work in *Tipping the Velvet* is that she challenges
this idea, and embeds an iconic representation of women as connected
to romance as life affirming and socially enabling. In doing this she foregrounds women and particularly lesbians, rather than solely men, as
forces within private and public spheres.

In *Tipping the Velvet* this is evident in the public display of affection
between Nan Astley and Kitty Butler in theatre performances (Kitty is
Nan's first romantic partner, who later rejects her – briefly discussed
above). In an early instance Kitty is dressed as a male impersonator and
openly displays affection for Nan who is in the audience, by kissing
and then throwing a red rose to her. Later when Nan has also taken
up a career in the theatre both are on stage dressed as men, and they
perform a song about finding sweethearts. In these instances we may
read that the romance is between two women, rather than offering
mainstream entertainment of sexual impersonation. Within the theatre, public space is used for the display of same-sex desire, challenging
dominant heterosexual narratives.

Also within *Tipping the Velvet,* challenges to male heterosexual order
are more directly foregrounded in the representation of Nan Astley, with
Florence Banner (her ultimate romantic partner) and Ralph Banner (Florence's brother, a political activist). We are presented with a scenario
where not only does Nan Astley prove her worthiness for the love of
Florence Banner involving domestic caretaking and family support (by
working in the Banner household in a manner that is highly efficient),
but also in a critical scene she rescues the political work of Florence's
brother. At a long-planned political meeting, when Ralph Banner is about

to speak to a large audience concerning the abject poverty of the disenfranchised and the need for social action he flounders, failing with nerves, and Nan Astley confidently speaks for him, stirring up the audience in support of their political cause. This places the lesbian heroine within the political and public frame. At the same time she is located within the heart of the domestic world, in her integration within the Banner family. This includes Nan and Florence as romantic partners, along with Ralph (Florence's brother) involved in constructing a 'family of choice' (Weston, 1991) together in the raising of a young orphaned child. Sarah Waters offers stature to lesbian identity within domestic and political worlds, placing this within the historical frame.

Armistead Maupin and Sarah Waters make new contexts for gay and lesbian identity, here offering new visions within historic and nostalgic settings. Whilst different strategies are involved, with Maupin favouring an open-ended ambiguous style and Waters offering more certain closure, both employ the setting of the past to reconfigure ideas of same-sex identity. Whilst it is possible to argue that the setting of the past offers 'safe distance' for the mainstream consumption of homosexual identity (it is not us), I would suggest conversely that it is through this method that contemporary ideas are explored. In this way, the struggles of Maupin's characters and the romantic closure of Waters' partners speak as much for the political advances which can be made as it reflects actual progress since the past, for example in terms of gay rights advances and civil progressions such as legal same-sex partnerships. Maupin and Waters do not reflect a different distant past, but construct a possible and already happening modified future through their progressive representations.

Our last case study within this chapter similarly contextualises the past, however with a more overt political agenda. Tony Kushner's work is not only more confrontational and rebellious, but also offers a cathartic experience and a catalyst for change.

Tony Kushner and *Angels in America*: community and transformation

In Tony Kushner's *Angels in America* (1995), the character of Harper, on a night flight to San Francisco referring to a prophetic dream concerning the damaged ozone layer of the earth's atmosphere, tells us:

> Souls were rising from the earth far below, souls of the dead, of people who had perished, from famine, from war, from the plague, and they

floated up, like skydivers in reverse, limbs all akimbo, wheeling and spinning. And the souls of these departed joined hands, clasped ankles and formed a web, a great net of souls, and the souls were three-atom oxygen molecules, of the stuff of ozone, and the outer rim absorbed them, and was repaired.

Nothing is lost forever. In this world, there is a kind of painful progress. Longing for what we've left behind, and dreaming ahead. (Kushner, 1995: 275)

These words near the close of the play (and the television drama) represent a metaphor for the political ideology expressed by Tony Kushner that community works together in complex ways and this transcends cultural, social, religious, political and scientific limitations and ideologies in the possibilities that may be offered (see Fisher, 2006; Geis and Kruger, 1997; Vorlicky, 1998); that the world is continuously in motion and that opportunity for progress and advancement is related to confronting our weaknesses and strengths, working together for the benefit of each other. In *Angels in America* this is represented through a complex relationship with the recent past in a setting of the mid 1980s, and the emergence of AIDS, which offers scope for future progress.

Set in New York and featuring the lead character of Prior Walter as a man who has recently discovered he has AIDS, the narrative focuses on confrontational reality and emotive fantasy in the trials and tribulations in which he is situated. This relates not only to his rejection by his partner Louis Ironson after the discovery of Prior's illness, but also after this in the visitation of an Angel who testifies that he is a prophet, and demands action. The dynamic between rejection and isolation from a loved one against visitation and expectation from a spectre forms an evocative narrative, oscillating between reality and fantasy, focusing on the onslaught of AIDS in America.

Within this, ideas of community and race are played out, offering a convergence of Christian, Jewish and Mormon religious ideologies, and the situation of non-belief. Community, belief and social action form the narrative threads through which ideas of nation and community are played out. AIDS is foregrounded, representing not only the sufferings and indictment of gay men who were devastated in the 1980s and were moved to social action, forming bonds and leadership, but also the plague-like onslaught which echoes previous social devastations such as worldwide epidemics and the context of war, which for humanity is non-discerning and punishes many. In this way gay men are situated at the centre of a diverse America which has suffered on many levels and there is a need to progress beyond this.

Progress is related to a need to combat AIDS, and the bringing together of communities and identities. *Angels in America* achieves this through representing complex social and racial relationships, which reflect the immigrant and minority constitution of the United States in settings of denial. Prior is Anglo-Saxon, and is abandoned by his partner Louis, a Jew. Belize, an ex-partner of Prior, is black, and as a nurse he cares for an AIDS sufferer Roy Cohen, a Jew who denies his homosexuality (Cohen is a character based on a real historical figure, who was a right-wing protagonist in the McCarthy era). Joe, Harper and Hannah Pitt (son, wife and mother respectively) are Mormons, torn apart by Joe's recently announced homosexuality, and Harper's drug addiction. Within this plot, five gay men (Prior, Louis, Belize, Joe and Roy Cohen), form the narrative contexts of engagement. This largely involves the themes of denial and the abdication of responsibility: Prior denies his celestial vision, Louis and Joe abandon their partners, and Roy rejects his homosexuality.

Such focus on denial, abandonment and tribulation is particularly evident in *Angels in America* in the representation of Prior and Louis. I argue that this foregrounds an oscillation between Apollonian and Dionysian sensibilities as exhibited in Greek drama (Nietzsche, 1995 [originally 1872]) in the confrontations that they face. The Apollonian drive is represented in Prior's attempts at self-control, ideal behaviour and sophistication in his attempts to maintain an aestheticism, genuineness and illusion of order: it is vivified in his struggles with the demands of the Angel, the loss of Louis, and the symptoms caused by AIDS. Conversely, Louis takes on a Dionysian persona in his drive towards free-spirited reactive behaviour without self-control or responsibility: it is evident in his apparent rejection of his partner whilst in trauma, his engagement in dangerous sexual exploits recklessly risking infection with AIDS, and in his inappropriate partnerships seen in his torrid relationship with the ideologically opposed Joe Pitt (Joe is a staunch Republican, and Louis a left-wing sympathiser). Prior tries to impose some order, knowing he is failing; Louis rejects order but recognises his human failing. Whilst James Miller (1997) has indicated that *Angels in America* offers 'a Nietzschean ... aestheticism–activism debate over the representation of AIDS in the arts [appearing as a] culture clash between Apollonian illusionism and Dionysian rage' (p. 60), I argue that this involves complex discursive moments which offer focus and control. Despite representing a dichotomy between order and free spirit, the seemingly opposed Apollonian and Dionysian characters of Prior and Louis are combined in political potential.

This is particularly evident where Prior and Louis are juxtaposed in different scenes, at a time where there is animosity between them. Whilst there is discord between the two we are presented with a collaborative message, exposing the denial of homosexual identity and its relationship to AIDS. In a scene where the vulnerable and diseased body of Prior is inspected by the nurse (played by Emma Thompson who also plays the Angel), this is juxtaposed with Louis in political conversation with Belize, at a diner. Prior's naked body is exposed revealing his Kaposi's sarcoma (cancerous lesions resulting from AIDS). Louis tells Belize:

> I mean it's really hard being Left in this country, the American Left can't help but trip over all those petrified little fetishes: Freedom that's the worst. . . . You have [George] Bush talking about human rights. . . . [T]hese people don't begin to know what, ontologically, freedom is or human rights, like they see these bourgeois property based Rights-of-Man but that's not enfranchisement. . . . That's just liberalism [and] bourgeois tolerance, and I think what AIDS shows us is the limits of tolerance, that it's not enough to be tolerated, because when the shit hits the fan you find out how much tolerance is worth. Nothing. And underneath the tolerance is intense passionate hatred. (Kushner, 1995: 95–6)

Prior is represented as ordered and provides the illusion of control, whilst foregrounding his body as a site of discourse. Louis is represented as emotive, aggressive and reactive, whilst expressing untrammelled political dissent. Such opposites of iconic presentation form contrast between Apollonian and Dionysian performance, yet combine one message: the failing of a political America to offer equality to all.

It is the combination of different voices, in different modes of delivery, which offers ultimately one voice in the establishment of a political agenda, asking for motion and progress. This is evident in a dream sequence where Prior comes to heaven to reject the role of prophet, and he makes a speech criticising God for abandoning humanity in the early nineteenth century at the time of the great San Francisco earthquake. Prior attests: 'We just can't stop. We're not rocks – progress, migration, motion is . . . modernity. It's *animate*; it's what living things do.' Furthermore, at the close of the text a coalition of apparently different voices come together in political union. Prior, Louis and Belize accompanied by Hannah Pitt (Joe's mother who had originally come to New York to sort out her son's failing marriage, but becomes politically active) gather at the Bethesda Fountain in Central Park, New York, in an epilogue,

. four years after Prior's trial by the Angel (when he is living with AIDS). Individual members of the group take turns in explaining the biblical prophecy of the Bethesda Fountain: that a miraculous fountain will flow again and it will have healing properties, indicating an optimistic future where man is helped by a divine force. At the same time such focus on the distant metaphysical is grounded in the present optimism of a unified humanity. Prior, now in better health, tells us:

> The disease will be the end of many of us, but not nearly all, and the dead will be commemorated and will struggle on with the living, and we are not going away. We won't die secret deaths anymore. The world only spins forward. We will be citizens. The time has come. . . . The Great Work Begins. (Kushner, 1995: 280)

Tony Kushner's focus on coalition, movement and citizenship forms the axis of his engagement. In *Angels in America* he places gay identity at the heart of a complex, fragmented and yet cohesive America. Whilst this is grounded in responses to AIDS, he reveals a coalition of minority identities working towards change and concerned for humanity.

This involves representing an order which might seem assimilationist and Apollonian, connecting to self-worth and the retrieval of citizenship rights. At the same time it reflects the discursive evocation of difference seen in pluralism, queer theory and the Dionysian, evident in free-spirited behaviour and seemingly disconnected confrontation. Through revealing the complex nature of the often disparate strands within America and the gay community, I argue that Tony Kushner presents not only conformity alongside rebellion, but also within this transgression and the move to transformation.

Conclusion

This chapter has focused on gay identity and self-reflexive storytelling relating the potential of community and history. Through examining diverse case studies it is revealed that progressions have been made which foreground a shift from concealing personal identity but expressing political needs, to challenging ideas within popular frames leading to transformation. In this way the case study on Dirk Bogarde as a non-affirmed homosexual, who despite this involved himself in the groundbreaking film *Victim*, set an agenda for change. Bogarde in his long-standing partnership with Tony Forwood also represented the discursive potential of same-sex life partners working together in media production. Through this iconic representation not only did they support homosexual political ideals, but also they ensured popular interest in their personal dedication. Dirk Bogarde has been discussed here, not so much because of his private or public sexual life, but because he represented a stealthy political force within homosexual identity and new storytelling.

The later case studies on Armistead Maupin, Sarah Waters and Tony Kushner have revealed an increasing shift towards unashamed intimate storytelling, where the personal self is foregrounded in the narrative. Through Maupin, Waters and Kushner involving themselves within the popular, historical and political frame, they engage in mainstream ideas, placing the homosexual at 'centre stage'. Maupin's nostalgic serialisation, Waters' historical reinvention, and Kushner's political event, rework and reconstruct popular ideas of gay and lesbian identity.

I have argued here that gay identity and new storytelling involve complex relations within the concept of the gay community. New storytellers engage in the idea of the imagined gay community, as this provides the foundation for identity ideals. At the same time this offers various potentials. Bogarde's personal life with his partner, the representations of community in *Victim*, Maupin's diverse social profiles, Waters' historic romance and Kushner's patchwork America, provide enticing liminal frames through which gay and lesbian lives are recomposed.

Ultimately I have proposed that this is enabled by a postmodern narrative engagement. Through the postmodern drive towards aesthetic and cellular collage, history itself is challenged, and no longer provides one continuous unified subject. Just as there are many gay communities, equally there are many histories. The new storytellers represented here capitalise on the postmodern ethic of stylistic reinterpretation and ready juxtaposition. They enable the creation of new forms through borrowing and reconstructing popular frames. *Victim* as a crime drama, *Tales of the City* as a serial journal, *Fingersmith* and *Tipping the Velvet* as period drama, and *Angels in America* as a spectacular event: these provide mainstream audience connections framing subaltern desire. The new storytellers discussed here reframe not only their lives, blurring the boundary between fictional work and their personal life chances, but also they foreground a potential for mobility and social advancement within diverse community forms.

Through new storytelling, political forces are evident within the discursive disseminations of writers, producers and performers, laying a pathway extending from personal and intimate selves. Whilst this inevitably involves rewriting history and community ideals, the audience is still distanced. The next chapter addresses this, and examines the issue of audience participation in new storytelling. Rather than possessing a minor role residing outside circuits of engagement, I argue conversely that new storytelling focuses equally on active audiences involved in personal narration and reinvention. This extends beyond self-reflexive desire in writing, production and performance, and extends to therapeutic potency.

4
Factual Media Space: Intimacy, Participation and Therapy

Introduction

Jermaine Peters, contributing to a web-based media forum offering responses to the film *Brokeback Mountain* (Ang Lee, 2005, US), tells us:

> I've never had a boyfriend, and the film makes me think that this is the way my life might be. I may eventually find someone, but we will be kept apart by society. That hurts, really deep down. I dreamt of having a husband/life partner/ ... and having a normal life where we both work, take holidays together, and sit and talk. Is that so much to ask? (Members of the Ultimate Brokeback Forum, 2007: 34)

As part of the Ultimate Brokeback Forum (discussed below), Jermaine's contribution reveals a personal intimacy in expressing possible life chances in contemporary online media forums. Expectations and shifts towards democracy are foregrounded by ordinary members of the public in the possibility of open access media spaces. Gay identity is presented as a normative social profile, representing shifts beyond the manufacture of non-heterosexual stereotypical forms produced historically within the media (Clum, 2000; Dyer, 2000; Russo, 1987).

This chapter focuses on gay identity within factual media forms, foregrounding potential within the talk show, documentary, reality television and online new media space. Focusing on case studies, an exploration is presented which traces the emergence of gay identity. This reveals factual media space as a prime opportunity for the exhibition of new gay and lesbian identity ideals. I argue that representational histories are challenged, largely by the efforts of ordinary citizens not necessarily in control of media production. This, I suggest, is enabled by a 'transformation in intimacy' (Giddens, 1995), where intimate storytelling offers contemporary potential to change social worlds. Furthermore, this reveals therapeutic benefits in the opportunity to work though identity issues. This, I argue, is relevant to the framework of the oppositional public sphere, contexts of intimacy and emotion, and Carl Rogers' (1983) idea of 'whole person learning'. Through these potentials (discussed below), social actors engage in political agency showcasing their work within various media forms. Despite their fragmented discursive potential, I argue that they are connected through the potential of 'performative space' (Pullen, 2007a) within factual media. This is evident within the following case studies, where performers and producers offer new stories of engagement.

I examine the impact of talk show host Russell Harty in the United Kingdom, with a particular focus on his interview with Dirk Bogarde (also discussed in Chapter 3). Whilst Harty was not openly gay (to the general audience), he was an iconic performer expressing a subliminal sexual diversity to the masses, enabling a certain connectivity which stimulated progressive ideas. Furthermore, in progressing the diversity of factual media space, I discuss the work of Peter Adair in *Word is Out: Stories of Our Lives* (1977, US), *The AIDS Show* (1986, US) and *Absolutely Positive* (1991, US) within the documentary genre. Adair encouraged gay and lesbian social actors to express their personal, community and relationship desires, foregrounding the context of AIDS. In addition I explore the impact of Pedro Zamora whose contribution to the reality series *The Real World* (Bunim-Murray for MTV, 1992–present, US) and the documentary *In Our Own Words: Teens and AIDS* (Jeanne Blake, 1995, US), offered powerful political discourse, coalescing his political work as an AIDS activist. Finally, in extending factual media to reveal the agency of the audience, I examine the impact of the film *Brokeback Mountain* with relation to the Ultimate Brokeback (web) Forum (briefly discussed above). Within this audience media producers express personal visions of connectivity to the film and its iconic meanings, extending the potential of the original text.

I will begin by contextualising these discursive possibilities, framing them within the context of the talk show. I argue that the talk show may be used as a model for what I term as 'factual media space' where intimate dialogue has foregrounded new stories connected to gay and lesbian lives.

Factual media space: Joshua Gamson, the talk show and vulnerability

Factual media space may largely be considered as 'talk show-like' in its propensity to offer discussion forums within various media. This is evident as documentary, reality television and online new media contributions similarly foreground 'everyday' conversation framed as 'factual' discussion. Furthermore, it is possible to argue that the contemporary idea of intimate dialogue within the media extends from, or at least has been influenced by, the impact of the talk show, progressing from the work of Phil Donahue and Oprah Winfrey in the 1970s and 1980s (see Gamson, 1998; Joyner Priest, 1995; Shattuc, 1997; Wilson, 2003). Although we may consider that there has been a historical development in the potential of talk shows (since Donahue and Winfrey) to offer discursive space for intimate storytelling, my focus does not address histories of development and form, but rather the progression and expanse of identity storytelling. I argue that the talk show has increasingly enabled the visibility of subaltern and disenfranchised identities, and potentially that this offers democracy to diverse identity forms. However, it is important to note that, conversely, through the demands of mainstream entertainment, talk shows often capitalise on stereotypical identity recognition, and that this can be retrogressive.

Joshua Gamson's work within *Freaks Talk Back: Tabloid Talk Shows and Sexual Nonconformity* (1998) reveals this ambivalence, and may be used as a historical and theoretical model to further contextualise factual media space. Gamson tells us:

> [T]alk shows shed a different kind of light on sex and gender conformity. They are spots not only of visibility but of the subsequent redrawing of the lines between the normal and the abnormal. They are, in a very real sense, battlegrounds over what sexuality and gender can be. (p. 5)

Through the analysis of a variety of contemporary talk shows and performances within these, Gamson explores the potential of discursive space. With regard to gender and sexuality, this reveals the opportunity to define the boundaries of normalcy. Similar to the observations by Patricia Joyner Priest (1995) where 'the Women's movement and gay rights advocacy groups ... have traditionally used self-disclosure [within talk shows] to highlight the connections between private realities and politics' (p. 105) and Jane Shattuc (1997) who consider this as 'consciousness raising' (p. 128), Gamson posits the idea of social agency. This may be seen in the proliferation of non-heterosexual identities given a platform in talk shows, a phenomenon which has developed over the years, extending to other media forms such as documentary, reality television and online new media (discussed below).

Joshua Gamson (1998) traces a history from early talk shows and the precedence of Phil Donahue working from the late 1960s in *The Phil Donahue Show* (1969–74, US) and *Donahue* (1974–96) which was 'remarkably consonant with the predominantly white and middle-class gay movement's agenda' (p. 49). Also he contextualises the significance of Oprah Winfrey and her varied talk show programming which offered further democratic scope.[1] However, the political potential of Donahue and Winfrey offering elucidation and education was eclipsed in favour of more commodity-based texts. Gamson postulates that 'the pursuit of truth [within the talk show was] abandoned' (p. 32), and was emblematic in the cancellation of *Donahue* in 1996.

Later contemporary talk shows (such as *Jerry Springer* and *Ricki*) involved increasing degrees of commodity use, and ultimately there is 'democratization [only] through exploitation' (Gamson, 1998: 19). In this way, rather than carefully examining the homosexual subject and offering favourable discursive space, there was a shift towards a postmodern deconstruction. Whilst I have argued earlier that in terms of storytelling, the postmodern ethos and its potential do allow diverse identities to be juxtaposed democratically (see Chapter 3), these have not necessarily been framed favourably in contemporary talk shows, where indifferent commentators rather than self-reflexive storytellers take hold. Gamson suggests that there is 'juxtapos[ition] rather than integrat[ion of] multiple heterogeneous, discontinuous elements' (Munson et al. cited in Gamson, 1998: 42), and this does not necessarily offer favourable political scope.

Consequently, whilst there is ambivalence in the contemporary talk show, involving a difficult relationship with commodity identity and postmodernity, at the same time there is a drive towards values: 'Talk shows cannot tolerate a crisis in meaning any more than the rest of culture' (Gamson, 1998: 168). This may engender vulnerability for homosexual identity, through prioritising dominant concerns and fears.

Joshua Gamson (1998) explores this, focusing on issues of vulnerability in the example of *The Jenny Jones Show* (1991–2003, US), which featured Scott Amedure and Jon Schmitz. Amedure had appeared on the show expressing a 'same-sex secret crush' for Schmitz who was unaware of the setting up. Shortly after the taping, Schmitz murdered Amedure, for his alleged humiliation in the show.[2] Whilst the episode was never actually broadcast, controversy surrounded the eventual trial of Schmitz and assumptions were made about the value of homosexual life. As Gamson (1998) reports:

> That most commentators (and to some degree, the jury) interpreted the event as public humiliation reveals not just blatant, unexamined heterosexism – in the assumption that same-sex desire degrades its object, while opposite-sex desire flatters it – but also a telling reaction to the integration of gays and lesbians into public media space. (p. 210)

In this way the equality of gay and lesbian life is rejected, suggesting that only heterosexual contexts of love and romance are worthy of mainstream contextualisation. Such rejection of homosexual intimacy but intense interest in its entertainment context is a contentious issue in examining social agency.

Whilst I discuss later that indeed there are instances of overt political potential, particularly within documentary, reality television and new media space, within the talk show there is often a tension and ambivalence between dominant and minority identities. At the same time, the context of emotion and the potential of the oppositional public sphere extending from theories foregrounding the potential of the talk show (discussed below), offer frameworks of progression for subaltern identities for homosexuals.

Oppositional public sphere, intimacy and emotion

Sonia Livingstone and Peter Lunt in *Talk on Television: Audience Participation and Public Debate* (1994) consider the potential of 'active' media viewers (p. 18), and the context of the 'oppositional public sphere'. Defining diverse theoretical frameworks which have considered the viewer in different ways, from economic and production contexts (Adorno and Horkenheimer, 1977) to cultural reading potential (Hall, 1980), they focus on the idea of the 'citizen-viewer' (p. 19) who potentially participates in democratic processes offered by the public sphere (Corner, 1991). Using the example of the talk show as a theoretical model they tell us: 'As more ordinary people participate in making television programmes as well as receiving them, this gives force to the concept of the active viewer' (p. 19). It is this focus on activity and citizenship which I argue is similarly embedded in the concept of factual media space as discussed here.

The context of 'intimate citizenship' (also discussed in Chapter 2) is also highly relevant within this, for its potential to describe the diverse

. actions of seemingly disconnected social actors who are working towards democracy. As Ken Plummer (1997) tells us:

> Intimate Citizenship does not imply one model, one pattern [and] one way. On the contrary, it is a loose term which comes to designate a field of stories, an array of tellings, out of which new lives, new communities and new politics may emerge. (p. 152)

Such a 'field of stories' may be considered to be contained within the generic confines of the talk show, the documentary, reality television and participatory media. This may be related to the potential of the 'oppositional public sphere', which Livingstone and Lunt extend from Jürgen Habermas' (1962) original concept of 'bourgeois public sphere'. Further developing Oskar Negt and Alexander Kluge's (1993 [originally 1972]) concept of 'proletarian' public sphere, they contextualise the contemporary work of Nancy Fraser (1989, 1997) and Chantal Mouffe (1988), telling us 'that the media can facilitate the expression of diverse political and social interests in order to form a compromise between negotiated positions' (p. 35). Livingstone and Lunt propose a concept for the public sphere extending beyond Habermas' original ideas which may only allow enfranchised citizens engagement in meaningful debate. The 'oppositional public sphere', similar to Negt and Kluge's 'proletarian' concept of this, allows dissenting voices valuable discursive space, not necessarily connected to 'authorised' citizenship status (see Pullen, 2007a).

The innovation of the oppositional (and proletarian) public sphere is that it brings together the idea of the private (family) and the public (work and social performance), allowing the idea that public debate can occur outside authorised government institutions and organisations. Furthermore, it displays 'resistance [to] the hegemony of the bourgeois public–private division and its conventions' (Van Zoonen, 2001: 675), which may be centred on authorised voices connected to property and social standing.

This, I argue, is largely achieved through the potential of intimacy and emotion, as expressed within contemporary society. Anthony Giddens (1995) tells us that:

> Emotion becomes a life-political issue in numerous ways with the latter-day development of modernity. In the realm of sexuality, emotion as a means of communication, as a commitment and cooperation with others, is especially important. The model of confluent love

suggests an ethical framework for the fostering of non-destructive emotion in the conduct of individual and communal life. (p. 202)

In contemporary society the expression of emotion (and intimacy) is a recognisable framework of engagement which encourages social connectivity and discursive flow. Within the oppositional public sphere this offers opportunities for expression and transgression. In this way gay and lesbian media performers express discourse through emotion, and this extends potential, as the 'central function of discourse is not to refer to the pre-existing world but to create and sustain the social order' (Livingstone and Lunt, 1994: 42). Consequently, I argue that the expression of emotion within the contemporary public sphere offers the potential to create new liminal spaces, rather than reinforcing old forms.

However, emotion and intimate display may not necessarily involve the direct expression of sexual identity and its potential in social constructionist terms. This is primarily evident in the following case study on Russell Harty, and the contextualisation of his interview with Dirk Bogarde (also discussed in Chapter 3). Whilst neither Harty nor Bogarde openly promoted homosexual identities, their discursive potential supported homosexual ideals, extending from themselves. This reveals a complex scenario where the signposting and potential fixing of sexual identity become prime concerns for audiences and performers alike.

Russell Harty and Dirk Bogarde: signposting, domesticity and humanity

Russell Harty (see Figure 4.1) was a television presenter who would develop a high-profile career as a talk show host from 1973 until his death in 1988.[3] He kept his sexuality private, yet his iconic identity was contiguous with homosexual ideals. This involved the audience reading him as homosexual, perhaps because of the way he presented himself and through interactions with his guests (involving camp humour and sexual innuendo). Later in his career, the mainstream press, most notably *The News of the World*, expressed an interest in fixing a particular homosexual identity upon him, attempting to connect him to male prostitutes. As Alan Bennett (1994) reports, this unfavourable pursuit even involved the journalist attributed to exposing Harty's imagined dalliances reiterating the story in the press whilst Harty was on his deathbed (p. 53). Such pernicious attention not only displays evidence of homosexual subjugation,

Figure 4.1   Russell Harty, talk show host and public figure. Image courtesy of Alan Bennett

but it demonstrates a general audience interest in the signposting, display and fixing of sexual identity.

My purpose here is to explore Russell Harty's relationship with homosexual identity, and the signposting of this within the media. Whilst he resisted broadcasting the details of a personal homosexual identity, he actively courted guests who could themselves be interpreted in this way, and thereby placed a focus on his own sexual life. This reveals a complex social state where Harty appears to be involved in subterfuge by not explicitly acknowledging his personal sexual identity, yet pursuing a political homosexual agenda. Whilst Alan Bennett (1994) reports that Russell Harty never denied that he was homosexual to his close friends (yet he was fearful of negative press which may have threatened his career), I believe that he presented a very open homosexual identity intended to be read by audiences and guests alike. This I would suggest offers a degree of subversion from within (see Chapter 2): Harty appeared to conform through not displaying a confrontational identity, yet he embedded his representations and discussions with homosexual discourse. In order to explore this I am contextualising his early talk show *Russell Harty Plus* (ITV, 1973–81, UK), and further examining his interview with Dirk Bogarde in *Dirk Bogarde: Above the Title – a Conversation with Russell Harty* (Nick Gray for Yorkshire Television, 1986, UK) (see also Chapter 3).

Evidence of Russell Harty's connection to homosexual identity may be seen not only in the audience reading his personal deportment and conversational style; it may be seen in his choice of interview guests. In the book of the television series *Russell Harty Plus* the selected guests include a number of gay-identified or sexually nonconformist interviewees,[4] such as April Ashley, who Harty introduces as:

> [First coming to] public notice when her name was blazoned across the front pages of the Sunday newspapers as the man who had the effrontery to undergo an operation to become a woman. Since then, she has undergone the even more painful process of divorcing the man she married, and being told by a judge that she didn't even measure up to being a woman anyway. (Harty, 1974: 49)

Harty progressively foregrounds the discourse of a sexual nonconformist member of the public, for what essentially was a show business entertainment magazine. It is notable that Ashley is introduced as challenging dominant sexual ideologies, and questioning the fixity of gender performance, in a way that positively frames her actions in becoming a transsexual. Furthermore, this is reiterated by Harty where he poses the question 'Do you believe that a man has to be a man and a woman has to be a woman, and there is not an area between those two in which the two may overlap?' (Harty, 1974: 51). Harty argues that there is a fluidity in gender performance, echoing Judith Butler's (1999 [originally 1990]) ideas that 'the repetition of heterosexual constructs within sexual cultures both gay and straight may well be the inevitable site for the denaturalisation and mobilisation of gender categories' (p. 41). Such radical positioning in examination of gender transgression is also evident with regards to the potential of homosexual lives. This is particularly apparent in Russell Harty's examination of Dirk Bogarde.

Russell Harty interviewed Dirk Bogarde at his home in Provence, France, staying with the film crew there for three days in June 1986 (Gray, 2007) (see Figure 4.2). In the eventual documentary *Dirk Bogarde: Above the Title – a Conversation with Russell Harty*, Harty (in collusion with director Nick Gray) posed deep and probing questions attempting to explore Bogarde's 40-year relationship with Tony Forwood (also discussed in Chapter 3). Set mostly in the house and garden of Bogarde and Forwood's home, Harty presents a domestic representation of the

Figure 4.2   Russell Harty (left) with Dirk Bogarde (right) and Amanda Wragg (centre). A casual photograph taken on location, whilst filming *Dirk Bogarde: Above the Title*. Photograph © Amanda Wragg

movie star. Whilst Bogarde at no point reveals the personal extents of his relationship with Forwood, Harty frames their lives together very sympathetically. This is particularly evident where there is a discussion on the decor of the house, as a metaphor for their relationship. This occurs after Harty persuades Bogarde to agree that they have 'more than an agent and client relationship' and that Dirk is 'blessed' in having Tony.

Harty   Whose house is it?

Bogarde   Mine!

Harty   And whose taste is reflected in the house?

Bogarde   Pah! Difficult to say really, it sort of grew like topsy, all around us.

Harty   It is a house of such exquisite taste, and it has a kind of unity on it, I wondered if you had created it together? . . .

Russell Harty ties their relationship together in the stylistic unity of the house, foregrounding the discursive potential of domesticity in the endurance and bonding of their lives. He uses this method to openly discuss Bogarde and Forwood's intimate connection, without confrontation or a sense of separation. In this way, whilst Harty presents Bogarde as possibly concealing his personal life, he offers a domestic image of Bogarde as strong and enduring.

This sense of strength and personal depth of emotion is contextualised in the early part of the documentary, where Harty investigates Bogarde's experiences in the Second World War, and the context of humanity. Whilst the premise for the documentary had been partially to advertise Bogarde's new autobiographical volume (Gray, 2007) *Backcloth* (Bogarde, 1986) in which he discusses his experiences in the war, Harty foregrounds the context of the war to illuminate Bogarde's comprehension of the failure of humanity in times of conflict. This, I argue, presents evidence of Bogarde's reasoning in wishing to conceal his personal self from the public world, after having witnessed unconscionable human behaviour during the Second World War. In discussing his arrival at the liberation of the concentration camp of Belsen, witnessing 'mountains of dead people', he emotionally discloses:

> I went through some of the huts, and there were tiers and tiers of rotting people, but some of them were alive underneath the rot. And some were lifting their heads trying to do the victory thing.
>
> [Awkwardly lifts his hand to his head and presents the war time victory sign, with two fingers]
>
> That was the worst.
>
> [Bogarde emotionally breaks down briefly, and apologises to Harty]

This sequence is the culmination of a conversation where Bogarde discusses the atrocities of war, and his situation at one time as an officer involved in selecting targets to be bombed. Bogarde's situation as agent and witness of war engenders an identity which is strong and sympathetic, and reveals the depth of his humanity. Harty frames this identity, not only reiterating that the war had made him stronger, but also that Bogarde is now aware of the vulnerability of the disenfranchised.

I would argue that Bogarde's experiences in the war enabled his full understanding of the potential moral failure of society, and that Harty foregrounded this as a valid reason why he preferred not to disclose his personal, and potentially vulnerable, identity. Harty even persuades Bogarde to admit that he is covert. In discussing the burning of his diaries, which included full details of his wartime life and possibly more about his relationship with Tony Forwood, Bogarde admits: 'I think it's the attitude of someone covering up. Covering up from some people who don't know, and don't understand, and never have known, a generation that thinks that's what you must have been like, and you weren't like that at all.' Bogarde rejects an intimate interpretation of his life, which might be reductive. As echoed in an earlier comment to Harty about his personal life with Tony Forwood: 'if you think that we sit down knitting and pulling rugs, forget it!' in this way distancing himself from an effeminised homosexual identity which might be seen as disempowered (see Bergling, 2001).

Such vulnerability is echoed in Russell Harty's own life where the popular press unfavourably pursued him (discussed above). This inevitably exerted pressure on him, to the extent that although *Above the Title* had been nominated for a BAFTA award he stayed away from the ceremony for fear of negative exposure (Gray, 2007). When he later became critically ill (with hepatitis), Alan Bennett and Nick Gray both report that *The News of the World* set up a cruel strategy involving the covert observation of his hospital room from outside the building and attempts to bribe hospital staff to provide 'useful' information. Such pernicious attention and abject inhumanity were further impacted with tragic irony, in that Harty passed away just at the moment that a helicopter was arriving with a transplant liver which may have saved his life (Gray, 2007), here focusing on the drama and vulnerability of Harty's life.

Whilst Russell Harty and Dirk Bogarde (also discussed in Chapter 3) were seen as vulnerable men, who could be represented as avoiding some imagined truth about their lives, I have argued that they employed powerful iconic and discursive strategies. Through the display of emotion and intimate connectivity, Russell Harty and Dirk Bogarde produce engaging discourse which encouraged contemporary audiences to connect to their personal stories. Even in the context of partially disclosed identity, through audiences witnessing intimate and emotive display there is an encouragement to make connections and evaluations. This, I argue, displays evidence of the potential of intimacy within factual media space, and its situation within an oppositional public sphere.

However, the full expression of intimate and emotive display which might include the open testament of personal sexuality, offers more intensity for social agency and active discursive power. This is particularly evident in the following case study, where the expression of the intimate (homosexual) self is embedded in the work of documentary film maker Peter Adair and political activist Pedro Zamora, here relating not only to the context of gay and lesbian community, but also the issue of AIDS and personal identity.

Peter Adair and Pedro Zamora: whole person learning and AIDS

Peter Adair (1943–96, see Figure 4.3) was involved (as a producer and editor) in the groundbreaking documentary film *Word is Out: Stories of Our Lives* (The Mariposa Film Group, 1977, US) (see Pullen, 2007a). Reaching wide audiences through the American Public Broadcasting Service network, this may be regarded as one of the first documentaries to record affirmative performances of gay men and lesbians, foregrounding the positive potential of non-heterosexual lives.[5] Later, Adair produced *The AIDS Show* with Rob Epstein (1986, US) which was a documentary adaptation of a theatre performance of the same name. This was a major break in tone with earlier representations of people with AIDS as victims (see Román, 1998). It provided an 'invocation of humour and camp mixed

Figure 4.3 Documentary maker Peter Adair depicted early in his career, 'adjusting the light'. Photograph © Veronica Selver

with the emotions of suffering and loss' (Román, 1998: 54), thereby representing a therapeutic performance of transgression. Furthermore with HIV positive status, Peter Adair produced and directed the self-reflexive documentary *Absolutely Positive* (1990, US) (Adair died in 1996). In this he not only presents interviews from a wide range of people who were HIV positive (or had AIDS), but also he contextualises their stories in relation to his life.

Pedro Zamora (1972–94) was a young AIDS activist of Cuban descent (see Munoz, 1998; Pullen, 2004, 2005, 2007a). After discovering the disease in himself at the age of 18, he embarked on a humanitarian mission to educate audiences concerning his personal experience as a gay youth with AIDS (Brownworth, 1992; Pullen, 2004, 2005, 2007a). In 1991 his outstanding focus on AIDS education was reported on the front page of *The Wall Street Journal* (Morgenthaler, 1991), and later he testified before the American Congress (12 July 1993) and spoke at a Capitol Hill reception (1 November 1993). His work was further broadcast in the educational documentary *In Our Own Words: Teens and AIDS* (Jeanne Blake, 1995, US), and in his high-profile participation in the MTV reality television series *The Real World*, San Francisco (Bunim Murray for MTV, 1994, US). In *The Real World* Pedro with boyfriend Sean Sasser represented an apparently normative romantically entwined couple who just happened to be gay, non-white and HIV positive or had AIDS (Sean was HIV positive and Pedro had AIDS). Whilst Pedro died shortly after the series was filmed (just after the final episode was broadcast), his lasting legacy was his connection with large audiences, which included personal support by President Bill Clinton near the time of his death (see Pullen, 2007a). Pedro became an icon not only representing people with AIDS, but also through the exposure of his intimate and frail life he presented a resilience and a resistance to subjugation, revealing a personal integrity and humanity which would challenge dominant ideas.

Peter Adair and Pedro Zamora are discussed here together not just for their status as openly gay men and their connection to AIDS education, but for their performance of self-reflexive storytelling in media participation. Adair as a documentary producer and Zamora as a public speaker, both crossing the producer and performer divide, developed strategies which capitalised on their emerging public profiles. Here Adair extends his documentary work in *Word is Out* to later more personal AIDS-focused texts, and Zamora publicises his political work, which had been apparent within the press and at educational venues, through personal exposure in documentary film. In this way both expose their intimate lives within the media, challenging issues of subjugation surrounding AIDS and gay identity, progressing discursive ideas.

Peter Adair and Pedro Zamora are politically enabled, foregrounding the potential of self-reflexive performance in the construction of social knowledge. As Anthony Giddens (1995) tells us: 'The continual reflexive incorporation of knowledge not only steps into the breach; it provides precisely a basic impetus to the changes which sweep through personal, as well as global, contexts of action' (p. 29). Such agency is presented in the work of Peter Adair and Pedro Zamora, making connections to global issues, such as the issue of AIDS or the context of non-heterosexual identity, through the unpeeling of the personal self. Capitalising on 'institutional reflexivity' (see Chapter 3) in the construction of knowledge, Adair and Zamora present the potential of homosexual lives, relating issues such as personal value, commitment, demand for equality and integrity. Whilst they are represented foregrounding the issues of AIDS, at the same time they frame this within the liminal context of homosexual desire. In order to discuss this further I will first examine work of Peter Adair, and then contextualise Pedro Zamora.

Peter Adair tells us in the opening sequence of *Absolutely Positive*:

> I've been making films for 30 years. My movies have always been a way of exploring personal interest. When I worried about religion, I made a film about it. When I realised I was gay, I made a film about it. When I worried about the 'bomb', I made a film about it. This has become a very expensive form of therapy.

Adair adds that when he tested positive for HIV, he decided again to investigate this through film in *Absolutely Positive*. Self-reflexive personalisation foregrounding issues of social concern forms the central narrative within *Absolutely Positive*, and is evident in Adair's previous work.

Peter Adair had been working for KQED (public broadcasting) in California in 1975, when he 'became dissatisfied with the quality of work there' (Atwell, 1988: 572) and made attempts to 'get into some sort of social film making' (Adair cited in Atwell, 1988: 572). This became the impetus for what would later develop into *Word is Out*, which Adair produced with the Mariposa Group interviewing 26 subjects. Whilst Lee Atwell (1988) notes that the interviewees were 'carefully chosen to display a richly diverse and contrasting series of views and lifestyles, [yet] no apparent structural pattern emerge[d] in the editing scheme' (p. 573), it is precisely the lack of 'expository' documentary focus (see Nichols, 2001) which might reveal a particular bias or argument, which engenders this as an early reflexive project. *Word is Out* is organised in an emotive sense, dividing the text into three areas of 'Early Years', 'Growing Up' and From Now On', rather than a dialectic sense with contrasting and oppositional views. The focus on experience, feelings and aspirations takes precedence over any obvious political drive or goal. This is emblematic of the potential of intimacy and postmodern narratives, where there is a collage of ideas, but also there is a democratisation of identity (see Chapter 3). This occurs too in *Absolutely Positive*, where the stories of heterosexual and homosexual lives are juxtaposed.

Such juxtaposition, however, is imbued with the overarching narrative of Peter Adair's identity as a gay man. There is a prioritisation which transcends the postmodern ethic, and foregrounds homosexual potential. I argue that whilst *Absolutely Positive* places equal attention on heterosexual and homosexual storytellers, the embedded persona of Peter Adair frames the narratives of the gay men represented there. This is apparent in an early part of the documentary where Adair advises us that the testimonies of the gay men offer a 'familiar ring, because these are my story'. Adair shared the same experiences with these subjects, as they too had announced their sexuality and had tested positive for AIDS. Consequently the narratives of gay men provide the most emotive sequences, due to their intimate connection to the documentary maker, Adair.

Therefore Peter Adair employs the narratives of gay men in self-reflection, offering an intimate realisation of situation, and potential for transformation and affirmation. This is evident in the testimony of a Gregg Cassin (Cole, 2007) in *Absolutely Positive* who after the first time he encounters a man with AIDS records his feelings of shame for being afraid to touch that person. Gregg describes how after shaking the man's hand, that he concealed his hand in his pocket and waited until he could go to a bathroom to wash his hands thoroughly. He adds that his behaviour was shameful, and considered that the man in question was incredibly brave in announcing his AIDS status, through unashamedly proffering his hand to a group of friends to be shaken (knowing the likely responses).

This realisation is further impacted where Gregg Cassin later affirms in a sense of transformation how he had helped a friend who was dying of complications resulting from AIDS, advising that not only was this a very emotional and loving time, but also that:

> Nobody knows what those people have gone through. Nobody knows the amazing strength, and the love and the generosity that those people have. Those awful gay people that this world thinks of, and the

amazing angels that they are, and the amazing love that they give to their friends.

This focuses on the potential of Kath Weston's (1991) concept of families of choice, where non-heterosexuals form friendship-based family-like networks of support. Also it foregrounds the failure of heterosexuals to be aware of homosexual worth. Such a focus embeds not only an emotive display, but also it sets a political agenda relating transformation. This foregrounds the issue of awareness of transformation in self, where one becomes more self-aware, realising previous failings. Also it signals a desire for transformation within society, where there is an awareness of the action that needs to be taken to improve social worlds. Such focus on transformation is evident in testimonies of personal change foregrounding self-reflexivity and a move to action, prioritising agency.

A similar focus on social agency is evident in the testimony of another young gay male called Eric. He recalls an intense attraction to a potential partner called Scott, and the discovery that Scott had been diagnosed with AIDS six weeks after he had met him. Eric expresses his deep loyalty for Scott, in the fact that he did not abandon him and cared for him until his death, telling us 'having Scott for two years would have been enough as having someone for 20 years'. This intense loyalty is transformed into a move to action with Eric telling us 'Losing Scott to AIDS made me realise that I needed to do something about AIDS, and [I] realised there was a real problem with homelessness among people with AIDS.' This agency is vividly represented with images of Eric holding a public meeting, where a number of homeless people with AIDS are present. This marks a progression from earlier images of Eric where he had been personally interviewed in a domestic environment, suggesting a shift from private to public sphere, and a call to action. Also this is emblematic of the oppositional public sphere (discussed earlier), where intimacy progresses into public social spaces and this possesses transgressive potential.

Ultimately Peter Adair employs representations within *Absolutely Positive* which relate the issue of affirmation and necessary agency. At the same time they clearly represent a therapeutic potential, and a coming to terms. This involves learning from self-realisation, and planning ahead. In this way *Absolutely Positive* builds on the metaphorical idea of discovery of illness (AIDS/HIV), and finding a way forward. This is apparent not only in Peter Adair's central role as lead storyteller and interpreter, but also is evident in the context of prioritising humanity over social standing or membership of dominant groupings. As Gregg Cassin tells us:

> My new goal is to be human; it is to really embrace myself. It's my right to have a shitty day. It's my right to have a cold. I am a human being. It's my right to be a bitch. It's my right to be less than perfect. It's my right to be HIV positive. Even there, I can be loved. Even there.

Acceptance of self, and one's imperfections, is presented as the way forward in dealing with HIV or AIDS status. This foregrounds the therapeutic nature of self-disclosure, and the potential of self-reflexive storytelling. Through Adair's performers exposing their personal selves, potential for change is presented in terms of an oppositional public sphere. Personal and intimate narratives stimulate public agency, in a drive to challenge ideas. Peter Adair uses personal narratives extending from his own story in a political drive to educate and reform. Pedro Zamora similarly foregrounds his personal story within diverse media, representing opportunities for change and issues of education.

Pedro Zamora, in an interview for *POZ Magazine* (a specialist HIV/AIDS publication which depicted Zamora on its front cover, see Figure 4.4), tells us:

> My greatest challenge in life has been to become an entire person. We fragment people, especially minorities, because we assume it's easier to deal with specific problems if we compartmentalize behaviour. Well I could deal with the fact that I was gay. I could deal with my being a Latino man in America. I could deal with having been sexually abused as a kid. I could deal with having HIV and AIDS. But I couldn't deal with them together at the same time. And you have to if you ever want to become a whole person. (Cited in Rubenstein, 1994: 79)

Zamora foregrounds the fragmented nature of disenfranchised identities, revealing how compartmentalisation is a dominant process which enables partial visibility; however, this maintains separation and reinforces the status quo. Zamora's key focus is to present the identity of a whole person, where the diverse aspects of his minority status are fully represented in order to achieve a sense of psychological completeness.

Through Pedro Zamora's foregrounding of his complete personal experience this is contiguous with Carl Rogers' (1971, 1983) ideas about the development of the self in 'becoming a person' and 'client centred therapy', where there is a focus on openness, personal feelings

Figure 4.4   Pedro Zamora on the cover of *POZ* magazine (a specialist publication focusing on HIV and AIDS). Image courtesy of *POZ*

and becoming self-aware. This may also be related to Rogers' (1983) idea of 'whole person learning', where education involves opportunities to extend beyond the normal schematic and curricular expectations, and there is a foregrounding of personal expectations and fulfilment. Furthermore, 'whole person learning' makes distinctions between left hemisphere brain activity which is considered to be logical and linear, and right hemisphere activity which is considered to be emotive and personal. Rogers suggests that education should not be reliant on left hemisphere associations which are about dominant order and the status quo, and that better self-improvement and fulfilment come from equal engagement with right hemisphere identifications which may be intuitive, metaphorical or aesthetic rather than logical. In this way education should concern the full potential of the self, and should not be inhibited by stereotypical concerns or dominant ideologies, which may not be beneficial to the individual.

Pedro Zamora's performance displays evidence of such creative educational potential, and this is particularly evident in his full expression of the diverse aspects of his identity. Whilst Zamora admitted that in the early stages of his educational teaching career he avoided talking about his sexual identity in order to disconnect the stereotypical association of the homosexual male and AIDS (cited in Rubenstein, 1994: 79), as his career developed he increasingly revealed more of his personal identity. This included (as discussed above) detail of his intimate sexual life, revealing the depth of his personal disclosures. Furthermore, as he began to achieve more media attention within the mainstream press, and this was further stimulated by his appearance in *The Real World*, he increasingly presented a candid, yet unashamed and complete identity. This included presenting aspects of his personal life, showcasing his romantic partnership with Sean Sasser.

Within *The Real World*, Pedro's potential to find romantic love with Sean comes as no surprise as it is foregrounded in the opening episode. We see his romantic potential in an edited forthcoming scene with Pedro saying to Sean: 'Do I plan on getting married?' As the relationship developed, it was represented in the classical form of desire, courtship and romance. Pedro and Sean are brought together by a third party (the AIDS educator group in San Francisco) with Pedro commenting that he had briefly met Sean (before San Francisco) and thought he was very desirable. Later, the relationship develops with them engaged in courtship, involving romantic dinner dates and walks together holding hands. Then Sean asks Pedro to marry him, and later they are both involved in planning the ceremony. Eventually the celebration takes place, where they are supported by friends. Within this we see *Real World* housemate Cory casually taking photographs of the couple, with intent to record the 'normative' romantic moment, and guests make statements of support to them. Furthermore, housemate Judd Winnick comments after witnessing Pedro and Sean's wedding ceremony that 'this is not something that I have ever encountered before, but it felt strangely right. This is an ordinary occurrence, or rather it should be.'

This focus on the potential of the coupling of Sean and Pedro connects with the potential of romance narratives in society. This forms a basis through which Pedro represents his coupling with Sean as normative, and progressive. As Anthony Giddens (1995) tells us: romantic love 'provides for a long term life trajectory, orientated to an anticipated yet malleable future; and it creates a "shared history"' (p. 45). Pedro showcases his relationship with Sean, foregrounding romance narratives which suggest stability, continuance and shared values. He does this by correlating his relationship with Sean as equivalent to hetero-sexual bonding, and frames this within a ritual ceremony where they exchange rings, echoing the institution of marriage. Pedro offers pro-gressive educational agency, revealing his 'whole person' identity. Such completeness of identity is further evident in his relationship to AIDS, and his educational value to society.

From the opening episodes of the *Real World*, Pedro reveals that he has AIDS. This creates narrative tension with Pedro as a central point of reference, and others are represented as either supporters or in opposi-tion. Whilst housemates Judd, Corey, Mohammed and Pam are instantly supportive, Rachel and Puck are represented in contrast or opposition. Rachel is initially concerned at the prospect of living in a household with someone who has AIDS, and is represented in the 'confessional' room at the close of the opening episode voicing concerns:

> I want to ask some 'hardcore' questions. About how [AIDS is] going to affect him, how it's going to affect us, as his roommates. None of those things were discussed, everybody was just in so much admiration of his accomplishments [if I had asked] a question at that point [I would have appeared like] the 'bitch'.[6]

Later as the series develops, Rachel gets closer to Pedro through friendship and the exploration of their shared Latino identity. She is represented as transformed and educated, although not necessarily foregrounding her open support of HIV/AIDS education.

Although Puck is largely represented as in a conflict of personality with Pedro, similarly we can read his distance from AIDS. Evidence of this is represented in Puck's apparent lack of concern for Pedro's condition as a vulnerable person with AIDS, demonstrated in his reckless attitude to hygiene, which could be perceived as a threat to someone vulnerable to infection. This occurs in the representation of Puck deliberately get-ting himself into dangerous scenarios where his skin is broken through careless bicycle riding in his job as a bicycle messenger. Through Puck's carefree exposure of blood leading to possible infections and in his unhy-gienic eating habits, including allowing a dog to eat from his plate, and plunging his dirty fingers into a pot of peanut butter belonging to Pedro, Puck is represented as lacking concern. Consequently, following a con-frontation between Puck and Pedro concerning this behaviour Puck is ejected from the house by a majority vote of the housemates (see Pullen, 2004, 2007a). Through the contrasting of Pedro and the issue of AIDS

Figure 4.5   Pedro Zamora photographed by Jeanne Blake in San Francisco during production of the DVD *In Our Own Words: Teens and AIDS*. (Available at www.wordscanwork.com)

in opposition to Rachel and Puck, these incidences are transformed into educational potential.

The support of education is further evident where Pedro is represented as working within AIDS education, and a number of the cast attend an event where Pedro makes a public address. Furthermore, Pedro's fluctuating health is used as an educational tool. In an instance where Pedro contracts PCP (pneumocystis pneumonia) and we discover that his T-cell count is dangerously low, we are presented with statistics and the likely prognosis. This highlights Pedro's physical vulnerability and courage, as he deals with the stresses participating in the programme, signalling his selfless contribution to AIDS education.

As further evidenced in *In Our Own Words: Teens and AIDS* (Jeanne Blake, 1995, US), Pedro Zamora is represented as a selfless role model educating the public, forming part of a small community of youths who are HIV positive but who selflessly give of themselves to AIDS education (see Figure 4.5). Within this it is notable that Pedro pays tribute to his good friend and peer David Kamens (see Pullen, 2007a) who died before the documentary was completed. Such physical frailty and vulnerability echo Pedro's own demise, which was recorded within the documentary *Tribute to Pedro Zamora* (Bunim Murray for MTV, 1994). Pedro became ill quite soon after *The Real World* was filmed, but he insisted that the producers record the final stages of his life. Within *Tribute to Pedro Zamora* we are party to the rapid deterioration of his health. In a sequence where Pedro tries to vocalise his feelings, due to a neurological disease he is unable to speak fluently. Despite starting a dialogue quite coherently where we see glimpses of his eloquent self, he stops in mid-sentence, there is a void and we are aware that the disease has taken hold. Later scenes reveal Pedro as immobile and in the last stages of life, with his head partially shaven from a neurological procedure, and he is emaciated. This powerfully marks an emotive transformation from his earlier 'healthy appearing' charismatic identity.

Such willingness to reveal his 'whole person' identity, including the tragic details of his decline, offers an inspiring story aimed at changing the world. This was also echoed in President Bill Clinton's tribute to Pedro at the time of his death:

> In his short life, Pedro educated and enlightened our nation. He taught all of us that AIDS is a disease with a human face and one that affects every American, indeed every citizen of the world. And he taught people living with AIDS how to fight for their rights and live with dignity. (Clinton, 1994)

Pedro Zamora's educational potential and evident personal strength reveal not only the social agency of self-reflexive storytelling where people may influence ideas, but also that this offers therapeutic potential. In a similar manner to Mimi White's (1992) idea of 'therapeutic discourse' (see Chapter 2), audiences may connect to the discursive ideas and they may interpret issues in relation to their personal identity. Therefore Pedro Zamora not only presents his 'whole person' identity, intimately disclosing his personal and social life, but also there is a process of 'discovery of self in experience' (Rogers, 1971: 113) where audiences may engage with this too. Pedro Zamora relates his psychological identity, willingly offering his personal expressions of self, rather than accommodating dominant expectations of how he should be. As discussed above, he avoids compartmentalisation where he might conceal the diverse parts of his identity and he exposes his intimate and vulnerable life in order to present a sense of personal wholeness.

This is evident in both the work of Peter Adair and Pedro Zamora, where there is psychological openness. As Carl Rogers (1971) tells us concerning the development of personal identity in *Becoming a Person*:

> [I]n this process the individual becomes more open to his experience. . . . It is the opposite of defensiveness. . . . The individual becomes more aware of his own feelings and attributes as they exist in an organic level, [becoming] more aware of reality as it exists outside of himself, instead of perceiving it in preconceived categories. (p. 115)

Although Rogers cites this concerning development within close relationships, such 'whole person' identity potential may be evident within media forms. Through Adair and Zamora opening up their personal lives and encouraging responses or performances around them, they stimulate a shift away from stereotypical and dominant concerns, offering self-reflexive potential. This is particularly evident within the final case study of this chapter on the Ultimate Brokeback Forum. Within this there is a focus on personal experience in responses to media texts. This makes connections between the performer and audience divide, revealing progressive agency within participatory media.

The Ultimate Brokeback Forum: therapy and agency

The Ultimate Brokeback Forum is a discussion board website which was generated in response to the film adaptation of Annie Proulx's novella *Brokeback Mountain* (Ang Lee, 2005, US) (Pullen, 2008).[7] As a groundbreaking tale set in the rural idyll of the American Midwest and focusing on a powerful love story between two young men, who whilst working together as cowboys find brief romantic and sexual satisfaction before being parted by the convention of their society, it inevitably became a controversial, provocative and stimulating text. Journalist Dave Cullen produced an online blog post in anticipation of the release of the film (in September 2005), which was eventually transformed into the Ultimate Brokeback web forum with the help of enthusiastic supporters. Drawing more than half a million posts in the first year (Cullen, cited in Members of the Ultimate Brokeback Forum, 2007), it exceeded the expectations of those involved in producing the discussion board, revealing a substantial need in the audience to respond to the content of the film. Therefore the imagined impact of *Brokeback Mountain* as a challenging Hollywood film situating a gay male romance, homophobia and hate crime murder within the heart of rural America, extended beyond this.

Figure 4.6 A small gathering of members of the Ultimate Brokeback Forum, just after the production of their book (May 2007, Estes Park Colorado): Dave Cullen (front row, second from left), Lydia Sledge Wells (front row, third from left), Jonathan Mortimer (senior editor) (front row, fourth from left) and Betty Greene Salwak (front row, fourth from right). They are posed in front of a truck which was used in the film *Brokeback Mountain* (owned by a forum member). Image © Jan Geyer

It stimulated innumerable discursive and cathartic responses through the web forum. This led not only to the popularity of the Ultimate Brokeback Forum, but also to the publication of a book called *Beyond Brokeback: the Impact of a Film* (2007) featuring contributions to the site, and additional commissioned work. This was produced in a large-scale collaboration between various supporters led by Lydia Wells Sledge and Dave Cullen (see Figure 4.6).

Within *Beyond Brokeback* (Members of the Ultimate Brokeback Forum, 2007) Dave Cullen tells us:

> Initially, 90 percent of the discussion was about the film – what was happening on the screen versus down in the audience. But there was a fascinating undercurrent about what it was doing to us. The film discussion died down eventually, and the personal stories edged their way to the forefront. (Cited in MUBF, 2007: xvii)[8]

This revealed an increasing focus of web contributors not only talking about the emotive impact of the film, but also about how this stimulated reflections in personal memory and experience often involving a reassessment of past events and a coming to terms. As Dave Cullen tells us:

> So many people were overcome by the experience [of watching *Broke-back Mountain*] they were searching the web and finding my site after they saw the film. Many of them had no idea what they were looking for, they were just grasping around. (Cited in MUBF, 2007: 2007: xviii)

A need in the audience to find an outlet for their responses to the film was evident in the vast support for, and connection to, the web-site, which also included an estimated 50,000–100,000 users each month who did not post but simply witnessed the contributions (Cullen, cited in MUBF, 2007). As Cullen indicates, the film raised issues which numerous members of the audience were attempting to explore with others. The discussion which follows examines the performances as represented within *Beyond Brokeback*, focusing on the identity potential of the Ultimate Brokeback Forum.

Whilst the book *Beyond Brokeback* (based on the discussion board) reveals many instances of personal lives which we may verify with regards to the expression of ages, professions and locations of living, due to the casual nature of web contributions and the lack of indexical evidence we are unable in every instance to authenticate actual identity (see Turkle, 1995; Gauntlett and Horsley, 2004). Consequently my focus here is on the discursive possibilities produced, outside of needs to ascertain the actual identity of contributors. I argue that the discursive potential is enabled by the web producers and editors (such as Lydia Wells Sledge and Dave Cullen) relating the content of the original forum, and that discovering the actual identity of the various contributors is less important. Through examining the discursive productions within the Ultimate Brokeback Forum, there is a possibility to explore coalescent social agency which foregrounds the potential for connectivity, democracy and therapy. At the same time the discursive performances produced provide possibilities in 'intuitional reflexivity' (see Chapter 3) revealing personal agency and self-reflexivity, offering therapeutic and democratic community ideals.

John McLeod (1997), writing about the therapeutic potential of narrative, tells us that:

> The telling of personal stories, tales of 'who I am,' 'what I want to be,' or 'what troubles me,' to a listener or audience mandated by the culture to hear such stories, is an essential mechanism through

which individual lives become and can remain aligned with collective realities [and works towards cohesion]. (p. 2)

This engenders a therapeutic possibility for minority identities, offering the reinterpretation of social lives and the challenging of dominant norms with regard to acceptance, equality and empowerment. I argue that the Ultimate Brokeback Forum offers such potential through its discussion forum basis, allowing diverse members of the public to present their personal interests and stories. This ultimately extends to the possibility to construct networks of connectivity where democratic communities may be formed.

Furthermore, I would argue that in terms of offering a participatory democratic public sphere, the Ultimate Brokeback Forum conforms to Robert W. McChesney's (1997) imagined criteria for this, constructing a 'sense of community [through] an effective system of political communication, broadly construed, that engages the citizenry' (p. 5). Whilst in terms of media this is not the mass communication hypothesis proposed by McChesney as ideal for national political democracy, in terms of a gay-identified communities (see Chapter 3) the Ultimate Brokeback Forum offers similar progressive scope. In this way the contributors may see themselves part of an imagined gay community and the forum constructs a resonant public sphere which not only connects diasporic gay identities (see Chapters 3 and 7), but showcases personal narratives to the larger world, offering transgressive potential.

Such formations of community and democracy may be produced in prioritising issues of personal liberty, indicating a desire for improved social worlds. As evidenced in the opening quote to this chapter, Jermaine Peters (web identity 'jermainep' – who is indicated as 20 years old, employed in retail and resident in Australia) there is hope for fulfilment in his entry entitled 'Is That so Much to Ask?' (cited in MUBF, 2007: 33). This also involves realisation, and citation of dominant social failing. Jermaine tells us:

[D]espite living in a small town, I have been fairly shielded. Some people refuse to serve me; I get called 'faggot' occasionally. I sort of shrug it off but I wonder how those people can do that. They don't seem to realize how much it hurts and they are hurting another human being. (Cited in MUBF, 2007: 33)

Personalisation indicating human needs in failing social worlds, offers a therapeutic scope where ideas are played out and imagined scenarios are relayed. Similar to the discussion above concerning Pedro Zamora and Peter Adair, humanitarian ideals are presented in the desires and observations of the web contributors, revealing the advent of watching the film as stimulating a catharsis for change.

Whilst I have discussed elsewhere the impact of *Brokeback Mountain* in relation to the iconic denial of homosexual domestic lives (Pullen, 2008) which is evident in the film's narrative construction by foregrounding society's failure to offer a safe place where lead characters Ennis and Jack may live together, I argue here that such denial forms the rhetorical impetus for web contributors to engage. This is particularly evident if we consider the contribution of Tom Gibson (web identity 'Wtg02'). Evaluating his own experiences in relationships as similar to those represented in *Brokeback Mountain* which reveal the dilemma of married men who repress same-sex desire yet engage in unsatisfying homosexual relationships, he postulates 'What I have come to understand is that not only were those relationships not very fulfilling – even though they were exhilarating – but there was never any real closure' (cited in MUBF, 2007: 76). Such foregrounding reveals not only the denial of domesticity for homosexual men in the representations of the film, but also the denial of psychological closure which could be related to the audience's personal experiences. This extends beyond personal dissatisfaction with intended suitors or partners, relating the problematic nature of dominant social confines.

As Tom Gibson suggests, this inevitably involves indicating the failings of everyday social and cultural worlds: 'How do you realise your hopes, dreams and desires in a culture that denies or marginalises and ultimately refuses to legitimize your experiences' (cited in MUBF, 2007: 77). In this way I argue that a large part of the emotive and therapeutic text within the Ultimate Brokeback Forum forms a drive for change, echoing personal memories and similar experiences. Evidence of this may be seen in contributions from Betty Greene Salwak (web identity 'neatfreak') and Glenn (web identity 'BrokenOkie'). Betty Greene Salwak's testimony relates to a letter she was inspired to write to a pastor in charge of Christian education at her church:

> My brother was a victim of homophobia. He died ten years ago from AIDS. For most of his life he never came out to his family. ... [*Brokeback Mountain*] clearly shows the disastrous results wrought by homophobia. Can we at least talk about it? (Cited in MUBF, 2007: 42)

Glenn relates the murder of a friend and ex-lover who '[w]as one of many innocent victims. The attack on him was similar to Jack's. He was dragged to a remote area, then stabbed and left to drown in his own blood; his body not found for days' (cited in MUBF, 2007: 32). Relating the experience of a brother rejected by family and church, and remembering a close friend who was murdered in a hate crime, reveals intimate levels of disclosure in attempting to explore the failings of humanity and dominant social worlds. Furthermore, it indicates a need for change.

The personal testaments of the Ultimate Brokeback Forum are not simply therapeutic and cathartic moments of reflection; they are frameworks of political desire constructed by a coalescent minority community involved in social agency. Whilst we are unable to fix indexical social identities to all the contributors, they generate discursive potential which bonds a potential gay community together. This offers not only therapeutic potentials, but also meaningful social connections and identifications.

Conclusion

Factual media space within the talk show, the documentary, reality television and online new media offers discursive possibilities for gay and lesbian lives. Whilst this has provided opportunity arising from talk shows relating the difference or intrigue of sexual nonconformity, audience focus has been creatively placed on subaltern identities. As we have seen in the groundbreaking work of Joshua Gamson (1998), the talk show provided a space for new discussions to take place, yet later contemporary formats have increasingly relied on commodity use. However, factual media space offers the opportunity of the oppositional public sphere (Livingstone and Lunt, 1994), where disenfranchised identities may engage in discursive potential. As exhibited in the case study on Russell Harty and Dirk Bogarde, the signposting of homosexual identity and the context of domesticity and humanity do not necessarily involve the open testament of personal lives. Such possibility, whether overtly commodified or subtly veiled, still produces discursive performativity.

As evidenced in the examination of Peter Adair and Pedro Zamora, through the display of intimate lives political agency is presented. Within documentary and reality television, discursive ideas are expressed working through from various media. The personal identity of Adair as a documentary maker, and Zamora as a political activist, both in relation to HIV/AIDS and gay identity, challenges social ideas through the foregrounding of their intimate lives. Such potential springs from the impetus to peel back the layers of identity, revealing humanity and personal strength. This, I argue, is related to the expression of 'whole person

. identity' (Rogers, 1983) where ideas of fulfilment are foregrounded. Adair and Zamora gave selflessly of themselves, changing the world through the agency of self-reflexive storytelling.

Such potential is further evident with the new media discussion board the Ultimate Brokeback Forum, inspired by personal responses to the film *Brokeback Mountain*. Participatory new media stimulates the coalescence of an imagined gay community, formed through the sharing of narratives. Furthermore, the showcasing of personal stories inspired by viewing *Brokeback Mountain* revealed therapeutic potency, suggesting reflection and reinterpretation. I argue that such potential relates not only to the connections and reflections which can be made, but also that this reveals a coalescent humanity evident within gay and lesbian lives.

Factual media space opens up opportunities. Whilst earlier forms focused on diverse individuals seen as outsiders 'breaking their way in', later concepts increasingly involve media participation. The progressive and courageous appearance of gay men and lesbians within the talk show, the documentary and reality television is advanced by the community possibilities of online new media space. The community convergence of the Ultimate Brokeback Forum represents a vivid new social formation which echoes the reality of the gay community though new connectivities. Such group potential forges a way forward, building on the substantial work of those in isolated positions. Harty, Bogarde, Adair and Zamora in various 'isolated' ways have extended the possibilities of gay community within factual media space. The promise of the Ultimate Brokeback Forum is not only that it is community based and contributes to a sense of collective homosexual identity, but also that this involves an awareness of group reflection working towards a political goal. Such an enabling force of togetherness inevitably leads to progress, foregrounding opportunities for participation and access to many individuals.

Access and participation are further discussed in the next chapter, where the commodity of the family, the community and relationship ideals offers scope to gay men and lesbians. This focuses less on the commodity access, as may be seen in the discussion on talk shows above, and instead foregrounds the commodity of identity with regard to use and exchange. Transactions occur where inspirational media producers offer not only self-reflexive stories, but also challenge archetypal iconic forms.

5
Commodity and Family

Introduction

Roger Wollen (1996) tells us in the introduction to *Derek Jarman: a Portrait*, that in Jarman's work: 'The use of home movies in [his] films recalls a sense of security in an England and an order of society that is past (*The Last of England, The Garden* and *Jubilee*) or creates a feeling of familiarity amidst alienation (*The Garden*)' (p. 18). This tension between security and alienation, played out within scenarios which contextualise the family and community, are not only evident within Jarman's work (discussed below), but also relate the larger issue of homosexuality aligned to or exposing the commodity of 'everyday' identity. Derek Jarman (see Figure 5.1) effectively reveals the rightful place of gay and lesbian identity as contextualised within normative family and community, juxtaposing memories of a traditional past against a challenging present. Whilst this dialectic does not integrate heterosexual and homosexual ideologies, through transformation and political juxtaposition we experience a reconstruction of historical and traditional identity forms. At the same time there is a foregrounding of the commodity of social identity, suggesting an exchangeability and recognisability in the stories which are told.

This chapter consequently explores homosexual identity from a commodity perspective, relating both the potential of non-heterosexual lives and the currency which may be offered from contextualising and re-inventing heterosexual ideals. In this way, gay and lesbian self-reflexive storytellers employ the commodity of family and community to challenge and transform ideas. I argue that this occurs not necessarily exclusively within artistic and 'queer' politicised arenas of conflict, as we may view Derek Jarman's *oeuvre* (within art house film or queer cinema), but also within domestic media forms focusing on drama, documentary

Figure 5.1   Derek Jarman, on 'Sainting day' at Dungeness. He was venerated by the 'Sisters of Perpetual Indulgence'. Image courtesy of Keith Collins, from Derek Jarman's personal collection

and community. There is a complex web of potential for gay and lesbian identity, echoing the context of family as representational and symbolic, and at the same time revealing it to be functional and real. Exchangeable commodities of identity are presented, foregrounding the family, community and relationships.

To illustrate this case studies from different forms of media will be explored, which whilst they might not appear to offer a specific historical progression, foreground the agency of gay and lesbian lives and the commodity potential of identity ideals. Therefore whilst the discussions of Derek Jarman, Russell T Davies and Debra Chasnoff could appear incongruent in generic and linear terms, I argue that cohesion may be found in their discursive potentials, extending beyond such limitations.

The work of Derek Jarman (discussed above) is foregrounded, particularly examining his use of 'Super 8' home movie footage supporting ideas of family and community in the construction of his films, alongside the significance of intimate couplings. Furthermore, the work of Russell T

Davies is contextualised, regarding his role as a groundbreaking writer and producer stimulating gay and lesbian identity as media commodity. Evidence of this is presented in examining Davies' influential television drama *Queer as Folk* (Channel 4, 1999, UK) which created new space for gay and lesbian identity, at the same time challenging histories of shame. Within *Doctor Who* (BBC, 2005–present, UK) and *Torchwood* (BBC, 2006–present, UK), Davies addresses mainstream and family audiences, foregrounding gay and bisexual themes. Within Jarman's and Davies' work, there is a reinvention of family and community ideals, which foregrounds the agency, value and recognisability of non-heterosexual lives.

Such a focus on the reconstruction of domestic and community ideals is further evident in the work of Debra Chasnoff within educational documentary. As the initial case study, this offers a template and hypothesis for the commodity potential of non-heterosexual storytelling within family and community forms. These ideas are echoed within the later analysis of Derek Jarman and Russell T Davies, working towards a collective movement which offers sociopolitical potential. This is particularly apparent in the work of Chasnoff, where family is represented as including non-heterosexual forms.

Family values and Debra Chasnoff

Ken Plummer tells us that 'the lives of lesbians and gays touch upon "family" in every direction, but stories of this diversity have rarely, until recently been told' (Plummer, 1997: 154). Central in Plummer's thesis within his groundbreaking book *Telling Sexual Stories* and his discussion of 'intimate citizenship' (see Chapter 2), is the new emergence of intimate storytelling which offers discursive space for gay men and lesbians to express their connectivity to family. This challenges the historical disconnection of homosexual identity from normative family life, opening up new ways of looking at or constructing, family. Gay men and lesbians have always been part of families, but traditional representations have involved denial of potential through rejection from family, rather than the centring of homosexual identity within family. Whilst I have discussed this idea elsewhere with regard to documentary and reality television (Pullen, 2007a), this chapter explores a wider storytelling base covering diverse aspects within the media. To this end I examine the work of writers and producers who provide self-reflexive narratives of engagement, further embedding gay and lesbian family life in the stories that they tell within both fictional and factual media forms. Central to this

Figure 5.2   Academy Award-winning documentary maker Debra Chasnoff. Image courtesy of GroundSpark ·

is the foregrounding of self within storytelling, revealing new narratives about the commodity of family, relationships and community.

Such potential is highly evident in the work of Debra Chasnoff (discussed in depth below, see Figure 5.2), who as a documentary maker locates gay and lesbian identity as equal and normative within educational and institutional environs. Her work includes a political drive aimed at the educational system. This is primarily evident in *It's Elementary; Talking about Gay Issues in School* (1996, US), *That's a Family* (2000, US) and *Let's Get Real* (2003, US), with all three texts placing an educational focus on gay and lesbian identity, the construction of diverse families and anti-bullying strategies, respectively. Furthermore, her work also includes wider perspectives in texts such as *Choosing Children* (1984, US) which presented an early account of the possibility of gay and lesbian parenthood, and *One Wedding and a Revolution* (2004, US) which reported on the issuing of marriage licences in San Francisco to same-sex couples (later revoked).[1] Central in Chasnoff's political drive is the 'Respect for All' project, which was formulated by her own production company Women's Educational Media (established in 1978) now known as GroundSpark. With high-profile support from charitable foundations, the Respect for All project works in coalition with national health and educational institutions, towards '[building safer and] more inclusive school environments for all children, foster[ing] respect for diverse families [by] strengthen[ing] the link between family school and community' (GroundSpark, 2007). The connectivity of these ideas, leading to a politicisation of gay and lesbian identity within normative productive social bases, is the essence of Chasnoff's strategy in attempting to influence established ideas. This I argue focuses on the use and exchange of narratives.

Commodity: use and exchange

Within Debra Chasnoff's work and the later case studies, community, family and everyday relationships are represented in terms of commodity value and use, foregrounding recognisability and exchange. This, I argue, reflects a shift in identification possibilities for gay men and lesbians, marking a progression away from leisure and consumption-based identifications towards those which may be considered as active and productive.

As Alan Sinfield (1994) notes in his discussions within *The Wilde Century* exploring the impact of Oscar Wilde (see Chapter 2) and the emergence of 'queer' identity, there was a focus on 'leisure, idleness, immorality, luxury, insouciance, decadence and aestheticism' (Sinfield, 1994: 3). This foundation was established and it progressed through the last century (as Sinfield reflects in the title of his work), perpetuating a stereotype of non-heterosexual identities as disconnected from meaningful contexts of social reproduction. Whilst gay identities and communities progressed in various socio-reproductive contexts, such as contributions to the war effort (Berube, 1990) and development of their own communities (D'Emilio, 1983; 1990; Le Vay and Nonas, 1995; Beemyn, 1997), general media representations denied non-heterosexual identity as a positive contributor to society.

Evidence of this may be seen in the rejection of homosexual identity within mainstream theatre, which John M. Clum (2000) reports through the Lord Chamberlain's Office in the UK. Similarly the New York Padlock rule in the US punished theatres which openly represented homosexual identities (see Chapter 2). Furthermore, in Hollywood cinema, gay and lesbian identities were represented as subordinate, 'other' or a threat to community. As Vito Russo (1987) reports, the gay man as the 'sissy' was an entertainment commodity never allowed to have a meaningful social life. Gay and lesbian characters were generally cast as antagonists and outsiders. They were not only oppositional to the leading characters, but also textual resolution was often achieved by the punishment or disposal of them. Evidence of this is apparent in films such as *Suddenly Last Summer* (Mankiewicz, 1959, US) and *The Children's Hour* (Wyler, 1961, US), with the former depicting a covert gay man who is expelled from a town and is murdered, and the latter representing a young lesbian teacher who is denied a potential lover and resorts to suicide.[2] In addition to these, Vito Russo catalogues numerous Hollywood films where gay and lesbian characters are either victims or perpetrators of murder. In these instances, the commodity of gay and lesbian identity is deployed in the service of dominant sensibilities and fears, reflecting the labelling of homosexual deviancy (see Pullen, 2007a) and punishments for this.

Whilst such representations foreground gay and lesbian identity within mainstream media, and some gay activists have stated that 'any' visibility is valuable (rather than denial),[3] in these terms non-heterosexual identity is valued as a commodity for entertainment, rather than as a social profile with commodity assets. Any commodity exchange value might be related to a need for homosexual identities to express certain peripheral or 'other' traits, to encourage mass identification and consumption. In Stuart Hall's (1980 [originally 1973]) terms, the message would be 'encoded' with the imagined archetypal norms of non-homosexuals such as stereotyping, labelling of deviancy and distance from everyday life, in order to be readily consumed by the mainstream.

However, audiences can, in Hall's terms, 'decode' and interpret the message in a form that they might find psychologically beneficial. With regard to gay male (or lesbian) identification with Hollywood cinema, through fantasy and spectator positioning (Farmer, 2000) it is possible to decode an image in positive terms. Brett Farmer (2000) provides evidence of this, through examining the image of film star Mae West. He suggests that this offers excessive spectacle and personal identification to gay men through 'camp excess', which potentially 'disrupts and refigures dominant cultural forms' (p. 111). Despite this such readings or transactions involve 'disparity' between the representational image and the subject it relates to. Dominant female movie stars may offer potential 'camp' readings to gay men in their excess of performed female identity, but in essence this image is distanced from the real productive social lives of male homosexuals. Consequently despite the potential to identify with disparate images, Hollywood has denied the social potentials of gay men and lesbians, including their imagined productive and economic lives. For example, an examination of Hollywood film reveals a failure to represent the domestic lives of homosexuals with equality.[4]

Despite this, gay and lesbian identity has increasingly been valued in terms of personal or community economic potential. Whilst this might not be related to a proliferation of new representations which more closely map the 'real' extent of gay and lesbian social lives, it does explore the economic power of the pink dollar (or pink pound). Homosexuals are often considered as not having the economic pressures of raising children, or the financial ramifications of close integration with (extended) family. This suggests that many (Western) gay men and lesbians are more independent in financial terms, and possess more potential buying power as consumers.

In cultural terms, evidence of this is vividly presented within the media, not only with reference to the 'pink dollar' and advertising strategies aimed at gay and lesbian audiences (such as may appear in the gay and lesbian press, e.g. *Advocate* and *Out*), but also within general advertising. As evidenced in *The Commercial Closet* (2008), a website focusing on television adverts depicting non-heterosexuality, there is recognition in LGBT identity related to financial commodity, suggesting consumer power. *The Commercial Closet* expressly supports the usefulness of LGBT identity, specifically addressing potential corporate clients with marketing advice. They tell us (within the mission and vision statement):

> Commercial Closet Association advocates for advertising that respects the diversity of all, specifically gender identity/expression and sexual orientation, for a more accepting society and better business results. ... We see LGBT inclusion and equality as commonplace in society through effective advertising. (Commercial Closet, 2008)

Such a focus on effectiveness reveals not only commodity value, but also exchange value. This is not necessarily connected to the personal assets and economic power of gay and lesbian identity revealing buying power, but it reveals the imagined efficiency of non-heterosexual identity in producing narratives offering selling power. As Paul Du Gay (1997) relates in connection with 'cultures of production':

> Meaning is produced at 'economic' sites (at work, in shops) and circulated through economic processes and practices (through economists' models of how economics work, through adverts, marketing materials

. and the very design of products) no less than in other domains of existence in other societies. (p. 4)

The economic sign value of gay and lesbian identity reveals potency in constructing cultural meaning. This progresses beyond personal finance and buying power, and extends to larger social identity and selling power, evident in the trading, or value, of stories.

Consequently although many theorists have explored the commodity of gay identity as connected to the ability to purchase, with financial and economic properties (see Chasin, 2000; Gluckman and Reed, 1997; Sender, 2004), I argue that usefulness and commodity could equally be appropriated to the exchangeability of the identities that they possess or the stories that they tell. This might be related to the commodity of the sign, and the exchange value of stories which would be recognised as exchangeable in dominant value terms, foregrounding stories of family, relationships and community.

Economy of narratives, shared experience and the real

This is evident if we consider Jean Baudrillard's (1981 [originally 1972]) concept of the 'political economy of the sign'. Within this, use and exchange value are related to 'the logic of ambivalence, which corresponds to symbolic exchange [and] the logic of difference which corresponds to sign-value' (Lechte, 2000 [originally 1994]: 61). This equates to the potential of the symbol and what it may offer (symbolic exchange) and what status may be provided by the sign (sign value). Whilst Baudrillard's work focuses mostly on the culture of consumption, and the consumer's imagined lack of potential within modern marketplaces, and also the issue of simulacra (discussed below), I argue that contemporary narratives' employment of sign values enables the exchange of stories as commodity. As Sean Nixon (1997) relates within Baudrillard's work: 'Drawing on his assertion about the centrality of the sign value of commodities and contemporary consumption, Baudrillard suggests that one principal effect of this "play of signs" is to constitute a new dominant form of social communication' (p. 184). In this way the following case studies engage in new modes of communication which evoke a 'play of signs' foregrounding the sign and its exchange value. The sign of family, community and everyday relationship may be seen as a commodity through recognisability. Furthermore, this may be related to homophyly which Kylo-Patrick

R. Hart (2000) reminds us (drawing upon the work of Rogers and Shefner-Rogers):

> [Defines] the degree to which [representational] characters [within fiction and documentary] are similar to the viewer. The greater the homophyly between the central characters in a narrative work and the individual viewing the work, the greater the chance that the work will be considered credible by that viewer, and the greater the chance that the viewer will be influenced personally by it. (p. 59)

This does not support a 'media effects' debate which supposes that audiences may in some way be transformed by what they view (and this is fraught with the difficulty of proof (Gauntlett, 1995)). The representation of similarity in appearance is contiguous with the idea of usefulness in the recognition and exchange of ideas. The self-reflexive storytellers below present similarities of self which are addressed to audiences who are able to recognise shared experience.

However, it is important to note that Jean Baudrillard's (1994 [originally 1981]) concept of 'simulacra' reveals complex scenarios in the representation of identity. Although the audience may recognise the similitude of the representation to their own identity, as a reconstruction and reformation it may appear larger than, or beyond, real life. Baudrillard tells us: 'Simulation is no longer that of a territory, a referential being, or a substance. It is the generation by models of a real without origin or reality: a hyperreal' (p. 1), revealing the distance between the original and the copy (or the hyperreal which is reproduced). Furthermore, with regard to the potency of media representations as 'holograms' and the 'imaginary aura of the double' he attests:

> Similitude is a dream and must remain one, in order for a modicum of illusion and a stage of the imaginary to exist. One must never pass over to the side of the real, the side of the exact resemblance of the world to itself, of the subject to itself. Because then the image disappears. One must never pass over to the side of the double, because then the dual relation disappears, and with it all seduction. (p. 105)

Consequently, whilst it is evident that similarity or homophyly might generate empathy and shared experience, suggesting exchangeability, at the same time the issue of reproduction is contentious. Baudrillard suggests that visual representation within contemporary media offers evocation though its disconnection from the real.

Nevertheless I would argue that the tension played out between the imagined and the real is exactly what stimulates audience engagement. Considering the relationship between homosexual identity producing new family, and traditional family as the authentic original, it is the similarities and the contrasts between the two which enable the vividity. Whilst Baudrillard suggests that the original and the copy are disconnected, it is the philosophical imaginings between the original and the modified copy which, I argue, enables gay identity to be situated and exchanged with commodity ideas of family. This may be seen in audience evaluations of the traits of gay and lesbian families in comparison with traditional equivalents. Non-heterosexual 'new' families may reveal dedication and commitment similar to heterosexual 'originals'; however, they may extend this by foregrounding democracy and equality in evaluation of their same-sex status parity. This enables an exchange and revaluation, prioritising a consensus to review family roles and evident values.

I relate this kind of agency to the commodity of the self, and architectures of narrative reinvention which may extend concepts of family. Within this constructed and potentially exchanged environment, strategies may be executed which drive the discursive possibilities. As Ruth Finnegan (1997) tells us:

> The self is inevitably storied and identity lies in the narratives constructed by the storytelling self. Structuring experience in narrative terms creates order out of chaos and gives meaning to what would be experienced as anarchic or fragmented. (p. 76)

Such potency in storytelling, and drive to cohesion, is highly evident in Debra Chasnoff's work. In the educational documentary *It's Elementary; Talking about Gay Issues in School* (1996, US) shared experience and humanist educational ideals are foregrounded in challenging concepts of identity and family.

Debra Chasnoff: school, narratives and humanist education

The opening sequence of *It's Elementary; Talking about Gay Issues in School* presents a transgressive juxtaposition: optimistic and enlightened dialogue from children at school is contrasted with a stultified diatribe from a politician (Senator Robert Smith (Republican, New Hampshire)):

> "Homosexuality is [an] essential quality of humanness and that its expression is the right of every human being". ... We must protect

the taxpayers by keeping this kind of trash outside of our schools. That is exactly what it is, trash. [Do not] let this filth come into our classrooms.

Forming part of a Senate debate on the potential to withhold funding to schools that support homosexual identity within teaching, Debra Chasnoff sets the tone of her documentary by illustrating the superior emotional intelligence of ascending young citizens, compared with elder figures in dominant positions of power. Unlike Chasnoff's later work *That's a Family* (see Pullen, 2007a) where the voices of children are imaginatively used to form a dominant narrative about the diverse constitution of contemporary family (including those headed by gay men and lesbians), *It's Elementary* presents a coherent political debate revealing young students to be fully able to learn about social diversity outside of family. Exhibiting evidence from various schools in the United States from kindergarten level and above, a central premise in *It's Elementary* is the exchangeability and value of stories and learning experiences in transforming established assumptions about education in the context of identity and social diversity.

This occurs on various levels, with participants including schoolchildren, teachers and parents contributing to the debate. From the outset, it is stated that sexual activity (or practices) never form part of these discussions: rather it is the social existence of gay and lesbian people in communities and support for the children of gay and lesbian parents which inspire debate. Equally, through the stories of teachers, attention to the welfare of gay and lesbian children (whose identities we may not yet be aware of) is emphasised. To this end, Scott Hirschfield, a teacher of grade three (8–9-year-olds), expresses the value of his participation in school as an openly gay man, revealing his positive role model to children who may be questioning their sexual identity.

Whilst many gay and lesbian identified teachers are represented, attention is also focused upon those who are identified as heterosexual (or indeterminate), suggesting a powerful alliance between gay and straight identities. Through an expression of the views of heterosexual supporters, we are presented with potentially objective political support. This is particularly evident if we consider the discussions within Manhattan County School (an independent school in New York) in grade eight (13–14-year-olds), where students debate the appropriate age to start teaching gay and lesbian issues in school. One female student comments in response to earlier dissent:

> If kids are too young to be taught about homosexuality, they are too young to be taught about heterosexuality. And you've got to teach

the equality, and instil the equality from the very beginning. Say if you are going to read Cinderella, you should read the one where two princesses go to the ball, fall in love and live happily ever after.

Through defining equality as a key issue, and the careful juxtaposition of the Cinderella narrative, the student imaginatively provides a story with recognisability and consequently exchange currency. This type of idealism is further impacted with self-reflective narratives from students, indicating a weakness in resisting homophobic tendencies. A grade eight Latino male student from Luther Burbank Middle School (in San Francisco) in response to a task in which he was asked to compose thoughts on gay and lesbian issues tells us (reading out his script): 'Most of the time I put gays and lesbians down: I know it's not right, but I do it anyway. I say things like gay men molest children, but that is not true. Most of the time I don't even know what I am saying.' Through revealing a self-awareness of homophobic behaviour, this student foregrounds peer pressures to reject outsiders. At the same time this presents a human transparency, offering a willingness to consider alternative behaviour.

Awareness of human failing is also indicated with regard to teachers. In Cambridge Friends School (a Quaker school in Cambridge, Massachusetts) where an annual gay and lesbian pride day is held, one young female student tells us (in the presence of her class, and teacher): 'At this school "fag" and "faggot" have been used. It's amazing how teachers (no offence) don't notice all the stuff that's going on. ... They don't necessarily use the word fag, but they say "are you gay or something?"' Furthermore, this is impacted by teachers themselves who reveal discriminatory behaviour, and this is contended. At a staff meeting, a teacher suggests that student resistance to gay and lesbian issues should be given fair attention, in opposition of this a fellow teacher articulates: 'I don't know if it works for you, but I think we are asking them to believe that [it is right to support sexual diversity], not [just] as a matter of world principle. ... We are educating them, and this is part of what we consider as a healthy education.' A foregrounding of failing behaviour in the teaching body and a resistance to change is juxtaposed with caring and illuminated responses from students and teachers striving for improvements.

Exchange of narratives such as 'failure' versus 'insight', however, does not indicate merely right and wrong dynamics, it constructs therapeutic scenarios where ideas are played out and discussed. In this way, unlike the opposition between unenlightened politicians and educated pupils (see above) which cites politics as resistant and school as engaging (opposites or contrasts), the dynamic played out in the school discussions within *It's Elementary; Talking about Gay Issues in School* reveals a potential to learn or adapt beyond personal knowledge or traditional foundations. Similar to Carl Rogers' (1983) idea of whole person learning (discussed in Chapter 4) this concerns humanity and comprehension through exploring personal potentials, and valuing the self in the context of the larger world.

As Carl Rogers (2005 [originally 1967]) tells us evoking this potential: '[N]o knowledge is secure, ... only the process of *seeking* knowledge gives a basis for security. Changingness, a reliance on process rather than statistic knowledge, is the only thing that makes any sense as a goal for education on the modern world' (p. 304). A focus on 'process' rather than 'statistic knowledge', similar to Jeffrey Weeks et al.'s (2001) findings on 'practice' over 'institution' (with relation to the performative potential of same-sex family and community constructions), reveals a fluidity in the construction of knowledge and educational ideals. Debra Chasnoff's work engages with such a drive towards understanding which reflects uncertainty and changingness in self-education. Her depiction of teachers, students and parents who are willing to consider alternative modes of identity, extended from traditional forms of family, community and relationship, reveals a humanist approach in education which foregrounds change and progress.

Progress, change and the humanist ideal are further evident in the following case study which juxtaposes the work of Derek Jarman within 'art house' cinema, and Russell T Davies within mainstream television. Whilst they have produced work within different generic forms, they similarly reconstruct identity ideals, offering commodities of use and exchange.

Derek Jarman and Russell T Davies: domesticity, exchange and transformation

Derek Jarman (1942–94) was a political icon for gay identity, reaching wide audiences through his role as a progressive film-maker and author. Also he received heightened media attention (after 1986) through openly discussing his condition as a person with AIDS. From Jarman's first feature length film *Sebastiane* (1976, UK) through to his last *Blue* (1993, UK) (and his autobiographical books),[5] he foregrounded his sexual identity, and (latterly) his condition of AIDS. This represented a politicised self-reflexivity where Jarman and the gay community were creatively cast within artistic, intimate and often abstract frames. His work resonated with the displacement and vulnerability felt by sexual outsiders, at the same time foregrounding the ultimate resistance and strength of gay men, and all sexual outsiders. This is particularly evident within *Sebastiane* where Jarman recontextualises the biblical story of Saint Sebastiane, cast in Jarman's screenplay as a figurehead within an eroticised 'homosexual' community who is persecuted and finally, was tortured to death in the well-known story (famously depicted in the last throes of life with arrows piercing his body). Furthermore, it is evident within *Blue* where Jarman represents his final personal vision, of a constant vivid blue screen depicting his own blindness resulting from AIDS. Jarman used his artistic work not only as a metaphor for the trial and accomplishments of homosexual identity, but also he situated his personal vision and iconic identity within the frame. My focus (below) explores Jarman's work in this context, particularly relating his engagement with issues of domesticity, and the representation of intimate male couples. This, I argue, may be contextualised through examining his use of 'Super 8' (and 16 mm) movie footage and the aesthetics associated with this, foregrounding domestic and community ideals within political and commodity settings.

While Derek Jarman challenged ideas of homosexual identity within cinema, later Russell T Davies similarly provoked the representational landscape within television. In his groundbreaking drama *Queer as Folk* (Channel 4, 1999) he depicted a friendship group of openly gay men (and lesbians) in Manchester (in the UK). The programme became the first popular media drama to foreground homosexual identity as shame free, content and productive. This not only influenced media representations in the United Kingdom which would centralise non-homosexual identity within mainstream settings,[6] it also stimulated a US version of *Queer as Folk* (Showtime, 2000–7), which through employing the domestic parameters of the soap opera genre similarly influenced representational possibilities (discussed below). Russell T Davies further capitalised on his status as an openly gay television auteur, not only developing mainstream dramas such as *Bob and Rose* (ITV, 2001, UK) which explored potential sexual engagements between homosexual (or bisexual) men and heterosexual women, revealing pressures from dominant and minority communities to adhere to specific roles, but also through his reinvention of the family drama *Doctor Who* (BBC, 1963–present, UK) in 2005, he influenced youth television further embedding homosexual themes (Harold, 2005).[7] I argue that Russell T Davies' contribution extends beyond the catalytic spectacle of *Queer as Folk*, and that his work within *Doctor Who* and *Torchwood* (a popular *Doctor Who* spin-off) reveals a mainstream address, which through the genre of science fiction and family television stimulates homosexual domestic currency.

Whilst Derek Jarman and Russell T Davies have worked within different artistic and textual arenas, art house cinema and mainstream television respectively (briefly discussed above), suggesting different production approaches and diverse discursive potentials, they are discussed here together for their reconfiguration of community and partnership possibilities for non-heterosexuals. Both Jarman and Davies have produced transgressive discourse, situating homosexual stories and identity possibilities at the centre of their texts. Whilst inevitably Jarman as a film auteur is likely to be perceived as closer to his texts, I argue that the engagement of Davies as writer and producer, extending from *Queer as Folk* to later progressive texts, bears similar connotation in transgressive media potency.

Although many theorists may consider this juxtaposition as ignoring the historical significance of Jarman's work within 'New Queer Cinema' (Aaron, 2004; Benshoff and Griffin, 2004; Hanson, 1999), my approach explores the power of discourse more than the possibilities (or constraints) of genre. Hence although Jarman may be perceived as a proponent of 'New Queer Cinema' which may not be 'burdened by the approval seeking sackcloth of positive imagery' (Aaron, 2004: 2), inevitably such potential crosses boundaries in form and context. Furthermore, boundary crossing forms the life blood of both Jarman's and Davies' work. With Jarman extending his capacity from fine arts to cinema, and Davies from screenwriter to producer, both cross imagined parameters of containment. This occurs not only in terms of artistic progression/development, but also in terms of exploring divisions (and connections) between communities and individuals within dominant and minority contexts. In order to discuss this further I will first examine the work of Derek Jarman, and then contextualise that of Russell T Davies.

Derek Jarman: domesticity under construction

Although we may not immediately consider domesticity and its connotations of homemaking at the forefront of Jarman's work, which often focuses on the alienation of homosexual identity, I argue that it is evident in his methods of production, and his iconic foregrounding of entwined male lovers. His use of the 'Super 8' (and 16 mm) home movie camera, and the interweaving of his own home movies within his films (notably in *The Last of England* (1988, UK)), present a sense of

. domesticity in style and form. Furthermore, his persistent representation of devoted and inseparable youthful male lovers, notably evident within *The Garden* and *The Angelic Conversation*, bears a connotation of romance, dedication and intensity. As Anthony Giddens (1995) tells us of the iconic significance of romance in contemporary society, this 'provides for a long term life trajectory, orientated to an anticipated yet malleable future; and it creates a "shared history"' (p. 45) (see also Chapter 4). The intense connection within romantic scenarios expresses not only desire and engagement, but also production, continuity and substance.

As Derek Jarman tells us within the book of *The Last of England*:[8] 'The home movie is the bedrock, it records the landscape of leisure; the beach, the garden, the swimming pool. In all home movies is a longing for paradise' (Jarman, 1987: 4). Jarman indicates the significance of home movies to evoke the longing for an ideal world (a paradise), foregrounding their iconic value as the staple of identity pursuits and desires. Jarman's specific use of home movies in this context may be related to actual home movie film in the traditional sense with the recording of family and friends within casual and domestic scenarios; also it may be related to the technique and aesthetics of home movie footage conveying intimacy and immediacy within film production and cinematic appearance. In turn these processes and aesthetics may resonate with the larger idea of intimate (and reflexive) storytelling, expressing a personal connection between the film-maker and the recorded image, evoking affinity and desire.

Jarman's aesthetic use of home movies not only offers new ways of seeing and connecting, but also offers new potentials for discourse and performativity. As Jim Ellis prophetically notes in exploring Jarman's early Super 8 films which centred on his friendship networks: 'By filming the denizens of the London counter culture in Super 8 and calling them home movies, Jarman [challenged] the definition of home and family' (Ellis, 2008). Jarman's cinema explores contexts of family life and domesticity overlapping boundaries between establishments and challenging voices. He does this through foregrounding past and present scenarios, relating politics (and religion, discussed below) to family.

Within the book and the film of *The Last of England*, Jarman presents an autobiographical account centred on intimate storytelling largely mediated through reflections on a traditional family past, in relation to a contemporary political and family present. Jarman offers contrasting and contextual visions of his birth family within archive family photos and home movies, in relation to his 'new' constructed family (discussed below). This is framed within allegorical political settings, criticising

Margaret Thatcher's government of the UK in the 1980s, through the representation of diverse iconography such as wastelands, disused factories, burning fires, terrorism, refugees and the destruction of fine art. Jarman foregrounds contemporary concerns for the loss of industry, and the demise of social and cultural networks of production and connectivity, focusing on erosion and transgression. Most notably this may be seen in the representation of Tilda Swinton, attempting to rip a wedding dress from her body, depicted in slow motion and abstract framing. The iconic representation of normative social production and the institution of marriage is deconstructed within this performance, with Swinton in agitation, ripping the dress apart, consuming a fabric rose as part of it, then using a pair of garden shears to cut the fabric. Paul Dave (2006) notes that this representation, 'the bride's dance', may be related to Jarman's knowledge of the poet Blake, and Swinton's character 'allegorically evokes the biblical figure of Jerusalem' (p. 155), echoing concerns for the destruction and loss of England under Thatcherite rule. However, whilst Paul Dave (2006) affirms that *The Last of England* 'projects "terminal visions" of England ... when, as [Jarman] saw it, [Margaret Thatcher's] neo-liberal political order threatened to irrevocably poison Englishness with philistinism, homophobia, greed and xenophobia' (p. 154), at the same time this apocalypse is counterpointed with reference to the historical context of the birth family, and the relevance of new family-like networks.

Within the book *The Last of England* this is evident in the inclusion of affectionate images of Jarman's family, including the representation of his father in wartime and the young Jarman with his mother and sister at home (see Figure 5.3). This is juxtaposed not only with political images (discussed above), but also with images of young lovers, such as those from *The Angelic Conversation* (discussed below), and Jarman with lovers, within intimate settings evoking his new family. Similarly, sequences of archive family home movie footage (which Jarman preserved for the family),[9] are fragmented and inter-dispersed among contemporary images. This interjection provides contextual readings which juxtapose past and present comparisons, foregrounding family and domestic life.

Within an early part of the film, we are presented with a 'pastoral' versus 'industrial' sequence, which could be read 'literally' as: yearning for the lost pastoral youth, and echoing concerns for an industrial and decaying present. Music denotes the extent of this sequence, accompanying the images with melodic arpeggio acoustic guitar, possibly evoking summer and leisure. We are presented with Derek Jarman's archive home movie footage including representations of a butterfly,

Figure 5.3   Derek Jarman as a youth (right), at home with his family. Image courtesy of Keith Collins, from Derek Jarman's personal collection

a child on a swing, and a picnic at home with Jarman as a child with his mother. This is intercut with images from the 'present', including a disused factory, a youth walking through rubble climbing to a high point and looking out, and Jarman at his desk sensing the aroma from a flower. Whilst inevitably such a succession of disparate juxtaposed images draws immediate conclusions such as idyllic past versus troubling present (briefly alluded to above), contrary to this I argue that a potential reading may be the coming of age, or identity under construction. The idyllic childhood scenes may signify a well-balanced foundation of contentment empowering Jarman to deal with the present rather than a yearning for the past. Furthermore, the representation of the youth traversing the desolate landscape may more likely represent the triumphs which can be enabled, rather than the character's apparent dilemma. This type of reading is preferred as not only does this sequence close with Jarman remembering the past through sensing the scent of a flower, but also this directly connects to the agency of the present with the iconography of a hand-held flare (with sound linking the two), suggesting potential to light the way forward.

The closing of this sequence with a bearer of light evokes a central iconic device in many of Jarman's films where characters similarly possess fire, connecting with Jarman's interest in fire and alchemy, and the potential for transformation (Ellis, 1999). In this way whilst *The Last of England* does represent discontent with political ideologies, at the same time I argue that it forms a foundation for Jarman's progressive self-reflexive film-making foregrounding domesticity and agency to transform ideas. Evidence of this may be seen within *The Garden*, where Derek Jarman builds on the domestic contexts of *The Last of England* (discussed above), resituating the gay male couple first depicted within *The Angelic Conversation*.

The Garden may be seen as a progression of *The Angelic Conversation* which foregrounded intimate dedication between two male characters providing poetic emotional imagery accompanied by the reading of Shakespeare's sonnets by actress Judi Dench. Whilst *The Angelic Conversation* almost entirely devotes its narrative to the bond between male lovers, *The Garden* foregrounds this idea, framing this within narratives from Jarman's own life. Filmed at Derek Jarman's beach house in Dungeness, and in the surrounding environs, it provides an emotive setting for the male lovers, connecting with Jarman's personal life in a number of sequences and referencing his status as a person living with AIDS (most notably evident in a scene with Jarman in a hospital bed on the beach as the tide comes in).[10] Whilst *The Garden* also foregrounds the familiar gay couple within pseudo-religious scenarios, echoing the events in the life story of Jesus (e.g. they both are punished as they drag a wooden cross), I am concerned with the representation of domesticity and agency.

In order to discuss this further I would like to consider two sequences from *The Garden*. One offers idyllic scenes of carefree male love, evoking naturalism through the aesthetics of home movies, and the other focuses on vulnerability and alienation, evoking realism through a constructed scenario of displacement. In the first scene, two male lovers are dressed in casual clothes and they are represented in emotional harmony on the beach; seated back to back, throwing stones in the sea and embraced in the shelter of a rowing boat kissing each other affectionately. This is accompanied by gentle accordion music, situating this as a sensitive domestic environment. In the second scene, the same two men are dressed in business suits set within the confines of a sauna, and the issue of alienation is foregrounded. They are standing awkwardly with heads close together appearing to feel threatened, around them are semi-clad men represented in a scene reminiscent of a Roman orgy. Members of the crowd gaze with desire at the couple and laugh, suggesting humiliation. One central figure washes his hands in a reference to Pontius Pilate and the biblical story, allegedly relinquishing responsibility for Jesus' crucifixion. The music accompanying this sequence is disturbing, reminiscent of music used in horror films.

In keeping with the allusion to Christianity and the story of Jesus, we may read these scenes as representing the early more carefree life of Jesus, juxtaposed with his later capture, persecution and eventual crucifixion, and how here this is used to represent the trial of homosexuality. This is particularly evident in the second scene where direct references are made to the act of being crucified, as one irreverent sauna-goer points at his hands and feet and emulates the process of being nailed to a cross. However, despite such a direct and controversial allusion to religion and the trial of Christ (read as homosexuality), I would argue that these scenes are indicative of Jarman's interest in depicting the potential of domestic and romantic couples, more than their vulnerability. Whilst the transition from unfettered idealistic potential by the sea, to capture and confinement within the sauna, suggests loss and trial, equally it could represent a preservation of cohesion despite adverse circumstances. Whilst inevitably the allusion to religion counterpoints Jarman's concern for dominant oppression, I suggest this largely represents a continuing reinforcement of his interest in the domestic potential of gay men, not necessarily their oppression. As Jarman says himself of *The Angelic Conversation*, which I argue was a foundation for the representation of intimacy between gay men within *The Garden*: '[Whilst this was the] most austere [of my] work, ... [it was] also the closest to my heart' (Jarman cited in MacCabe, 2007: 2). The representation of romanticised gay men within Jarman's work is less about 'queering' identity norms; it is an affirmative and robust social construction.

Whilst it is likely that this reading of Jarman is controversial, as he was considered as a prophetic 'queer' film-maker who offered up challenge more than solution (Aaron, 2004; Benshoff and Griffin, 2004; Hanson, 1999), I argue that his iconic use of domesticity was embedded with identity constructions and aspirations. Inevitably this may extend from his personal desires for new community and partnership potentials. This is something equally apparent within the work of Russell T Davies. However, unlike Jarman, Davies appears to more openly engage with commodity. Nevertheless as I argue below, issues of use and exchange are embedded in both.

Russell T Davies: commodity identity

Russell T Davies (speaking in 2004) tells us:

> I never planned to go public [and become an icon for gay identity] . . .
> but there was just so much misrepresentation [of gay and lesbian sex-
> uality] flying around [within the media]. The poor actors were made
> responsible for the words and actions I had written for them and a lot
> of the time they didn't know what they were talking about. So I never
> had a choice, really. (Cited in Duerden, 2007)

In an article (published within *The Observer* newspaper) focusing on Russell T Davies' emerging role in reinventing the long-standing science
fiction television series *Doctor Who* (BBC1, 1963–present), we are presented with the affirmation of his sexual identity linked to his potential
for new storytelling (see Figure 5.4). This was largely extended from
Davies' groundbreaking work within *Queer as Folk* (including *Queer as
Folk 2*) which focused on a friendship group of gay men, who were unfettered in expressing their sexuality within contemporary social worlds.
Through *Queer as Folk* Davies placed himself in the limelight, becoming

Figure 5.4   Russell T Davies depicted on home ground in Cardiff. Image courtesy
of Russell T Davies

an icon for gay and lesbian storytelling. Whilst Davies' work within *Doctor Who* is discussed below, with particular regard to his potential influence within family television, it is first necessary to discuss the significance of *Queer as Folk*. This was a groundbreaking text which influenced the way in which gay and lesbian identity would be represented on television. Furthermore, it provided commodity value for non-heterosexual identity, enabling not only mainstream demand, but also outsider potency.

Queer as Folk displays the commodity of homosexual identity, often relating the primacy of a hedonistic gay male sexuality. This is largely evident within the foregrounding of central character Stuart (aged 29), who displays the stereotypical identity traits of a promiscuous gay man. Stuart is related as a powerful icon for gay sexuality (alongside success in finance and career), and is contextualised with the characters of Vince (Stuart's best friend, also gay) and Nathan, a gay youth (aged 15) who is attracted to Stuart. Within the drama, homosexual identity is played out between these three characters, with Stuart and Nathan representing hedonistic carefree sexuality, and Vince standing for monogamy and domesticity. *Queer as Folk's* central narrative dynamic occurs in the tension between the characters of Stuart and Nathan, whilst prioritising the themes of promiscuity and hedonism. *Queer as Folk 2* shifts the focus towards a 'Stuart and Vince' dynamic by exploring monogamy and domesticity. *Queer as Folk* was largely considered to be groundbreaking for its representation of underage gay sex, as the character of Nathan, aged 15, was three years below the age of male homosexual consent at the time of broadcast. The representation of hedonistic homosexuality was less controversial, as this conformed to the dominant stereotype of gay men as sexually unfettered. More challenging was *Queer as Folk's* questioning of monogamy, and the issue of domesticity, which were embedded as possibilities or challenges for gay men. This raised questions about the progress and determination of gay identity, relating stereotypes, challenges and achievements.

Within *Queer as Folk* I argue that Russell T Davies evokes homosexual social worlds, exploring concerns such as achieving or rejecting identity, and the problematic nature of imposed identity traits. Achievement of identity is demonstrated within characters who express (or work towards) the maintenance of an imagined homosexual identity. This may be apparent where Stuart desires to maintain his sexual primacy as a promiscuous gay man, and Nathan follows this ideal. This is particularly notable within *Queer as Folk 2*, where Nathan triumphs in sexual encounters and he displaces Stuart as the lead (sexual) protagonist. Rejection of identity is explored through strategies to reject ideals, such as Stuart rejecting a monogamous life, or Vince a promiscuous one. Furthermore, rejection of identity is also related to the need to confront and expel stereotypes and deviant labels which may surround homosexuality. This is particularly notable with regard to rejecting shame.

Within *Queer as Folk*, Stuart continually rejects the concept of homosexual shame. Evidence of this may be found in a seminal sequence of the drama where after sleeping with Nathan the night before, Stuart (with Vince) drives him to school the next morning. This occurs, however, not only in plain view of a mass of onlookers at the entrance to the school (who may be aware that Stuart and Vince are not Nathan's parents), but also with the word 'Queers' scrawled on the side of Stuart's Jeep (which was vandalised the night before). The sequence foregrounds the defiant, proud identity of Stuart (along with Nathan, and to a degree Vince), who are seen to confront and reject labels of abjection.

However, as Sally Munt (2000) points out in her examination of *Queer as Folk*, whilst it is beneficial to reject the imposition of shame, at the same time she acknowledges that such strategies involve a perpetuation of the need to reject myths of shame (see also Chapter 1, where myths are discussed in more depth). Evidence of this contention may be found within *Queer as Folk 2* where Stuart is threatened with financial blackmail by his ten-year-old nephew, Thomas. In a cathartic sequence where Stuart confronts Thomas in the presence of Stuart's parents, who are apparently unaware of their son's sexuality, Stuart proclaims (in response to his father's request to help him with DIY):

Stuart: We don't do hammers and nails or saws, we do joints and screws, but that's different.

Mother: Who does?

Stuart: Queers, ... because I'm queer. I am gay, I am homosexual. I am a poof, I am a poofter, I am a ponce. I am a bum boy, batty boy, back sided artist, bugger, I am bent. I am that arse bandit. I lift those shirts. I am a faggot arsed, fudge packing shit stabbing uphill gardener. I dine at the downstairs restaurant. I dance at the other end of the ballroom. I am Moses at the parting of the red cheeks. I fuck and I am fucked. I suck and I am sucked. I rim them and wank them, and every single man has had the time of his life. And I am not a pervert. If there is one twisted bastard in this family, it is this little blackmailer here. So congratulations Thomas, I have just officially outed you.

. This scene reveals the dramatic power of rejecting deviant labels. Stuart addresses and parodies terms of abuse, repositioning the culpable parties not as those assigned as 'deviant', but those who would punish difference. However, whilst this scene is evocative, it also stimulates responsive strategies needed to reproduce a homosexual identity within drama, which relies on the recognisability of shame within the homosexual identity. As we know in Foucaultian terms of power (see Chapter 3) such direct resistance partially re-energises the challenging voices.

Consequently, whilst Russell T Davies' strategies are dramatically powerful, at the same time they reconstruct issues of the rejection and oppression of difference. This is further evident within *Queer as Folk 2*, where Stuart punishes the mother of a friend for rejecting her son. Alexander's mother has denied her son's inheritance, upon the death of his father. Stuart initially confronts Alexander's mother in the hospital, pointing a finger to her head implying that he will execute her, and then later he sets fire to her BMW, which we imagine she has purchased with the inheritance. He does this deliberately in her presence to affirm his fitting revenge. However, whilst this reveals issues to be dealt with, and sites of culpability, similarly it reframes homosexual identity within reactive, rather than productive scenarios.

Therefore I argue that *Queer as Folk* is an ambivalent text. It does deal with identity issues offering the commodity of gay identity, but at the same time it frames such commodity in terms of working towards dealing with problems, more than creating new space. Although it does reveal a shame-free gay community, its axis is generally centred on the need to overcome imposed shame and issues of rejection.

Queer as Folk was a stimulus for change, but it was also awkwardly placed at a crossroads of representational development, and consequently needed to reflect back on histories of homosexual discontent. Whilst its focus on shame-free homosexual identity provoked change, other texts extending from Russell T Davies' *Queer as Folk* would be more subversive and possess more enduring impact, moving beyond shame. As intimated above, the American adaptation of *Queer as Folk* produced by Ron Cowen and Daniel Lipman for Showtime (2000–5), would offer more longevity in its enduring domestic focus (see Ruditis, 2003). Similarly it addressed issues which were missing from the original text such as the depiction of gay men and lesbians working productively in social and political union, and exploring the impact of AIDS. Furthermore, the success of the American adaptation in turn would stimulate the production of other equally influential texts such as the lesbian drama *The L Word* (Showtime, 2004) (see Akass and McCabe, 2006). The impact of Russell T Davies from *Queer as Folk* would not only extend to the American adaptation and other following texts, it would be within his own developing work aimed at further integrating gay identity within the mainstream, as evident in *Doctor Who* and *Torchwood*.

Notably (as discussed above) Russell T Davies' participation within *Doctor Who* provided an opportunity for gay identity. As an openly gay writer given the challenge to bring back an enduringly popular 'cult' television drama series which had been a staple of children's and family viewing from the early 1960s to the late 1980s (Howe and Walker, 2003), this allowed him a high-profile arena for his work. Described as 'The saviour of Saturday night drama' (Bryne, 2007), Davies' success was evident not only in achieving large audience figures, but also in presenting progressive ideas extending the seemingly well-worn format of *Doctor Who* (Russell, 2006). Through reinventing the *Doctor Who* series, Davies was able to rewrite the story of a time traveller (Doctor Who) who whilst he is not human (but appears so) has a particular mission for saving the human race. Progressive within his adaptation was the subtle development of a modern depiction of diverse sexuality. This is mostly evident in the creation of the character Captain Jack Harkness (played by openly gay actor John Barrowman), who is signified as bisexual and becomes the central protagonist in the spin-off series *Torchwood* (discussed below). Harkness' bisexuality is clearly evident in the finale of the first series produced by Russell T Davies, when he kisses Doctor Who (and the Doctor's female assistant), and later becomes a recurring character. However, the narratives within *Doctor Who* have also addressed the issue of homosexual youth.

Under the direction of Russell T Davies as executive producer, Mark Gattis (who is also openly gay) wrote the episode 'The Idiot's Lantern' (*Doctor Who* series 2 episode 7). Clearly aimed at younger audiences, this episode creatively foregrounds a youth, Tommy, who is signified as gay within the narrative, through an allusion to his sensitive nature and his imagined status as a 'mummy's boy'. Set in early 1950s Britain, relating the advancing technology of television in offering an opportunity to witness the coronation of Queen Elizabeth II, the science fiction narrative explores an extraterrestrial force transforming television audiences into faceless apparitions. Central within this is the gay-identified character of Tommy who saves the world from the alien force, when he uses his intelligence to repair a technical device designed by the lead protagonist (Doctor Who). This occurs at a crucial moment when only Tommy can provide a solution, and consequently he restores the lost identities of the masses. The episode achieved an audience of 6.76 million viewers

(Russell, 2006) consisting largely of children. Characters like Tommy (intelligent, proactive yet sensitive) help to dispel myths surrounding homosexuality (see Chapter 1) which are often absorbed by young people viewing unsympathetic, ill-informed media.[11] Davies addresses the contentious nature of stereotyping, inverting the idea that sensitive and homosexual equals weak and superfluous. However, positive representations within *Doctor Who* alluding to homosexuality (such as Tommy within 'The Idiot's Lantern') appear more subtle than those within the spin-off *Torchwood*.[12]

The series *Torchwood* places bisexuality and homosexuality clearly within the frame. This is largely evident in the role of the leading protagonist Jack Harkness who exhibits bisexual desire, including a casual homosexual coupling with Ianto Jones, a regular member of his extraterrestrial policing force (see Pullen, 2010a). Furthermore, it is evident within the casting of openly gay John Barrowman in the leading role of Jack Harkness, who has become as an icon of gay identity (see Krochmal, 2007).[13] Notable within the series is an episode entitled 'Captain Jack Harkness' which is written by Catherine Tregenna under Russell T Davies as executive producer, where we are presented with a romantic vision which intensifies homosexual desire. Set in Cardiff (Wales) during the Second World War, this episode appears to present a pastiche on the romance narrative of the film *Brief Encounter* (David Lean, 1945), where sexual tension with a stranger is foregrounded, but ultimate happiness (and sexual fulfilment) is denied. Through Davies offering a vision of two men who are both signified as bisexual but are drawn together through homosexual desire, we are presented with an engaging filmic intensity. When *Torchwood's* Jack Harkness travels back in time (to the 1940s) he encounters an army officer also called Captain Jack Harkness, at a dance hall. This unlikely coincidence occurs as the *Torchwood* protagonist had assumed the name of Jack Harkness to conceal his real identity, taking the name from official records recording deaths during wartime. When Jack Harkness meets his namesake, we discover that the original Harkness would die the following day on a training mission. The tension played out is that both men become aware that one will die shortly, and in order to give meaning to their lives they are naturally drawn together. The evident display of affection involving slow dancing, embracing and kissing, represents the iconic romantic and sexual tension similar to that played out in *Brief Encounter*. However, instead of the atmospherics of a train station and the beckoning responsibility of marriage (imagined between actors Celia Johnson and Trevor Howard in the film), the original Jack Harkness is inevitably drawn to his death, and *Torchwood's* Jack Harkness must return to his duty in his own time, transported through a space and time portal emitting light and mist, here providing similar atmospherics to that of the train station (steam and light) within *Brief Encounter*. Such a pastiche involves not only 'accentuation, exaggeration [and possibly] anachronism [and] stylistic inconsistency' (Dyer, 2007: 137), it also contextualises dominant narratives of engagement and redesign. Davies' work within *Torchwood* provides new expressions for romantic love displacing and reinventing heterosexual norms in favour of sexual diversity.

Whilst Russell T Davies' representations within *Doctor Who* and *Torchwood* seem less provocative than *Queer as Folk* in showcasing sexual community, through his direct access to mainstream and domestic audiences which may accept subtle, and possibly evocative, transformations in identity ideals, this paves a more accessible way to understanding. Although *Queer as Folk* inevitably provided the catalyst for these conditions to occur, Davies understands that the progression of ideas depends less on looking back and dealing with old issues such as rejecting deviant labels (as discussed above), than it concerns stimulating a modified future, which might offer more integration between gay and straight identities. This is not to say that histories should be ignored and ignorance forgotten, but that the ability to move forward depends on constructing accommodating pathways. In Davies' new work this involves creating media dramas which frame gay identity within wider perspectives.

Conclusion

The case studies reveal the progressive agency of openly gay and lesbian new storytellers, extending narratives of self-identity to wider public arenas. Debra Chasnoff, Derek Jarman and Russell T Davies construct iconic representations of family, community and partnership, foregrounding homosexual ideals. Whilst I have discussed their work within various genres, such as documentary and fiction, within film and television, I argue that their self-reflexive storytelling produces discourse beyond the limits of form.

The production of discourse inevitably touches upon its commodity value in use and exchange. Whilst (as discussed above) the commodity of gay identity has tended to be connected to its use to mainstream audiences as entertainment, and recently the emergence of economic power connected to gay and lesbian lives has substantiated identity potential, equally we may consider the 'sign' value of non-heterosexual storytelling. This offers recognisability and exchangeability, revealing similar, or contextual, experience in comparing aspects of heterosexual and homosexual life. Although the historical usefulness and exchange value of gay and lesbian identity have generally served mass audiences' imaginings of social type, the new storytellers discussed in this book challenge these forms. Through offering not only the commodity of themselves, but also the expression of new forms of family, community and partnerships, they stimulate transactions forming wider scope. This relates to the exchange value of signs, and the economy of narratives which might reveal shared experience, in the use and reception of stories. I have argued that new expressions of gay and lesbian lives offering new transactions, reveal commodity potential in the manufacture and progression of new stories. The diverse work of Debra Chasnoff, Derek Jarman and Russell T Davies offers this potential, foregrounding identity cohesion as much as philosophical debate.

Debra Chasnoff's work within educational documentary set an agenda for understanding by revealing the potential of humanist education. Through constructing school as an environment for debate as much as teaching, Chasnoff stimulates the potential of education to be viewed as a work in progress, rather than as a monolith cast in stone. This model of understanding allows the exchange and transference of ideas, whereby young people can reconstruct family and community norms.

Whilst Derek Jarman similarly foregrounds domesticity with his use of home movies, at the same time he presents an evocation of homosexual intimacy and partnerships. We are presented with the construction of family, community and relationships, within complex, and often political, iconic juxtapositions. Whilst Jarman's work has tended to be associated with 'queer theory' and identity deconstruction (and he clearly foregrounds alienation and subjugation), at the same time he provides constructions of new family, community and relationships. Jarman looks forward more than back, and in many ways provides premonitions for Russell T Davies' work within domestic television.

Russell T Davies' groundbreaking work within *Queer as Folk* stimulated a new era in televisual representation for gay and lesbian identity. Although in its rejection of shame it is reactive more than constructive, it provided a foundation for new domestic representations. Whilst Davies' *Doctor Who* and *Torchwood* are clearly not exclusively gay and lesbian texts, they offer shared experience over confrontation, representing a positive move beyond queer identity politics.

Challenging norms, offering new stories and providing a pathway: new storytellers are now progressing beyond identity histories. Debra

Chasnoff, Derek Jarman and Russell T Davies integrated family, partnership and community ideals, offering exchange and recognisability, echoing dominant forms. To further contemporise and extend this debate, the following chapter explores a 'post gay' (Sinfield, 1998) world beyond history and situation, where expectation and possibility are foregrounded within the iconography of gay and lesbian youth. This relates less to the reconstruction of equivalents (to be exchanged), more to the potential of youth within storytelling, seemingly unfettered by histories of denial.

6
Teenage Identity and Ritual

Introduction

Marcos Brito (2007), an openly gay rapper (also known as Q Boy, see Figure 6.1) and the force behind the revolutionary educational documentary *Coming Out to Class* (Channel 4, 2007, UK) (discussed below), affirms that:

> The internet is amazing [for gay and lesbian youth] because they can find information that I couldn't find when I was young, they can find other teenagers going through similar experiences to them, and speak to them. They can find dates which is wholly important. When you are a teenager, everybody pairs off. Everybody has a boyfriend or a girlfriend: Its part of growing up.

Finding a partner, and taking part in the ritual of dating and romance, are often distanced from gay and lesbian youth. As Brito foregrounds, the Internet and diverse forms of related new media (such as Internet social networking, discussed below), have recently offered new life chances for gay and lesbian youth. This has not only enabled new connectivities, but also it has stimulated performative possibilities. Gay and lesbian youth have constructed new social worlds challenging repressive heteronormative constraints, where romance, desire and the ability to naturally engage take centre stage.

This chapter explores the construction of this optimistic new world, which for gay and lesbian youth offers the potential to participate in everyday teen rituals, including social development and finding a partner. Through allowing themselves the possibility of success (and failure) in social networking and aspirations for romance, gay and lesbian youths

Figure 6.1 Marcos Brito, also known as 'Q Boy', is a gay youth music rapper. His contribution in the documentary *Coming Out to Class* (Channel 4, 2007, UK) reveals his status as a role model. Image courtesy of Marcos Brito, © Greg Frederick (gregfrederick.com).

are reconstructing frames of social possibility normally open only to heterosexuals. This leads to the construction of new social worlds, revealing new gay communities through the advent of storytelling. Gay and lesbian youth echo and transgress normative ritual events such as dating and romance, through coming out and the affirmation of self-identity.

The work of Marcos Brito forms a case study later in this chapter exploring the representations within *Coming Out to Class*, alongside analysis of the supporting Internet content in *LGB Teens* and the new media social networking site Gay Youth Corner which foreground new technologies. Also it will be necessary to consider the context of gay and lesbian youth within storytelling. Consequently the first case study explores the work of Jonathan Harvey in the groundbreaking play and film *Beautiful Thing* (Hettie Macdonald, 1995, UK), which I argue, through a tradition in cinema realism, presents a new level of progressive engagement. Furthermore, I examine the work of Todd Haynes in *Velvet Goldmine* (Todd Haynes, 1998, US), and Alan Bennett in *The History Boys* (Nicholas

. Hytner, 2006, UK), which both relate identity issues within the ritual of growing up gay (or lesbian). These case studies reveal the inherent tension of coming out, and the expression of identity, as much as a new social stimulation for diverse sexuality.

However before embarking on this discussion, I would like to contextualise social identity issues surrounding gay and lesbian youth, revealing the exposed and vulnerable context of gay youth in attempts to find identity, often where normative rites of passage, such as romance, are denied. Furthermore, I argue later that issues of performance (the actions which may be taken) and performativity (the potential to transform or influence) are evident in the ritual expressions of non-heterosexual youth, and Victor Turner's (1982) work relating liminal frameworks provides analysis of this potential. Gay and lesbian youth involved in new storytelling provide intimate expressions of self, and lay a pathway to new social worlds.

Gay teen identity: similar experiences and expectations

Ritch Savin-Williams tells us in his groundbreaking book *And then I became Gay: Young Men's Stories* (1998) that: 'Despite the inherent value of romantic relationships, many [gay male] adolescents despair of being given the opportunity to establish anything other than clandestine sexual intimacies with another male' (p. 160). Through the presentation of personal narratives, Savin-Williams reveals not only the desire of gay male youths to find romantic partners but also that opportunities for engagement rarely occur. As outsiders to dominant expressions of romance which reveal the binary dynamic as centred on male and female, same-sex potential is denied. When gay and lesbian youths challenge the normative rules of romance, this lays them vulnerable to the threat posed by peers, with 'the penalty for crossing the line of "normalcy" [resulting] in emotional and physical pain' (Savin-Williams, 1998: 161). However, I argue that the case studies below foreground expressions from performers who challenge these ideas, revealing positive and affirmative opportunities for gay and lesbian youth.

Whilst later I discuss the impact of Marcos Brito's documentary *Coming Out to Class* and the significance of the website the Gay Youth Corner for their potential to reinvent storytelling, the issue of support for youth identity needs to be explored first. As Gerald Unks (1995) observes:

[A major] factor contributing to the marginalisation of homosexual adolescents is their lack of viable support groups. While virtually all students of any other identifiable group have advocates and support in the high school, homosexual students typically have none. (p. 7)

This leads not only to a failure for the gay teen to find a positive sense of homosexual identity, but also it reveals the disparity in experience and expectation offered to non-heterosexuals. As evidenced in the work of Debra Chasnoff (discussed in Chapter 5, and the case studies below), gay and lesbian youth are often situated (particularly within school) in an environment which locates them as outsiders.

Gay and lesbian youths are constrained by 'normative' teen peer groups, finding themselves isolated from networks of support. This occurs not only at the level of lack of peer or friendship affirmation, but also lack of institutional and discursive support. Generally in school, there are not adequate social mechanisms designed to protect emerging gay and lesbian citizens. Debates within 'normative' family and society practically ignore the existence of the gay teen. This is particularly relevant with the issue of growing up at home where, as Ryan Caitlin and Diane Futterman (1998) report:

As [gay and lesbian youth] develop cognitively many ... begin to understand the nature of their difference and society's negative reaction to it. In identifying and learning to manage stigma, lesbian and gay adolescents face additional, highly complex challenges and tasks. Unlike their heterosexual peers, lesbian and gay adolescents are the only social minority who must learn to manage a stigmatised identity without active support and modelling from parents and family. (p. 9)

Gay and lesbian youth are subject to stigma, and find ways to deal with this often in isolation. This relates to a sense of trying to find an identity, in an arena where there are few role models, and one's personal sense of self is labelled as deviant. As Ritch Savin-Williams (1998) affirms: 'Falling in love with someone of the same sex and sustaining an emotional investment with that person suggest to many Americans an irreversible deviancy. So, too, youths may come to believe that a gay relationship is an oxymoron' (p. 160). Gay and lesbian youths (in school) are often situated within non-affirming educational institutions. Furthermore, dominant society and normative family reject the potential offered by gay and lesbian youth. This not only impacts on identity possibilities, but also situates gay and lesbian identity as outside normative relationship structures. This limits potentials, and denies obvious pathways to fulfilment. Evidence of this may be seen in the groundbreaking work of Gore Vidal in his novel *The City and the Pillar* (1997 [originally 1948]) (discussed in the introduction), where despite attempts by the young lead character Jim Willard to connect with his potential soul mate Bob Ford, societal oppression ignores the idea of same-sex romance and denies any opportunity of fulfilment.

Despite such obstacles, Ritch Savin-Williams (1998) reports (citing the research of Eric Dubé) that there is substantial evidence that young gay men are able to pursue romantic partnerships, and intimate same-sex relationships are not that dissimilar from those of heterosexual youths (p. 162). Also he tells us that:

> Although only a few published studies of same-sex oriented teens focus primarily on their romantic relationships, suggestive data [such as Eric Dubé's study] debunk the myth that youths neither want nor maintain steady, loving same-sex relationships. [Furthermore] Tony D'Auguelli at Penn State University reports that one-half of his sample of gay/bisexual youths were 'partnered' and that their most troubling mental health concern was termination of a close relationship, ranking just ahead of telling parents about their homosexuality. (Savin-Williams, 1998: 162)

In forming and conducting romantic partnerships, a surprising similarity between homosexual and heterosexual experience is revealed. Furthermore, there may be a drive towards parity in the narrative performances of gay youths. This may be evident in expectations of youths wishing to participate in social ritual events with equality (to heterosexual peers).

This is apparent in the groundbreaking work of Aaron Fricke recorded within his autobiography *Reflections of a Rock Lobster* (1981). Fricke provides a personal account of his homosexuality and coming out, recording his romantic coupling with fellow student Paul. He expresses a desire to attend the school prom with Paul as a same-sex couple. Whilst the drama may have been centred on the court case brought by Fricke against his faculty, which had denied him access to the prom with his same-sex partner, its discursive potential is evident. As Fricke (1981) reports:

> Heterosexuals learn early in life what is expected of them. They get practice in their early teens having crushes, talking to their friends about their feelings. Paul and I hadn't got all that practice; our relationship was formed without much of a model to base it on. It was

the first time that either of us had been in love like this and we spent much of our time just figuring what that meant for us. (p. 46)

Such performative potential in storytelling, revealing the explorative and reflective nature of self-investigation, is indicative of new storytelling, and the performances discussed below. Fricke not only challenged political authorities in demanding equality to attend the prom with his partner (which he won), at the same time he redefined the ritual potential of the prom for gay and lesbian youth. In these instances, gay and lesbian youth place themselves within the frame and question ideas of normality.

Whilst elsewhere (Carrington, 1999; Weston, 1991; Weeks et al., 2001) the revelation of the non-heterosexual family and community has been discussed with regard to the potential of friendship, partnerships and social networks, there has been little discussion of the positive potential of gay and lesbian teens. Furthermore, although the work of Gerald Unks (1995), Ryan Caitlin and Diane Futterman (1998) and Ritch Savin-Williams (1998) is discussed above in relation to the educational, psychological and narrative context of gay and lesbian youth revealing lack of potential, the issue of performance and potential within media storytelling merits further investigation. Consequently, the discussion below develops work I have stimulated elsewhere (Pullen, 2004, 2005, 2007a) regarding the significance of 'coming out' and romance narratives within documentary, further exploring the potential of performance within storytelling. This, I argue, is related to the context of ritual and its employment in gay youth narratives.

Ritual and performance: liminality, participation and antistructure

Victor Turner's (1982) interpretations of the terms 'liminal' and 'liminoid' are useful in discussing the performative potential of gay and lesbian youth with regard to ritual transition or progression (see also Pullen, 2007a). This may also relate to participation, coalescence and 'antistructure' (Turner, 1982) within ritual transitions (discussed below). Whilst the work of Turner emerges from his analysis of 'traditional anthropological studies of ritual performance [related to] modern theatre [and] experimental theatre' (p. 7), his ideas might easily be applicable to media performances involving identity reconstructions. The concepts of framing performances and the transitional potential outside, or beyond, the frame are evident in 'liminal' and 'liminoid' contexts of ritual progressions.

As Richard Schechner (2002) suggests, 'liminal' is derived from the Latin word *limen* meaning 'literally a threshold or sill, an architectural feature linking one space to another, [providing] a passageway between places [rather] than a place itself' (p. 58). This involves the framing of a story and a performance, and a process of transition leading to a new place or progression. In ritual terms, this translates as leading to a new identity such as sexual maturity or accomplishments in partnership finding. For gay and lesbian youth this could involve contextualising yourself within the frame of dominant identity, and progressing towards acceptance of your outsider identity. Liminal performances inevitably involve having to produce plausible recognisability, usually associated with the liminal frame. For gay and lesbian youth to evoke the context of romance, it would be necessary to express relationships equivalent to dominant ideas of intimate engagement, such as contextualising heterosexual coupling. Where 'liminal' performances frame the 'recognisable' leading to a ritual transition (within the frame), liminoid performances extend beyond the frame and lead to new ways of seeing.

Lesbian and gay youth involved in liminoid performance rather than necessarily reproducing heterosexual ideas would challenge or extend potential. As Victor Turner (1982) tells us, considering contemporary society and culture: '... liminoid phenomena are often parts of social critiques or even evolutionary manifestos – books, plays, paintings, films etc., exposing the injustices, and immoralities of the mainstream economic and political structures' (p. 54). Liminoid performance often involves more free expression, connecting the aims of performers more directly to the idea of dealing with contentious issues, rather than conforming to liminal framework expectations. This suggests a type of free expression, and potential play in performance in a similar manner to Mikhail Bakhtin's (1965) idea of carnival play and 'carnivalesque ambivalence' where identity might challenge ideas (see also Morris, 1994; Pullen, 2007a).

Furthermore, liminoid performance might involve ascribing 'meaning' to identity, relevant to progress and movement rather than conforming to established goals. This may involve exhibiting details of 'lived' experience, which also connects to the idea of reflection and the achievement of goals. As Turner (1982) tells us: 'Thus experience is both "living through" and "thinking back". It is also "willing and wishing forward", i.e., establishing goals and models for future experience in which, hopefully, the errors and perils of past experience will be avoided or eliminated' (p. 18). In liminoid performance, gay and lesbian youth potentially transcend the subaltern role of the 'disenfranchised'. Through exhibiting ideal goals and models representing political potential, they emerge through ritual beyond the frame, making new space.

Consequently, we may consider that liminal performances reflect and reinscribe the norm, whereas liminoid performances challenge structures. As Marvin Carlson (1996) tells us, although liminal performance: '... might seem to mark sites where conventional structure is challenged, this structure is ultimately re-affirmed. ... Liminal performance may invert the established order, but never subverts it' (p. 23). In these terms, liminal performance for gay identity might possess discursive power in recognisability through expressing equivalence to heterosexuality; however, it may not subvert power in necessarily having to contextualise heterosexual ideas. Therefore liminoid performance might be more transgressive in extending potential. For gay and lesbian youth, this may be seen in evoking the democracy of same-sex engagements which offer more potential than heterosexual equivalents, as they do not need to follow specific gender roles in social and sexual engagements.

However, I would argue that the transgressive potential of gay and lesbian youth owes less to same-sex improvements on heterosexual models leading to comparative outcomes, than it does to interactions and discursive engagements which produce new space. Although gay and lesbian youth display the potential to transform identity through ritual engagements (which appears to be evident in dating and romance reinventions), the focus is less on movement to one point, and more on the process of participation leading to change. As Felicia Hughes-Freeland and Mary M. Crain (1998) tell us within *Recasting Ritual: Performance, Media, Identity*:

> Instead of a ritual process which moves from one movement to another in time and space, ritualised performative practices embody creativity and constraint to be thought of as simultaneous, co-present, and co-dependent, and embodied in different forms of participation. This entails a shift in focus from form and meaning in ritual, to different aspects of participation. (p. 3)

The participatory aspect of gay and lesbian youth performance involves different levels of engagement which cross the production and audience divide. It is evident in the discursive connectivity between film-makers and audience social identities, leading a pathway to potential social change through connectivity and resonance. Furthermore, it is apparent in new media social networking for gay and lesbian youth such as Gay Youth Corner (discussed below), where new connections and participations foreground coalescent and free-flowing opportunities.

Whilst this suggests fluidity removed from ideology, I believe that this is indicative of Victor Turner's (1982) ideas of 'antistructure', which stimulates the performance of counter-cultural ideology, or actions against dominant structure. In these terms:

> 'Antistructure,' ... can generate and store a plurality of alternative models for living, from utopias to programs, which are capable of influencing the behavior of those in the mainstream social and political roles (whether authoritative or dependent, in control or rebelling against it) in the direction of radical change. (p. 33)

Through participatory modes of engagement, gay and lesbian youth performers offer new scope though questioning and challenging ritual norms connected to social networking, dating and romance. This might not lead to a new specific place defined by the liminal expectations of heterosexual normality, but instead enables 'antistructure' in discursive scope working towards change.

Antistructure is evident in the narrative performances of Jonathan Harvey, Todd Haynes and Alan Bennett, with regard to the representation of gay youth within film. Whilst Harvey, Haynes and Bennett come from entirely different backgrounds (and sensibilities regarding gay identity – discussed below), they are brought together for their focus on youth ritual, performance and realism, expressing not only the positive nature of gay youth coming of age, but also in the construction of realism and integrity.

Jonathan Harvey, *Beautiful Thing* and reflective realism

Jonathan Harvey (see Figure 6.2) is an openly gay playwright and media producer. He has achieved considerable success on British television, including the establishment of his own production company (6th Floor Productions). He has written three series of the situation comedy *Gimme Gimme Gimme* (BBC, 1999–2001, UK), which focuses on a dysfunctional relationship between a gay man and a female best friend who share a flat together. Also he has achieved notable status on the writing team for the long-standing soap opera *Coronation Street* (Granada, 1960–present, UK), which has increasingly included sexual diversity.[1] I argue that Jonathan Harvey's play *Beautiful Thing* represented not only an impetus to his later work (discussed briefly above), but also that it offered new landscapes of film realism for gay identity.

Jonathan Harvey's play *Beautiful Thing* was written in 1993, winning the prestigious John Whiting Award the following year, meeting the

Figure 6.2 Jonathan Harvey, creator of *Beautiful Thing*. Image courtesy of 6th Floor Productions.

criteria as 'an original and distinctive development in dramatic writing' (BBC, 2008a). A film version was produced in 1995, with an adapted screenplay by Harvey, foregrounding the music of Cass Elliot (popularly known as Mama Cass) of the 1960s American group The Mamas and the Papas. This involved Hettie MacDonald as director, and Bill Shapter and Tony Garnett as producers. As a film production of Channel 4 television which had originally been intended as a television drama, and with the participation of Tony Garnett, a producer renowned for realist discourse (Bennett et al., 1985), *Beautiful Thing* offers an intimate connection between television and film realism. This is apparent in Channel 4's public service remit as a broadcaster and film producer to be innovative and to reflect public diversity (Annan Committee, 1977), evident in Channel 4's early development through groundbreaking programming (Hobson, 2008). This included the production of the film *My Beautiful Launderette* (Stephen Frears, 1985, UK) (Geraghty, 2005), which focused on Hanif Kurishi's exploration of homosexuality, race and contemporary politics in the 1980s. *Beautiful Thing* conveys optimism

Figure 6.3   Jamie (left, played by Glen Berry) and Ste (right, played by Scott Neal) in scene from Jonathan Harvey's *Beautiful Thing* (Hettie MacDonald, 1996, UK), sharing a carefree moment. Image courtesy of Channel 4 and Film 4.

and youthfulness in representations of growing up and self-discovery, contextualising contemporary narratives and precedents of early realism in British cinema (discussed below).

Beautiful Thing represents the narrative of two teenagers, Jamie and 'Ste' (Steve), who develop a same-sex romantic and sexual attachment (see Figure 6.3). They are situated as neighbours within the setting of a low-income council housing 'tower block' estate (filmed in Thamesmead, south-east London). We discover that Jamie harbours an internalised romantic affection for his schoolmate Ste, which is then realised. Through a series of events, where Ste's oppressive family, headed by his abusive father, punish him for failing to maintain the household in the absence of his mother, Jamie and Ste are further drawn together. This is largely stimulated by Jamie's mother (a single parent), who offers to protect Ste, suggesting that he should stay with her family, sharing Jamie's bedroom. Jamie and Ste have to share a bed together (because of a lack of space), and this stimulates a physical closeness, where Jamie discovers the signs of physical abuse on Ste's body, in bruises inflicted by his brother and father. Through Jamie offering to apply 'peppermint' ointment to soothe Ste's bruised body, the two become physically and emotionally close, resulting in an intimate relationship. Jamie and Ste embark on a secret romantic journey, which although it is troubled for fear of exposure to family and peers, offers insight into the first stages of a relationship and finding a partner. Although Jamie's mother discovers the relationship, and is initially upset, the film ends with a positive scene of defiance where Jamie and Ste dance together in a romantic embrace in front of their neighbours (discussed in the introduction to this book, and represented in Figure 0.1), supported by Jamie's mother, and their neighbour, Leah. This realism supports homosexual identity, connecting issues of social class and location.

Beautiful Thing reveals not only contiguity with contemporary realism (discussed above), but also develops earlier expressions of social representation. It is resonant with the movement towards realism in 'British cinema [evident within] the late 1950s and early 1960s [which offered] a breakthrough, surfacing, first, as a series of documentaries screened at the National Film Theatre under the banner of "Free Cinema"' (Hill, 1986: 127). Films inspired by this such as *Room at the Top* (Jack Clayton, 1959, UK) and *Look Back in Anger* (Tony Richardson, 1959, UK) offered the promise of realism, in their focus on class issues, social changes and poverty. Also films such as *Victim* (Basil Dearden, 1961, UK) (discussed in Chapter 3) and *A Taste of Honey* (Tony Richardson, 1961, UK) explored homosexual identity, with the former exposing the problem of homosexuals blackmailed for their illegal status in society, and the latter depicting a young gay man who forms a partnership with a pregnant girl, against an oppressive world.

I argue that *Beautiful Thing* further develops the discourses of *A Taste of Honey*, progressing homosexual identity and expressing contemporary realism. *Taste of Honey* reveals a closeted gay youth, Geoffrey, limiting his life expectations by embarking on a dysfunctional but worthy partnership with a girl, and supporting the raising of her child. *Beautiful Thing* offers visions of personal rather than a social fulfilment in comparison, foregrounding the achievement of a developed same-sex partnership between Jamie and Ste. Robert Murphy (1992) tells us that '*A Taste of Honey* inherits the "poetic realism" of Free Cinema [evident] in its playground-game theme' (p. 22), focusing on youth and romanticised play. I argue that *Beautiful Thing* extends such poeticism, fulfilling the optimism of youthful and playful characters, evident in the accompaniment of an affirmative soundtrack such as 'Make Your Own Kind of Music' by The Mamas and the Papas.[2] Geoffrey in *A Taste of Honey* (1961) and Jamie and Ste in *Beautiful Thing* (1995) are reflected in working-class and impoverished settings marking a connection with realism. Despite this, Jamie and Ste eventually triumph, displaying their mutual affection in a public place (within the housing estate), while Geoffrey remained hidden but was regarded as noble and useful, though an outcast. This shift to exposure and the progression to public space are resonant of Jonathan Harvey's contribution.

As an openly gay writer, Jonathan Harvey further progresses the potential of the early realist films, where there was often a distance between the writer, producer and/or performer, and the textual subject. John Hill (1986) tells us of the early realist texts, where the 'outsider's view' is 'inscribed in the films . . . articulate[ing] a clear distance between observer and observed' (p. 133). In contrast, Jonathan Harvey presents a self-reflexive vision of sexual identity in *Beautiful Thing*, offering narratives which might seem autobiographical. He presents the ritual of growing up as a gay youth, in terms which may be close to his own experiences as a gay man. This represents a reflective realism where concepts of the outsider are not exclusively distant, and the subject involves the writer potentially as part of the text. I argue that Jonathan Harvey establishes a personal voice as a new storyteller, exploring issues of teen identity in the exposure of a valued and liberated gay and lesbian life.

Todd Haynes and Alan Bennett similarly foreground their personal identities within their text. However, rather than offering discursive realism, they focus more squarely on ritual events and the potential of individual character.

Todd Haynes and Alan Bennett: gay youth narratives in film

Todd Haynes is an 'auteur' film director with a distinctive and often confrontational style. Crossing varying generic boundaries within art house and mainstream cinema, he addresses multifarious audiences with homosexual (and sexual nonconformity) themes. James Morrison (2007) tells us: 'Haynes' work is indispensable in considering some of the most pressing [issues within] contemporary culture [foregrounding] ... the proper social role of art ... [and its relationship to] mass production and commodity fetishism' (p. 1). Haynes focuses on the aesthetic pleasure of viewing, commodifying sexual identity within popular cultural themes. From films addressing the perceived threat of consumerism (and the fear of contamination or disease) to everyday life (*Safe*, 1995, US) to those reconfiguring popular music cultures (*Velvet Goldmine* (1998, US) discussed below, and *I'm Not There* (2007, US)), Haynes engages popular art in commodity-based settings. Furthermore, Haynes foregrounds gay identity reconstructing contemporary voices. This occurs in texts as diverse as *Poison* (1991, US), a three-narrative evocation including a tribute to homosexual French writer Jean Genet (1910–86) depicting erotic sexuality within military and criminal confines (see Ishii-Gonzales, 2007), and *Far from Heaven* (2002, US), a tribute to the work of 1950s director Douglas Sirk within melodrama, further exploring male homosexual desire repressed within the confines of (heterosexual) marriage. Also in providing postmodern and pastiche-like collages of narrative (see Dyer, 2007) he brings together the previously unexplored (or disconnected), and places a focus on the ritual of growing up for 'queer' youth. This is primarily evident in *Dottie Gets Spanked* (1993, US) and *Velvet Goldmine* (1998), with the former exploring the emerging queer identification of a six-year-old child, and the latter the ritual of coming out and gay sexuality enabled through identification with popular music culture (discussed below).

Alan Bennett is a leading author and playwright within contemporary British culture. A former Oxford university scholar in history who abandoned a developing career in his field to work in radio and television, and originally formed part of the satirical comedy group *Beyond the Fringe* in the early 1960s (see Bennett and Cook, 2003), he has become a household name in the United Kingdom (and is well known in the United States of America). Although he has only recently confirmed his homosexuality in an autobiographical text where he records an incidence of a personal hate crime against him and his partner (Bennett, 2004),[3] he has written celebrated texts which have dealt with the subject of gay sexuality. Most notably, Alan Bennett's *An Englishman Abroad* (BBC, 1983, UK) explored the life of Guy Burgess, an upper-class British spy, exiled to Moscow after supplying secrets to the Russians in the 1950s. This play partly established his reputation within television, and at the same time it recorded the restricted yet tragicomic life of Burgess as a homosexual in 'cold war' Russia (in the late 1950s). Within Bennett's wider work there are many incidences where covert or subtle homosexual identity might be read though his focus on sentimental, camp and effeminate male identity;[4] however, his most recent notable film *The History Boys* (Nicholas Hytner, 2006, UK) provides his most confrontational account of gay sexuality (discussed below). *The History Boys,* similarly to Todd Haynes' work, records issues of coming of age as a gay person.

Todd Haynes and Alan Bennett within *Velvet Goldmine* and *The History Boys* (respectively) both locate the sexuality of young gay men as interwoven within normative and everyday popular frameworks. I argue that this is established through framing identity by aesthetic and discursive means. As Mary Ann Doane (2004) tells us of Todd Haynes' work: 'Haynes' tracking shots are saturated with subjectivity' (p. 2) where the protagonist's ideas are foregrounded, intensifying personal feelings. As Doane explains with reference to Todd Haynes' *Far From Heaven* and the dilemma felt by the lead female character on the discovery of her husband's homosexuality, the aesthetic device of gazing through household or car windows connotes and intensifies a longing to understand and explore other worlds. Furthermore, Doane (2004) indicates the discursive context of the child, or youth, as an emblematic theme within Haynes' *oeuvre* and I argue that this is also evident with Bennett's work. As Lucas Hilderbrand (2007) affirms, Haynes' *Dottie Gets Spanked* (1993) portrays a pop culture site where a child (yet to be identified as gay) 'vicariously experiences desires and genders in the absence of other identificatory frameworks' (p. 43).[5] Consequently, I argue that Haynes and Bennett both foreground subjectivity through aesthetic and discursive means, revealing the progression of gay youth towards imagined adulthood status. This occurs through the portrayal of subjectivity, evoking the emerging citizenship status of young homosexuals with equality to heterosexual peers. I argue that this idea might extend from Gore Vidal's novel *The City and The Pillar* (1948) (briefly discussed above, and in the introduction), where notions of self- worth are foregrounded in establishing the equality of gay citizenship. In order to discuss this further I will first contextualise *Velvet Goldmine* and then examine *The History Boys*.

Whilst Lucas Hilderbrand (2007) considers *Dottie Gets Spanked* (discussed briefly above) as Todd Haynes' 'most autobiographical film [for its] narrative of a proto-gay boy's identification with a female television character' (p. 42), I would argue that *Velvet Goldmine* offers more developed scope for, as Nick Davis (2007) identifies, the 'unburying of queer desire' (p. 88) which intensifies Haynes' narrative self-reflexivity. Although located in a popular music cultural past, reinventing glam rock narratives of the UK in the early 1970s which surrounded performers such as David Bowie, Brian Eno and Iggy Pop (replacing these with fictional yet evocative reconstructions),[6] the central protagonist is a contemporary journalist who reappraises his emerging homosexual self-awareness in flashback.

In a setting of the mid 1980s and reflecting on the 1970s, Arthur Stuart (played by Christian Bale) is set a task of researching the story of glam rock star Brian Slade on the tenth anniversary of his disappearance. The central focus appears to be the story of Brian Slade, exploring his possible whereabouts, and the philosophy behind the staged assassination attempt which hastened the end of his career. At the same time Brian Slade's homosexual relationship with Curt Wild is contextualized. Despite this gravity towards celebrity, the narrative axis is firmly located on journalist Arthur Stuart and his personal reflections on his sexual awakening in the early 1970s. Arthur Stuart's identification with Slade and Wild for their avowed bisexual/homosexual tendencies is vividly portrayed in a scene where at school a teacher is reading extracts from Oscar Wilde's *The Picture of Dorian Gray* (1891) to a seemingly uninterested class. While this occurs Arthur Stuart is affectionately drawing a portrait of Brian Slade in his exercise book, initially oblivious to the teacher's reading:

> There were times when it appeared to Dorian Gray that the whole of history was merely a record of his own life. Not as he had lived it in act and circumstance, but as his imagination had created it for him, as it has been in his brain and in his passions. He felt that he had known them all, those strange, terrible figures that had passed along the stage of life, and made sin so marvellous and evil so full of subtlety. It seemed that in some mysterious way, their lives had been his own.

Arthur Stuart suddenly takes notice, looking up at the teacher after the reference to the ambiguity of sin and evil, and the soundtrack plays the pop song 'Coz I Love You' (by the actual pop group Slade in 1971). In foregrounding the identification between the character Arthur Stuart and the pop music world representing diverse sexuality, Haynes provides a rich discursive moment where emerging sexuality is represented as potentially fulfilled through engagement with popular culture. Arthur Stuart is located outside the pop world, but he takes part in it through identification.

Furthermore, this identification process is vivified near the close of the film where Arthur Stuart experiences a sexual rite of passage through a sexual/romantic connection with Curt Wild (Brian Slade's former homosexual lover). Also Curt Wild passes on a green emerald to Stuart, which is traced in the film from original possession by Oscar Wilde and then to leading members of the glam rock movement before him (initially with the character Jack Fairy),[7] connoting the iconography of sexual difference and creativity. These liminoid transitions (extending liminal frameworks) stimulate a positivist aesthetic and discursive dynamic, supporting homosexual identity. Through foregrounding both distance and fulfilment of experience, issues of alienation are framed, and identifications are resolved. This occurs also within Alan Bennett's *The History Boys*, at the same time relating the teacher–student dynamic.

The film of *The History Boys* was adapted by Alan Bennett from his original play and theatre production which had been an enduring success.[8]

Figure 6.4 The student cast of *The History Boys* (Nicholas Hytner, 2007, UK). Gay student Posner (fourth from the right) is represented as the intellectual leader of the group. Image courtesy of Kevin Loader, © Alex Bailey/History Boys Ltd.

The adaptation into film seemed not only a natural progression, but also it capitalised on its highly successful theatre cast by employing the central performers in the film version. Consequently, the cast of the film (and the previous theatre production) expressed a common bonding, revealing their work as a unified project supported by the actors.[9] Although the central narrative concerns attempts by talented grammar school students to gain entrance to Oxford University aided by inspirational teachers, its focus equally relates issues surrounding teen sexuality and the ritual of growing up. Central within this is the issue of homosexual identity, with three central characters signified as gay. Irwin is a young visiting teacher who helps the students with their studies for Oxford, and is seen as a progressive and revolutionary force. Hector is an elder teacher forming part of the permanent staff, and is seen as 'old world' yet entirely supportive and inspirational. Posner (see Figure 6.4) is one of the students attempting to gain access to Oxford, and is portrayed as sensitive, artistic and troubled with unrequited love for classmate, Dakin. Dakin, also a student, is signified as heterosexual, yet represents the object of desire for all three gay characters.[10]

In a pivotal scene between Hector (played by Richard Griffiths) and Posner (played by Samuel Barnett) (see Figure 6.5), we are presented with two archetypes of homosexual identity, with the historically repressive,

Figure 6.5   Posner (left, played by Samuel Barnett) and Hector (right, played by Richard Griffiths) in a scene from *The History Boys* (Nicholas Hytner, 2007, UK). Posner as insightful student represents the potential of gay youth, and Hector as inspirational (gay) teacher, contextualizes loss. Image courtesy of Kevin Loader.

in contrast with the contemporary ideal. Hector is an older married man who cannot resist his homosexual inclinations, but does not wish to embark on a same-sex relationship, and Posner is a developing gay youth who contemplates his sexual desires and wishes for fulfilment. Just before this sequence, Hector has been accused by the headmaster of gross indecency with student Dakin (Hector fondled his genitals whilst giving him a motorcycle ride). Although Hector admits the 'alleged indecency' and apologises, he is about to be suspended from teaching. Dejected, Hector takes a tutorial with Posner, who is studying poetry relating the loss of soldiers in war. Prior to this Posner reads an extract from *Drummer Hodge* (1899) by Thomas Hardy (1840–1928). Hector reflects and opines:

> The important thing is he has a name. Say Hardy is writing about the Zulu Wars, or the Boer War, possibly, and these were the first campaigns where soldiers, common soldiers, were commemorated: the names of the dead recorded and inscribed on war memorials. Before this, private soldiers were *all* unknown soldiers. And so far

. from being revered, there was firm in Yorkshire *of course*, which swept up their bones from the battlefields in order to grind them down into fertiliser. So, thrown into a common grave he is, still Hodge the Drummer had a name. (Bennett, 2006: 60)

The distance and yet proximity of youth identity as forming the backbone of war, yet previously denied a rightful name, resonates with the issue of homosexual identity and youth in similar circumstances. Posner is related to the life of Drummer Hodge, suggesting his right to have a name, or a tangible identity, also. Furthermore, the context of remembrance and memorial is evident, relating a need to respect and support the identities of those who form an important part of society yet may easily be forgotten or written out. Drummer Hodge and Posner are connected through their age and standing as potentially lost identities within society, either through war or alienation.

Furthermore, Posner and Hector, in the context of Drummer Hodge, are represented as isolated figures, illuminating the rejection of homosexual identity. This is particularly evident where Hector discusses the term 'un-coffined' from the Thomas Hardy poem, as a compound adjective formed by prefixing a negative. Also within this Posner contextualises his unrequited love for Dakin. Hector expresses: 'Un-kissed, un-rejoicing, un-confessed, un-embraced. It's a turn of phrase that brings a sense of not sharing, being out of it . . . not being in the swim. Can you see that?' and Posner responds 'Yes Sir. I felt that a bit', echoing his feelings of rejection. Here juxtaposing Hector's and Posner's identities reveals their situation as outsiders.

The History Boys resolves this tension at its close by foregrounding Posner as not only successful in gaining access to Oxford University, but also in becoming an inspirational teacher, like Hector, and in this way, exceeding the achievements of his peers. Therefore a foregrounding of homosexual potential is evident, in positing Hector and Posner as excellent educators beyond the capacity of the norm. Furthermore, it is revealed in the postscript at the end of the film that Posner achieves (relative) content in his homosexuality, suggesting that there is hope for gay youth.

Alan Bennett's *The History Boys* and Todd Haynes' *Velvet Goldmine* both relate the need for an ascendancy of gay youth to adulthood, which foregrounds worthiness for enfranchised citizenship. By revealing the alienation of homosexual youth from normative ideas such as everyday romance, yet foregrounding their integral desire and identification with these issues, they present a liminal framework of understanding producing recognisability. Whilst Haynes relates homosexual potential and expectations through identifying with popular culture and music, and Bennett achieves this with literature and education, in similar ways they evoke a liminoid expectation for gay youth beyond normative frames.

Central within this potential are the imagined identification possibilities, evoking the potential of the audience to connect with the text. As Alan Bennett relates with reference to reading and identification, in the words of Hector to Posner:

> The best moments in reading are when you come across something, a thought a feeling, a way of looking at things, that you had thought special, *particular to you*. And [there] it is, set down by someone else, a person you have never met maybe even someone long dead. And it's as if a hand has reached out, has come out and taken yours. (Bennett, 2006: 60–1)

Haynes and Bennett display evidence of such connectivity to their potential gay and lesbian audiences, contextualising their experience as outsiders. As self-reflexive writers involved in new storytelling, they contextualise their identity in attempting to change social expectations. Reflecting on the formative potential of youth, and also its tribulation, they reveal new contexts for an imagined gay youth community. This extends the liminal frame, offering liminoid potential (discussed above) revealing new spaces for social possibility.

The next case study on the documentary *Coming Out to Class* and the accompanying new media content LGB Teens (2008a), leads to an analysis of the website Gay Youth Corner (discussed below). These texts display evidence of young audiences, providing confident performances of gay and lesbian identity, not necessarily already seen or defined by established older media forms.

Coming Out to Class and LGB Teens

Coming Out to Class (briefly discussed above) presented by Marcos Brito, an openly gay pop music rapper (also known as Q boy), is an educational documentary which explores sexual identity issues for gay and lesbian youth. Broadcast in late 2006 in the daytime and forming part of Channel 4's Learning Programmes[11] in a week-long series of documentaries, it evoked evidence of the station's public service remit to educate audiences about social diversity (Harvey, 2000), focusing on sexuality. Alongside other texts such as *Batty Boy* (an exposé of attitudes within the black community towards gay identity), *My Big Gay Prom* (an exploration of the preparations for a same-sex youth dating event) and *Gay to Zed* (an investigation of various young lesbian, gay and bisexual lives, including singles and couples), a prime focus is educating school audiences. This series also included web interface support from Channel 4, offering personal advice on a website entitled LGB Teens (2008a), and on an alternative educational website (Channel 4 Learning, 2008) designed for the provision of teaching and research resources.

My discussion continues below, first examining the performances in *Coming Out to Class*, and then progressing with an analysis of the accompanying web content largely examining LGB Teens. In these instances, new storytelling opportunities are foregrounded which reveal the determination of gay and lesbian youth to express positive identifications of self.

Marcos Brito's role as the narrator of *Coming Out to Class* is significant, as he may be regarded as an accessible iconic figure of popular youth music culture and homosexual identity. As the first mainstream openly gay rapper in the UK, the media attention drawn to him inevitably encouraged young gay men and lesbians to consider him as a positive source of identity. As we discover in *Coming Out to Class*, two of the main interviewees (Alex and Jamie) actively contacted Brito (via email and MySpace, respectively) to discuss identity issues, outside of the research base of the programme. Furthermore, in *Coming Out to Class* Brito shares his similar experiences of growing up gay within school, providing a supportive co-present environment. Brito aged 29, along with early teens Alex, Jamie and Jake, provide discursive moments of engagement, citing the school environment as often repressive to emerging homosexual identity.

Marcos Brito foregrounds the issue of school, asking Jamie (aged 15) who came out during his English class at the age of 13, to explain his reasons for doing this:

I didn't want to keep denying [my gay identity], I was denying [it] to people and myself. When I found the confidence not deny it to myself anymore, that also gave me the confidence to tell other people.... Even though things got worse [and I was bullied even more initially, and continued to self harm for a while] . . . I think it was better because people couldn't keep asking me if I was gay, because I had already given them the answer.

Jamie advises that answering pressure to reveal sexual identity often forms the reason for gay teenagers to announce their homosexuality. It is suggested that school environments distance gay and lesbian identity so much from the norm that the questioning of identity appears inevitable in order to appease confrontational peers, often involved in exposing outsiders. Jamie's personal dilemma initially got worse, but later it was resolved through finding a personal sense of strength in his own self. He tells us that 'you don't choose who you fall in love with', indicating an adult sensibility in his attitude to relationships.

However, Jamie's admission of self-harming as a way of dealing with the oppression from school peers suggests that support comes less from school authorities (who have the power to protect students), but more from friends, who provide a positive sense of identity. Marcos Brito interviews Jamie's friends to this end, revealing their role as confidants and enablers. As one (female) friend says of Jamie describing his current psychological state after coming out at school, '[He is] more like a person and less like a shadow of someone', suggesting that admission of (homosexual) identity leads to completion of self. Furthermore, as Alex, now aged 15 (who similarly came out at 13) attests: 'I have had a few people say that to me "Oh it's just a phase", "Oh don't worry about it", but then I thought to myself, it's not just a phase. I am liking who I am. I am not attracted to any girls, so I don't think it's just a phase.' Alex expresses a confidence in his homosexual self, which extends beyond transitory explorations of sexual identity. He rejects those who would suspend homosexual realisation until later in life, affirming the positive benefits of announcing gay identity when there is a personal sense of confidence in self. Jamie affirms that you should only announce your gay identity when 'you are secure with yourself [and] you can show that you are strong and proud' (of yourself).

Jake takes this confidence in identity to another level, where he reveals that he has enabled a positive sense of self through producing a school project on gay culture. He reports that peers responded 'quite positively' to this. We are presented with a papier-mâché construction representing a well-toned young male torso, and accompanying work. Jake discusses text he has inscribed on the torso which reflects his personal feelings regarding gay culture and his identity. Paraphrasing this he tells us: 'here I mention [that] I like to stay in my own world, because the bigger world, the full picture is full of hate and perfection, where everyone has to conform to people who are straight". The enabling of personal identification reveals Jake's transgressive agency, effectively inscribing the 'body' of gay identity with political text situated within the arena of the classroom. Through this Jake not only provides a therapeutic point of reference for himself, but also he argues convincingly for gay identity as a valued subject for analysis within school. This agency is further exhibited where Jake reveals that with the support of a schoolmaster (Mr Bogg) he had broached the difficult subject of defining a school policy towards homophobia, which is yet to be established. As Marcos Brito continually reiterates in *Coming Out to Class*, there needs to be a legal policy in the UK regarding the protection of gay and lesbian youth, and whilst guidelines are beginning to emerge (Bawden, 2008; Department of Health, 2008) there still are issues of resistance.

However, such lack of political mobility is not evident from broadcaster Channel 4; not only had they produced positive discourse within *Coming Out to Class* and the accompanying documentary texts, but the new media content of the series was highly supportive.

LGB Teens (2008a) is the public web interface for the series, providing audience advice for lesbian, gay and bisexual youth. Furthermore, Channel 4 provided a teaching and learning site constructed for *Coming Out to Class* (and the accompanying texts) (Channel 4 Learning, 2008), which included the PHSE (personal health and school education) learning notes for schools in the UK. Whilst LGB Teens offers a popular vision addressed to young web users, including text offering advice about assessing emerging sexual 'nonconformity', the learning site provides informative teaching support, including contextualising school curricular themes. Channel 4's construction of these sites clearly offers overarching support of the televisual content. On the one hand it provides popular cultural material embedding the affirmation of gay, lesbian and bisexual youth, and on the other it coherently defines the educational significance of the series. In both instances there is a political drive to provide discursive agency supporting lesbian, gay and bisexual identities.

However, an obvious omission is that LGB Teens and the educational site do not address transsexual identity possibilities. This is especially relevant as the normative term for sexual identity diversity is LGBT, and the employment of LGB without the T suggests a surprising exclusion. It is possible to speculate that the producers considered transsexual identity to be a more sensitive subject, and that school education could become over-politicised in a scenario where there is inadequate legislation supporting transsexual life. Despite this, the content provided supports 'limited' sexual diversity in a positive manner.[12] Whilst both sites are beneficial and illuminating, my discussion here continues with a focus on LGB Teens for its overt narrative drive in constructing new storytelling.

LGB Teens (2008a) sets out its positive popular political tone with an affirmative statement on the home page: 'There has never been a better time to be young and gay in the UK. But what if you're young and questioning your sexuality? You'll probably have loads of questions. How to tell people? How to meet people?' In an address which directly advertises the imagined emerging positive status of LGB identity, the new media content offers many informative contexts. Notably LGB Teens defines a pathway leading to either boys' or girls' home pages, with both options accommodating bisexuality pages below these. Furthermore, coming out advice is offered for the boys' and girls' options, providing moderated text and iconography within the two pathways. Also considering the vulnerable nature of emerging adults, the site includes information about sexual health and safe sex expectations, plus details on how to maintain anonymity if you are using a shared home computer, providing technical information on how to 'hide tracks'. However, negative issues are eclipsed by largely positive content, such as exploring coming out, where to meet people and what might be expected later in life.

LGB Teens' provision of the thread '10 years later' (LGB Teens, 2008b, 2008c) specifically relates changing legislative possibilities for gay and lesbian youth. Through reflecting the emerging parity of the age of sexual consent (16 in Scotland, England and Wales, the same as heterosexual relationships)[13] and the provision of data such as '15,672 [same sex] civil partnerships were formed between December 2005 and September 2006', a general tone of optimism is generated. Furthermore, personal narratives are recorded offering therapeutic identification to young audiences, potentially in similar situations to the writers. On the girls' page of '10 years later' (LGB Teens, 2008b) we are presented with 'Sam's Story':

> I came out when I was 17, a year after I left school. I never felt like a 'typical' girl, but in school everything was so split into what girls did and what boys did that I had to play along. ... I've been with my current girlfriend, Natalie, for a year and a half, and we work for the same hospital. I would like us to move in together at some point, but I don't think we'll ever get a civil partnership – we're just not that interested. ... My life doesn't revolve around the gay scene, I don't go clubbing or anything, but I still have a big social network of gay friends as well as straight ones, and I never feel like I'm in a minority.

This narrative presents an affirmative and carefree stance, which whilst it contextualises social options such as engaging in a civil partnership, or taking part in the gay scene, it avoids a determinist projection which might limit pathways. In this sense, LGB Teens focuses on maintaining the playfulness of youth in its narrative disseminations, keeping in mind its focus on a young audience. This is particularly evident where the idea of social networking is foregrounded as a way of bringing gay and straight identities together, avoiding establishing LGB as 'ghetto' centred 'minority' identities.

Furthermore, a primary focus is establishing connections within communities, evident in the support of online new media as a social networking tool. Whilst information is included for those considering visiting gay bars and clubs, within the thread 'sex and relationships' (LGB Teens, 2008d), it defines these as largely adult arenas advising us that 'The first time you go to a gay bar or club [it] can definitely be a bit of an eye-opener', advocating that 'Everyone's clicking their mouse and hooking up online these days. Most young gay people believe they'll meet their future partner online.' Consequently whilst LGB Teens provides very intelligent information about possible sexual encounters, such as 'You should never feel pressured into any sexual practices that you are not comfortable with' (LGB Teens, 2008d), its general axis is towards weighing up possibilities and considering identity issues more than advocating sexual agency. This is primarily evident within my last case study on the social networking site The Gay Youth Corner, which not only features in *Coming Out to Class*, but also provides an excellent point of positive identification for emerging gay and lesbian youth.

The Gay Youth Corner: affirmation, disclosure and agency

The Gay Youth Corner (2008a) is a revolutionary website which was created by Hamish Priest at the age of 16 in 2005 (as discussed above, featured in *Coming Out to Class*). It was designed to provide new media social networking opportunities for gay and lesbian youth striving to find a positive sense of identity. It features many new media layers, including chat rooms, web forums, a blog, and advice and information. Reaching a diverse worldwide audience and addressed to young users, a central premise is considering the announcement of homosexual identity to family, friends and peers. Hamish Priest (in *Coming Out to Class*) tells us: 'we're not helping you to come out, we're saying, well do you need to come out', revealing the therapeutic benefit of the site in offering a pressure-free environment. I argue that The Gay Youth Corner offers an affirmative and investigative arena, not necessarily addressed at fixing identity. It is therapeutically enabling, encouraging an understanding of personal identity concerns, which often leads to investigation, affirmation and change. This dynamic is apparent in its web forum and in its advice and information strands.

Within the web forum option there are many engaging and reflective subject areas. This provides an opportunity for users to compose their own concerns within a forum, and to view the responses, or to participate in discussion, testing out and questioning ideas. Under the strand 'The Gay Youth Forum – advice and personal matters – coming out' (Gay Youth Corner, 2008b) in a forum entitled 'The First Person you came out to' posted by G. Dizzle, we are told 'I was wondering if you came out to a friend or a family member? and what was it like? I personally came out to a friend first.' Various responses are listed below:

> I came out to my brothers first. They kinda already knew anyway plus we get on great so it didn't change anything. (Kalas, aged 17, gay male)

> I was kinda forced out of the closet. I wrote a love letter to a boy in my class, and my teacher found it, and told my parents. (Morgan05, aged 18, gay male)

> I came out to a couple of friends at first, who were really cool with it which was nice and kind of paved the way for me to come out to my mom. It was cute ... my mom said she already knew and I asked her how and she said she could just tell which shocked me. (Ktword, aged 16, lesbian)

> I came out to my mom, as she was so proud of me for it, at 17 she took me to my first gay club. (Bambie, aged 22, gay male)

These testaments reveal the potential of personal disclosure and intimacy in new storytelling. Through presenting positive or cautionary narratives of social agency to peers, they define a way forward for gay and lesbian youth. Whilst the social networking community provides instances of identity affirmation, the representation of role models within the media becomes a general point of reference.

Under the strand 'advice and information – life' (Gay Youth Corner, 2008c) we are presented with a lead article written by Sacha Howard

. entitled 'Homosexuality in the Media: is the Press Good?' and comments below from site users. It is notable that the article offers a basic historical account of the media, citing key contemporary texts which have portrayed gay and lesbian identity, and questions are posed. Central within this are attempts to stimulate a debate on the 'visibility issue', suggesting that a profusion of gay and lesbian identities within the media may not necessarily be beneficial. Directly addressing the commodity of gay identity (see Chapter 5) we are told, referencing two high-profile television texts:

> *Queer Eye* depicts homosexuals as human Barbie dolls (manicurists and personal shop assistants) and *Sex and the City* shows us pimped up gay guys whose only purpose is to be fashionable accessories to successful young arty women. What a depressing set of role models for young gay society, and what a pathetic example of homosexuality for society as a whole. ... This level of publicity doesn't mean that being gay is necessarily accepted, it's just popular like a new trend or a fashion statement.

Clearly providing a point of view, a consensus is presented which foregrounds the potentially negative currency of high-profile representations. Furthermore, the tone indicates the use of homosexual identity within dominant media as oppressive. Whilst many users might approve of the representations within *Queer Eye* and *Sex and the City*, the consensus of responses indicates agreement with the writer's argument, with one user (BAJ 103) (see also Gay Youth Corner, 2008g) telling us:

> Yes I agree with this. When I came out to one of my female friends the first thing she said was 'so now we can go shopping and you can tell me what looks good and everything'. And I seriously thought it was a joke, but she was dead serious.[14]

Through stimulating debate, the article encouraged responses which made users reflect on personal identity issues, indicating personal realisations. Whilst personal opinion is subjective, and the constitution of gay identity is various, the discourse encouraged users to affirm their identity preferences. This revealed a consensus of opinion that gay and lesbian youth are not necessarily reflected favourably within mainstream media (such as television and film), and intimated that online new media (such as The Gay Youth Corner and LGB Teens, discussed above) offers more scope for diversity and 'realism'. To this end, a plenitude of identity possibility may be seen in reviewing the user profiles and this may provide the closest evidence for diversity and 'realism' in the media for gay and lesbian youth.

The Gay Youth Corner attests to membership in excess of 45,000 users (Gay Youth Corner, 2008a). Whilst it is not possible in the remit of this book to review all members' profiles, an examination of sample content reveals an identity landscape rarely portrayed within mainstream television or film. As Priest reports (cited in *Coming Out to Class*), the youngest users start coming on to the site between the age 13 and 14, and evidence from the profiles reveals a certain confidence in identity aspirations at this age. Users 'brian3393' (Gay Youth Corner, 2008d) and 'jasom1p' (Gay Youth Corner, 2008e) both identified as gay males and aged 14, present a confidence in 'public identity'. Through foregrounding their personal photos set within school and the family home (respectively), normative and domestic arenas are revealed. Furthermore, the users display aspirations for relationship formation, expressing within their profiles an interest in 'long term relationships [and looking for someone that cares and loves me for who I am' (brian3393), and wishing to find a partner that 'likes to cuddle, has a sense of humour, likes to laugh but isn't ashamed to cry – he listens and talks to me' (jasom1p). In these instances, discourses which are usually connected with older people and stereotypically heterosexual romance, are made resonant by young gay teens. This provides not only transgressive discourse, but also offers opportunities for peers to find affirmative reflections of self. This also extends to networking connectivity, enabled for peer support. This is evident not only in encouraging connections to other users within collated profiles on the guest's link on the website, but also in the provision of links to web forums to which the members have contributed. Users view each other's profiles and make connections about contributions and interests, expanding their social possibilities.

Furthermore, there is a provision for members of The Gay Youth Corner to link to external pages which might more openly display their identities. This may be seen in many users providing the details of their personal blogs or MySpace profiles. If we consider the user 'travelinHom' (Gay Youth Corner, 2008f), a gale male aged 21, he links his profile to a 'blogspot' entitled 'Progressive Grass Roots Politics'(2008), more formally revealing his identity:

> I'm currently a junior in college, trying to figure out what my major should be. Well, it's more like, what I need to do with the rest of my life. Lately, I've been rather scattered because of some crazy

happenings in my life. I like to beat around the bush, but I won't do that today: I just came out to some close friends and family.

Whilst the blog is focused on his college project and the subject of politics, this further new media layer is interesting as it reveals an additional confirmation of his homosexual identity, this time within a social and educational context, furthering the dissemination of identity. Similarly, if we consider user 'BAJ 103' (discussed above), he provides his MySpace web link (Gay Youth Corner, 2008g). This then reveals his full name and more personal details, which in the context of MySpace allows for an active social connectivity with friends, at the same time foregrounding popular music and culture. Consequently, the networking possibilities are extended from The Gay Youth Corner, seeping into integration with more mainstream sites.[15]

The connectivity to extend beyond the personal allowing for a construction of an online new media community, both within and beyond The Gay Youth Corner, is a prime element in enabling new storytelling. Gay and lesbian youth move forward, beyond histories of oppressive representation within mainstream media, and define new pathways through self- and peer reflection.

Conclusion

The participation of gay and lesbian youth within the media is a contentious subject. Media producers within the mainstream are normally mature people who have worked for some time in dominant heteronormative media environments, suggesting apprenticeship and a certain need for (liminal) framing. The revolution discussed here is that increasingly young people involve themselves in self-reflexive media representation outside the frame, free from repressive conditioning. The case studies at the close of this chapter reveal this emerging, unfettered potential. Clearly this would not have been possible without the progression of online new media technologies, or, I argue, the precedence of gay and lesbian elders within media production (as discussed earlier in this book). Whilst new technology offers a discursive space, personal identification and confidence in self come from reflective experience, which may be relative be earlier foundational agency.

Therefore whilst emerging new storytellers often disapprove of mainstream media representations of gay and lesbian lives (discussed above), I would argue that self-confidence and optimism for the future, to a degree, extend from preceding storytellers. This may not be seen in a proliferation of everyday (fictional) role models, but rather in writers and producers who provide isolated yet affirmative narrative. Jonathan Harvey in *Beautiful Thing* has contextualised a sense of realism in film which echoes traditions from the past, generating optimism for gay youth. This extends to a self-reflexive vision where we may look to the future with hope and some confidence.

Todd Haynes and Alan Bennett have become iconic figures within the mainstream media, and their support for gay and lesbian identity inevitably has offered new ways of exploring narrative. Although Haynes may be viewed as a 'queer activist' film-maker, and Bennett may be considered as a celebrated playwright who plays down his sexual iden-tity, they both disseminate non-heterosexual identity with inspiration, persistence and force. Notable within this, as discussed above, is their reflection on what it may be like to grow up gay. Although Haynes and Bennett seem politically and generically incomparable, they are contigu-ous in their support of storytelling which portrays the possible extents of gay and lesbian life. They display the performative potential of the limi-nal frame, resulting in liminoid possibility, leading to change. Their focus on the experience of gay youth coming of age inevitably not only influ-ences storytelling ideas within film, but also it predicts wider narrative forms.

Jonathan Harvey, Todd Haynes and Alan Bennett offer self-reflexive narratives of fictional worlds which are embedded with 'antistructure' (discussed above). They are produced within the mainstream media system, yet they challenge dominant ideas of sexuality, romance and personal choice. Through displaying the alienation of gay youth, yet revealing the simple human similitude of homosexual feelings and aspi-rations to dominant ideas, both distance and proximity are framed. This locates gay and lesbian within, rather than outside, the frame.

The sense of proximity, optimism and domestic aspiration is equally evident within online new media and contemporary discourses of gay and lesbian youth. The participants in *Coming Out to Class* and The Gay Youth Corner realise they are stepping outside the dominant frame, yet they construct confident and illuminated pathways. A confidence in self, and an expectation of fulfilment, provides a realisation of the potential discussed by Harvey, Haynes and Bennett. As contemporary performances by social actors as youths involved in new storytelling, they do not necessarily have to reflect histories of denial or rejection, which contextualise the dominant frame. They move beyond the frame, realising that the participatory coalescence of social networking creates community from within. Gay and lesbian youth in new media do not need to justify their single place; they progress together in apparent social union, unfettered.

However a social union such as this, which relies on participation and mainstream understanding, does not necessarily encompass all. The next chapter explores the issue of other storytelling, largely told by those outside. Issues such as isolation and individual expression are foregrounded in examining the 'frameless', outside the imagined (Western) gay community.

7
Other Storytelling and the New Frontier

Introduction

Ashraf Zanati (see Figure 7.1), a former teacher and one of 52 men arrested in Cairo, Egypt, for 'debauchery' in 2001, in an incident which would stimulate worldwide attention concerning gay identity in the developing world, tells us (in the documentary *Dangerous Living: Coming Out in the Developing World* (John Scagliotti, 2001, US)):

> I stayed in prison for 13 months. I tried to make myself quite useful, I adapted myself. I thought that I am there for a reason so I started to teach people in prison, English. I taught about 50 people in prison.... Now I am leaving [my home] behind. I am leaving everything behind me, even my memories. My mum is very attached to me, and when I told her that I am leaving, she couldn't believe it, and she said to me 'try again to be here'. But I couldn't.

Zanati's testament reveals the vulnerable nature of sexual nonconformity within the developing world.[1] Not only was he arrested for simply attending a social event, and inordinately punished as part of a government campaign to limit gay visibility within Egypt, but also the context of imagined democracy within the Western (developed) world plays a significant role in his identity expectations. Unable to resolve the oppressive situation within his own country, in order to find a more fulfilled sense of self (as a gay man) he must leave for the West, eventually becoming a refugee in Canada. The affluent West plays a dynamic political role in the expression of sexual nonconformity within the developing world: although it offers a productive point of reference which stimulates possibility and agency, at the same time such expectations

Figure 7.1   Ashraf Zanati, depicted in a scene from *Coming Out in the Developing World* (John Scagliotti, 2004). Ashraf was one of the 'Cairo 52'. He was imprisoned for 13 months purely for attending a gay social event. Image courtesy of Michael Hanish and John Scagliotti

inevitably pose a challenge to local identity traditions which might not be accommodating.

This chapter consequently explores the representation and agency of gay and lesbian identities from the developing world, and the context of contemporary homosexual (Western) democratic ideals. However, whilst there may be a proliferation of homosexual behaviour within diverse communities around the world, it is important to note that my focus on identity is related to the contemporary concept of homosexuality and westernised social expectations of citizen equality. Furthermore, although Gilbert Herdt (1997) reveals that many non-Western societies occasionally are potentially 'more tolerant of variations across the spectrum of sexual behaviours [compared to] western cultures, since the early modern period, [who have] been more disapproving and punishing of all variations and domains of sexuality and gender, especially homosexuality' (p. 21), my investigation explores homosexual expectations of equality to heterosexual ideals. Consequently, although Herdt (1997) cites examples of liberated homosexual behaviour from the Sambia in New Guinea and the Zuni in pre-colonial North America, and we may also consider Lee Wallace's (2003) findings on the 'Fa'afafine' in Samoa (feminised gay males who are integrated into dominant heterosexual family life), my discussion here only considers links between a spectrum of homosexual identities which may be connected through identification to Western ideals of equality and liberty within democratic citizenship.

The potential of gay and lesbian identity within the developing world may be considered as a 'queer diaspora' (Patton and Sánchez Eppler, 2000), where diverse (Western orientated) non-heterosexual identity seems globally dispersed and disconnected, yet I argue that this offers new stories of political engagement and hope. Within this the performative potential of ritual and religion challenges the archetypal dominance of Western homosexual identity. In these terms new life chances are enabled through new forms of storytelling, revealing dispersed and localised identities as mobile, performative and inspirational. Consequently, rather than providing a Western focus revealing the developing world outside, this chapter foregrounds the diasporic potential of 'other' new storytellers as enabling change. This provides potentially therapeutic and socially enabling connective pathways, offering proactive agency which may be self-reflexive and socially rewarding. Although in these terms new storytelling might be inspired by Western (democratic) advances, at the same time it offers new definitions of social choice which extend global life chances for gay and lesbian people.[2]

This extension occurs where the political agency of new storytellers redefines social and ritual possibilities through personal identification and performance. It may be seen where gay men and lesbians capitalise on recent legislative opportunities offering same-sex civil unions and marriage, stimulating new ritual and performative possibilities, evident (for example) within the documentaries *World Weddings: Gay on the Cape* (South Africa) (Clifford Bestall for BBC, 2004, UK) and *Foreign Correspondent: Two to Tango* (Argentina) (ABC, 2004, Australia) (discussed below). Furthermore, it is apparent in those who want to find acceptance and equality through challenging authority and creating their own community, evident for example within the new media social networking website Iranian Queer Organisation (IRQO, 2008) and extensions of this reported in the documentary *Out in Iran: Inside Iran's Secret Gay World* (Farid Haerinejad for CBC, 2007, Canada) (both discussed below). In addition, gay men and lesbians define themselves as part of mainstream society in attempting to change their world. The documentary *Jihad for Love* (Parvez Sharma, 2007, US) (discussed below) offers expressions of connectivity to Islamic culture and religion, situating gay men and lesbians as part of dominant themes. In these instances, new storytelling is

. enabled through ritual and domestic expressions, revealing confidence in self and connections to theological norms.

However, the issue of otherness and its relationship to the West is paramount in examining constructions of homosexual identity within the 'developing world'. Whilst new discourses have emerged which foreground the new storytelling of 'other' gay and lesbian identities (discussed below), peripheral lives are still disempowered. Such opportunity, offering hope and evident denial, is revealed in John Scagilotti's *Dangerous Living: Coming Out in the Developing World* (discussed below), where brave participants stand up in an oppressive 'other' world. Yet new voices emerge challenging authority, offering intimate connectivity.

I argue that in terms of history and narrative archetype, the concept of the homosexual within the developing world has been established within certain iconic settings, and new storytellers engage and capitalise on these potentials. Julian Schnabel's autobiographical film (2001) of openly gay Cuban novelist Reinaldo Arenas' (1943–90) *Before Night Falls* (1993) (discussed below), reveals such an emergence contextualised within discourses of intimacy and resistance.

However, before exploring the case studies, it is first necessary to examine the context of homosexual identity within the developing world, and new stages of progression which have enabled fresh political, social and cultural possibilities, and expectations.

New identifications within the queer diaspora

The 'Cairo 52' court case (briefly discussed above) attracted worldwide press attention, and this stimulated social action. The inordinate punishment of 52 gay men, arrested, tried, tortured and imprisoned for alleged 'debauchery' in a government attempt to stifle an emerging (westernised) gay identity within Egypt, coalesced the worldwide international gay community (as it is perceived) and its supporters. The event produced new discourses of resistance, which might be compared to similar historical situations of oppression in Western society. As John Scagliotti argues in *Dangerous Living: Coming Out in the Developing World*, comparisons may be made with the police oppression resisted in the Stonewall riots by gay and transgendered people in the late 1960s, and with Anita Bryant's and the Christian right's campaign against homosexuality in the 1970s (see Gross, 2001; Clendinen and Nagourney, 1999). Whilst gay men and lesbians were punished and cited as outsiders, in resistance they seized opportunities of response, which stimulated change. Gay men and lesbians were projected into the limelight, various social forces came together, and ultimately this widened identity possibilities. In assessing Foucaultian terms of power, oppression of identity stimulates power resistance (see Chapter 3) and this often energises new forceful voices. John Scagliotti makes direct comparisons between Stonewall, which is cited as the Western gay breakthrough event, and the advent of the Cairo 52 as offering new hope for gay identity in the developing world.

Although the Cairo 52 event did focus attention in a similar manner to Stonewall, the stimulus for change in the developing world might more generally be seen in homosexual identifications of liberty, freedom and equality, disseminating from the West. This may be evident in new global cultural and social connectivities such as the advance of MTV and its support for gay and lesbian identity, responses to AIDS for its dissemination of (homo)sexual discourse, and new media Internet technology offering advanced social networking possibilities. Whilst the impact of MTV may be problematic for its propensity to dominate cultural emissions with westernised American ideals (Kaplan, 1989), and the impact of AIDS similarly provides skewed connotations of Western (homo)sexuality, in both instances we are presented with cultural and social iconography embedded with popular and intimate discursive potential. Consequently, through the hybrid and global disseminations of MTV, and scientific and social responses to AIDS, new contexts for homosexual identity have been engendered.

HIV and AIDS health education programmes have stimulated new awareness of homosexual lives, extending from purely medicinal responsive strategies to highlighting male homosexual social identities as part of a global productive community. As Simon Watney (2000) tells us:

> HIV has in many respects served to reconstitute homosexuality and identities founded on homosexual desire. This reconstitution involves many overlapping elements, from attitudes towards sex, towards illnesses and death, mourning and so on. It informs the totality of [gay] social and psychic lives in ways that we hardly begin to understand. (p. 130)

I believe that such an active social and psychological expression extends beyond the limits of individual people and communities, and inscribes a global potential for gay identity. This breaks down barriers of resistance, stimulating large audiences to understand or investigate homosexual desire. Whilst it is inevitable that many people will continue to 'other' homosexual identity, and the significance of AIDS as an illness stimulates repressive connotations (Sontag, 1989), at the same time this produces vivid identity profiles and structures. Such overt expression of a need to recognise homosexual identity is also evident within the cultural disseminations of MTV.

MTV has produced many progressive texts which have favourably represented gay men and lesbians. This is particularly evident within the reality documentary series *The Real World* (1992–present, US) where gay men and lesbians have been offered the lead role in the narrative construction: for example, many same-sex couples have been cast as the series romance (see Chapter 4, and Pullen, 2007a). Furthermore, it is apparent in MTV's advertising strategy, and is vividly displayed within a series in 2000 entitled 'Do You Speak MTV: the Language of Love' (Commercial Closet, 2003), situating gay and lesbian relationships as equal to heterosexual ideals. MTV's narrative strategies and the multivalent disseminations around AIDS are focused on the personal, at the same time indicating possible connections to 'other' social worlds. Just as Anthony Giddens (1992) describes the context of 'dissembedding mechanisms' (such as television, contemporary communication and the World Wide Web) as freeing the individual from the hold of the local and explains how this offers identification with the global, this engenders intimate identification and connectivity, beyond local restraints.

In addition, new media extends this possibility enabling performativity, merging the local with the global, and constructing new concepts of gay community. As Chris Berry, Fran Martin and Audrey Yue (2003) tell us, 'The recent emergence of gay and lesbian communities in Asia and its diaspora is intimately linked to the development of information technology in the region' (p. 1). This illuminates a progression of homosexual identity within new media as one 'from [originally] subcultural data [about health] to 'presentness' [and performativity] enabled by media synergy [evoking] libraries of imageworlds and signs' (Berry et al., 2003: 2). The Internet in its social networking capacity stimulates personal performances in the construction of a global, imagined gay community, through its connectivity.

Whilst Berry et al. (2003) are concerned for the homogenisation of worldwide sexual cultures, revealing this as a process which might prioritise those who are information rich (such as Western new media contributors), it is not the aim of this book to explore the complex issue of globalisation and its influence on sexual diversity. Rather, issues of global sexuality are related to the personal agency of media producers and their narrative performativity, working within, yet potentially challenging, Western hierarchies.

To this end the significance of the imagined gay community and the context of the 'queer diaspora' play a central role.[3] As Cindy Patton and Beningo Sánchez Eppler (2000) tell us:

> Sexuality is intimately and immediately felt, but publicly and interna-tionally described and mediated. Sexuality is not only not essence, not timeless, it also is not fixed in place; sexuality is on the move. With this new clarity we are in a better position to analyze the valences of body-in-place and consider the transformations in sexualities that move between – indeed, may have been produced at – the intersections of specific geopolitical territories. (p. 2)

Whilst gay and lesbian identity from various political and regional global areas evokes the diversity of sexuality, issues of social construction and group identification influence the potential in formations of self. As Patton and Sánchez Eppler suggest, these liberating 'transformations' may be produced through the complexity of locality and difference and responses to various political ideas, as much as extending from dominant (Western) ideas of a heterogeneous gay community. Whilst (other) devel-oping world gay and lesbian identities living within the 'queer diaspora' are located within different contexts, through mobility and transfor-mation they possess local experience and diverse political drive in the construction of self-reflective new storytelling. Therefore whilst we may consider developing world identities as 'other' within dominant western-ised concepts of gay and lesbian community, at the same time I believe that they possess extraordinary performative potential in the new stories that they tell.

The documentary *Dangerous Living* (briefly discussed above) provides illuminations on these ideas, in the discursive and archetypal expres-sion of gay and lesbian identity within the developing world. This may involve not only the context of the West, but also the individual agency of the 'other'.

Dangerous Living: other storytelling, colonialism and the new frontier

Lesbian activist Dilcia Molina (see Figure 7.2, also discussed in the intro-duction to this book) tells us in *Dangerous Living: Coming Out in the Developing World*, of an event which stimulated her need to ultimately leave her home country of Honduras:

> It happened on the 7th of November of 2001 [while I was absent]. Six heavily armed men came into my house. They entered looking for me

Figure 7.2 Dilcia Molina (also discussed in the introduction to this book), depicted in a scene from *Coming Out in the Developing World* (John Scagliotti, 2004, US). Dilcia recalls her family's torture by oppressors. Image courtesy of Michael Hanish and John Scagliotti

and asking after me, 'Where is this bull dyke? Where is the bitch? We are going to rape her so that she learns not to stick her nose in that business.'.... One of the men grabbed my son and cut his face with the knife. He tied him up and started to torture him, my son and the girl who looked after him.

Dilcia's family and allies had been punished possibly for no other reason than that she had presented her identity openly to the public in a demonstration at the first gay march in San Pedro Sula, Honduras, when others concealed themselves with masks or make-up.[4] The torture of her son revealed extreme abjection in the assailants, evoking a need to displace, eject and punish those not considered part of the normative world.

Although it is not the aim of this book to explore the psychological problems of those who would punish outsiders to the norm, it is important to contextualise the outsider identity and the focus of gay men and lesbians who are attempting to situate their identity within developing worlds. Whilst Dilcia, and Ashraf Zanati (discussed briefly at the head of this chapter), eventually had to find refuge in the West, their original intention had been to change their local worlds, not necessarily to depart. Consequently, although this book acknowledges that in many instances, an openly gay or lesbian identity leads to an untenable life in the developing world, the significance of new storytelling is to challenge these dynamics at home.

However, lesbians and gay men within the developing world are situated as outsiders at home, and as 'other' to the dominant Western gay and lesbian community worldwide. Democratic ideals of homosexual liberty have been promulgated in the West, and whilst the developing world may contextualise this, histories of otherness and colonial oppression reveal disparities. As Michael Pickering (2001) tells us: 'differences constructed in relation to myths of advancement in the [w]est during the nineteenth century have cast an extensive shadow' (p. 61), subjugating the other in racial and social terms in order to show progression and difference. Furthermore, this may connect to colonising processes whereby the inferiority of other identities is foregrounded. As Pickering (2001) affirms:

> The colonialist construction of the inferior Other contradicts the civilising mission of colonialism, which was predicated on making the colonised like the coloniser. The imperialist subject's sense of self was a denial of this sense for the colonial Other, who only existed in an incorporated, exterior racialised form, which he or she was required to enact. The othering of cultural difference in this way threw into doubt any attempt to prescribe or encourage identification with the coloniser whose identity depended on this projected Otherness of difference in every confirmation of itself. (p. 68)

Therefore a binary identification process exists whereby the situation of disempowered or emerging gay and lesbian identities within the developing world may be viewed as fixed in subjugation through Western (homosexual) narrative frames. This is a colonising process whereby, as Pickering indicates, the 'other' cannot be easily incorporated into the dominant frame unless they play a minor, 'inferior' role. The Western representation of 'other' gay and lesbian identities is problematic: in order to be empowered, narratives must be Western-focused, offering resolution and progression. This is evident within *Dangerous Living: Coming Out in the Developing World*, as the prime heroes are those depicted as departing for the West (such as Dilcia Molina and Ashraf Zanati, discussed above), or those who have followed the potential of westernised gay identity and its advances, suggesting a colonial hierarchy.[5]

However, whilst it is arguable that gay and lesbian identity within the developing world remains colonised, issues of post-colonial identity are also relevant. *Dangerous Living: Coming Out in the Developing World* does foreground a colonial liminal framework, yet at the same time it evokes a liminoid post-colonial philosophy, foregrounding discursive agency. As Helen Gilbert and Joanne Tompkins (1996) tell us:

> As a critical discourse, ... post-colonialism is both a textual effect and a reading strategy. Its theoretical practice often operates on two levels, attempting at once to elucidate the post-coloniality which inheres in certain texts, and to unveil and deconstruct any continuing colonialist power struggles and institutions. (p. 3)

Progressive 'other' storytelling inevitably should contextualise the past, revealing power dynamics and disparities. Gay and lesbian 'other' identities in post-colonial situations should be related to current circumstances and troubled histories. This occurs in *Dangerous Living* where histories of oppression are foregrounded, and culpable forces indicted.

Within *Dangerous Living,* Western historical influence is contextualised, suggesting that colonial rule introduced homophobia, and that it is not an indigenous thread. Through foregrounding a past before colonisation as stimulating sexual freedom, evident in figurative iconography displaying homosexual engagement and affection, it is suggested that colonisers and Western religion built the foundations of sexual oppression within the developing world. This reveals that although the West may have provided the extents of new liberty ideals, at the same time it was instrumental in fashioning the homosexual as 'other', worldwide.

The relationship between homosexual identity, the West and the developing world is revealed as complex and reflective. Whilst it is possible to argue that gay and lesbian identity within the developing world is inspired by advances made in the West, at the same time the developing world does not fully support a homogenised Western ideal which might stimulate a global sexual identity. This difficult contiguous relationship might be related to Homi Bhabha's (2004 [originally 1994]) context of borderline engagements between different cultures. As Bhabha tells us:

> The terms of cultural engagement, whether antagonistic or affirmative, are produced performatively.... The social articulation of difference, from a minority perspective, is a complex, on-going negotiation that seeks to authorise hybridities that emerge in moments of historical transformation.... The borderline engagements of cultural

difference may as often be consensual as conflictual; they may confound our definitions of tradition and modernity; realign the customary boundaries between the private and the public, high and low; and challenge normative expectations of development and progress. (p. 3)

The developing world may have a symbiotic relationship with the West; however, it is not simply a one-way exchange prioritising Western imperialism. Whilst inevitably there are disparities in power and cultural identification, discursive connections and political aspirations may be paralleled. As Bhabha suggests, this may involve hybrid identity engagements or transactions, and whilst the relationship between borderline cultures may not be mutually beneficial, discursive concepts may be progressed, or challenged, in the transference or exchange of ideas.

Therefore, whilst the performers in *Dangerous Living* foreground Western forces as culpable in establishing homophobia worldwide, suggesting that new storytellers in the developing world are divorced from an exclusive Western-centric union, at the same time a relationship exists which suggests a co-presence and learning advance. The 'articulation of difference' within *Dangerous Living* does not necessarily rely on the subjugation of gay and lesbian identity within the developing world; rather it is a transactional process, merging identities working towards hybridity. I believe that other storytellers inspired by the iconography of liberty, and advances made in the West, project their personal identity ideals through this liminal frame, changing its form rather than being shaped by it.

In the manner of liminoid potential (discussed in Chapter 6), this reveals the context of 'other' storytelling as interlaced with Western homosexual ideals, stimulating new hybrid forms of gay and lesbian possibility for a worldwide stage. Whilst this seems to follow a Western path, using building blocks already in place, I would argue conversely that new constructions are in place, offering new structures of engagement.

The following case studies reveal not an imperial Western gay identity, and distant cousins in subordination, but a new world order where other new storytellers are inspired by new potentials. Gay and lesbian new storytellers stake their claim, expressing their intimate lives within the new frontier of the developing world. They are pioneers in new identity expression, and confident enablers of change.

Nature and instinct in *Before Night Falls*

Julian Schnabel's film *Before Night Falls* (2001, US), adapted from gay Cuban literary icon Reinaldo Arenas' autobiography of the same name

. (1993), presents an iconic image of childhood within the developing world focusing on the context of the homosexual self in harmony with nature, and intimate senses. In the opening (and closing) sequences of the film we are presented with an image of a naked child playing outside in the dirt. Reframing Reinaldo Arenas' experiences of growing up gay in the Cuban countryside, we are told:

> Trees have a secret life that is only revealed to those willing to climb them.... I think the splendour of my childhood was unique because it was absolute poverty but also absolute freedom; out in the open, surrounded by trees, animals and apparitions and people who were indifferent toward me.

Represented as an unwanted child, brought to his grandparents' home by his mother as a sign of her failure, Reinaldo Arenas reveals himself within his poetry and literature (and echoed within the film *Before Night Falls*) as an isolated figure, yet intuitive with nature, senses and emotions. Whilst Arenas would achieve wider attention after his death (aged 47 after fleeing Cuba for America), his iconic presence within the film *Before Night Falls* is discussed for the contextualisation of gay identity within the developing world as contiguous with themes of nature, instinct and sensitivity.

The setting of Cuba (also original home to Pedro Zamora, discussed in Chapter 4) provides a rich pathway to an understanding of gay identity within the developing world, oppressed at home. I argue that 'other' gay and lesbian storytellers embed their stories with natural instincts of sexual freedom, against a setting of oppression and punishment.

The irony within *Before Night Falls* is that Reinaldo Arenas wishes to join the communist revolution in Cuba (in the late 1950s), and initially becomes an active supporter of this, yet later oppression by the revolutionary forces engenders a climate of homophobic anxiety. As Marvin Leiner (1994) reports:

> Homosexuality was ... condemned through association with the previous degenerate and corrupt world of Havana. Homosexual bars and cruising areas were viewed as centres of counterrevolutionary activities. Homosexuals not only suffered from traditional homophobia and prejudice; for a time they were considered enemies of the state because they could not fit into [a Marxist-Leninist] ideological social unity. (p. 27)

Within *Before Night Falls,* Arenas is situated in this repressive environment; however, he actively enables a personal sense of self through his literature. Nevertheless, despite Arenas' literary talent emerging whilst he worked within the Biblioteca Nacional José Martí, and his achievement of a commendation from the National Union of Cuban Writers and Artists, he only published one book in Cuba itself. His numerous other works were published outside of Cuba, due to the incompatibility of his ideas with the revolutionary regime.

As depicted in *Before Night Falls*, homosexual identity was repressed and contained, often leading to incarceration. After an incident where Reinaldo Arenas is represented as being framed for the sexual molestation of a minor, in a situation where young male criminals at a beach defend themselves alleging sexual impropriety, he is represented as a fugitive on the run in Cuba. Arenas tries to escape to Florida by attempting to sail there supported only by an inflated tyre tube, this fails and later he is in hiding in the Cuban countryside. Eventually he is caught and sent to the El Morro Castle, 'a fortress built by the Spaniards during colonial times that early in the revolution became a dungeon where homosexuals, political dissidents, and other undesirables were locked up' (Manrique, 2008). His imprisonment formed part of a larger oppression against dissidents and homosexuals.

As Marvin Leiner tells us:

> In 1965, homophobia reached an organized level of oppression. The military set up Military Units to Aid Protection (UMAP) camps as they came to be called. At this time homosexuals were not only being publicly and politically denounced as perverted and decadent, but viewed as social deviants. (p. 28)

As Leiner adds citing Dominguez (1978): 'Many were interned in these rehabilitation camps [because their] behaviour was not in accordance with good citizenship' (p. 28). Here the ideology that homosexuality is divorced from normative society and production is reinforced. Whilst Reinaldo Arenas' imprisonment occurred in 1973, and the UMAP camps had closed earlier in 1967, oppression continued for many years in Cuban society. Central within this was a concern for male effeminacy, indicated as irresolvable with masculine life.

Within *Before Night Falls* Reinaldo Arenas is represented as an effeminate male homosexual, in his connection with passive sexuality and confrontational sexual encounters. Through this he challenges issues of sexual identity, engendering a transgressive and political ideology. This is evident not only in his various casual sexual encounters where he takes a submissive role, but it may also be seen in iconic potential elsewhere.

Notably it is apparent in prison when he is aided by the transsexual Bonbon, who attempts to smuggle the original manuscript of *Before Night Falls* out of the prison (and is caught). This directly locates an effeminised passive gay man as a hero in a sexual transgressive agency. Arenas' opposition between feminine passivity and masculine order could be related to the imagined role of the homosexual at the time and to issues for 'machismo' in Latin male sexuality, and the suggestion of threat.

As Martin Leiner (1994) reports with regard to concerns within Cuban society just prior to the emergence of the UMAP camps (discussed above), 'a 1965 Ministry of Health report concluded that there were no known biological causes of homosexuality' (p. 33), and no effective biological treatment was possible. This report suggested that male homosexuality is learned, stimulated by excessive female identification from single mothers, where male role models are absent. Furthermore, there were concerns that the homosexual condition could spread among peers in childhood, through learned behaviour. Leiner reveals that special schools were established where:

> Children ... were divided up into groups according to five categories of behaviour problems: hyperactive and aggressive children; anxious and withdrawn children; boys with effeminate tendencies; bed wetters and children with eating disorders. Each group or brigade was identified with a colour. The effeminate boys were in the yellow brigade. (p. 34)

Through the segregation of outsiders to the norm, potential homosexual male children were subject to behavioural teaching, promoting 'normality'. Embedded within a masculinised culture, which directly signalled the feminised male as homosexual, systems were in place which repressed personal identity choices. I argue that Reinaldo Arenas challenges these ideas within his personal performance.

This is particularly evident in *Before Night Falls* where repressed identity is connected to both sensitivity to nature and the instinctive drive in sexuality. Within these two themes the personal self is enabled through intimate reflection and performance. Connoting Anthony Giddens' (1995) ideas concerning the discursive power of intimacy (discussed in Chapter 4), Reinaldo Arenas contextualises his reflections, senses and instincts. As discussed above, this occurs in the representation of his childhood and adult life as outside the norm, but in touch with nature and instinct. It is evident in his desire to climb trees and inscribe his poetry on them, and view the landscape below (Manrique, 2008). Furthermore, it is apparent in his unashamed expression of sexual liberty, related to opposing forces. As Ed Morales (2008) observes in reviewing *Before Night Falls*, 'For the late Reinaldo Arenas ... sex was the muse that allowed him to spirit his body out of an oppressive reality, and into a dream of freedom.' Arenas' expressions of sexual desire are represented not only in terms of personal fulfilment, but also in terms of challenge to social order. In a pivotal part of the film where Arenas signs a false declaration rejecting his work and beliefs to gain freedom from the El Morro Castle prison, he displays a sexual attraction to an oppressor. Whilst a brutal prison governor taunts Arenas, he becomes sexually aroused, and this appears agreeable to both parties, aware of the sexual tension, and their expectation to perform polarised masculine and feminine roles. This reveals not a moment of contrition and desperation, but a display of knowingness of inevitability. Arenas foregrounds stereotypical Latino machismo and enforced role playing, revealing a false world where homosexual desire is repressed, or hidden, in order to fulfil dominant social expectations.

Reinaldo Arenas' death in 1990 further contextualised his performative potential. After suffering from AIDS he took his own life, leaving a final message for the press:

> In a moving farewell letter sent to the Miami Spanish newspaper *Diario las Américas*, [Reinaldo Arenas] made it quite clear that his decision to take his life should not be interpreted or construed as defeat. 'My message is not a message of failure,' he declared, 'but rather one of struggle and hope. Cuba will be free, I already am.' (GLTBQ, 2008)

It is interesting to contrast this apparently direct political message, contextualising Arenas' imagined spiritual liberty, with the ending of Julian Schnabel's film. Arenas is depicted as taking a prescription overdose, in the company of his friend Gómez Carriles who assists in his suicide.[6] Carriles comforts Arenas just before he dies, by reading out his poem *My Lover Sea*. The close of the film brings us back to the image of the child playing in the dirt in Cuba (discussed above), and the poem continues. An edited extract of the poem *My Lover Sea* follows:

> I am that child with the round, dirty face who on every corner bothers you with his 'Can you spare a quarter?' I am that child with the dirty face, no doubt unwanted.... I am that child of always before the panorama of imminent terror, imminent leprosy, imminent fleas, of offences and the imminent crime. I am that repulsive child that improvises a bed out of an old cardboard box and waits, certain that you will accompany me.

Before Night Falls poeticises Arenas' life and death, foregrounding the identity of the vulnerable child who is in touch with nature, yet located as distant from supervision and proper care. This establishes a political message in the iconography presented, situating the developing world as a place of potential understanding and growth, possibly beyond the experience and comprehension of the affluent West. However, the poem also indicates the contiguous relationship between the impoverished and the well-off, suggesting potential in the affluent West to understand and progress. This locates the developing world as the site of discursive expression, and the dominant world as in stasis and needing development. I argue that where Arenas discusses his desire for a liberated Cuba, it is not in a future westernised form, but as a self-reflexive and intuitive state supporting humanity, diversity and potential.

Consequently other storytellers in the developing world lead the way for the affluent West: gay men and lesbians create new pathways through inspiration, personal bravery, intuition and reflection. This is particularly evident within *Gay on the Cape* and *Two to Tango*, where in South Africa and Argentina respectively, new legal forms of same-sex relationship offer ritual and social opportunities for change.

Uruguay, *Two to Tango* and *Gay on the Cape*

In January 2008, Uruguay became the first country in Latin America to introduce national same-sex civil partnership legislation offering property, family and healthcare rights. In a news feature on *BBC News 24* (2008) Ana Mora of the Uruguayan Lesbian Association tells us: 'It will give my partner and myself relative security. Because it will allow me to visit her in hospital without being thrown out. It will give me relative security in front of my family and in front of the state also.' The media representation showcases Ana Mora and Jacqueline Renati (her partner) at home, in the garden and reading books, foregrounding the everyday normality and domesticity of lesbian and gay identity. Furthermore, *BBC News 24* reporter Bill Hayton tells us that whilst Uruguay may not have been the first Latin American country to introduce such legislation as 'several cities in Mexico, Brazil and Argentina have similar laws', it was the first to embed same-sex rights in national law. Uruguay's leading role in offering new opportunities in Latin America reveals the engagement and opportunity of domestic same-sex partnerships, challenging normative ideas of family and relationship. However, as *BBC News 24* attests, contextualising the (female) author of the new legislation within

Uruguay who desires that same-sex couples should have equivalence to heterosexuals in the right to marry:

> *Reporter [Bill Hayton]*:   But the Catholic Church in Uruguay as in the rest of the world is heavily opposed. So the current law is a compromise, but in the capital [of Montevideo] at least it's popular.
>
> *Male passer-by*:   Correct, perfect, we all have the right to live the way we wish to, without affecting others.

Uruguay's example showcases the difficult position of gay and lesbian identity within the developing world: there is a tension between secular and religious forms, often leading to compromises for opportunity.[7] Whilst legal changes supporting homosexuals may achieve public support, often this involves challenging traditional elements of society where there is a deeper resistance. The liminal frame of opportunity and possibility is not necessarily formed by a popular mass, but it is influenced by a historical world which prioritises heteronormativity. These apparently immovable forces, however, may be stimulated through performative engagement. When gay men and lesbians engage in civil unions and performing the ritual of marriage, they challenge historical ideas and potentially remodel the liminal frame (see Chapter 6, and Pullen, 2007a).

In *World Weddings: Gay on the Cape*, producer and director Clifford Bestall presents the relationship between Mark and Cengay (see Figure 7.3) as they prepare for their wedding ceremony in South Africa. In *Foreign Correspondent: Two to Tango*, reporter Eric Campbell similarly introduces us to partners Leonardo Gorosito and Esteban Hubner (see Figure 7.4) in anticipation of their civil union in Buenos Aires, Argentina. Situated in South Africa and South America, both engagements reflect a growing emergence of same-sex couples in the developing world who are forming partnerships, stimulating new ritual and legislative possibilities. Both couples reveal similar aspirations to Ana Mora and Jacqueline Renati from Uruguay (discussed above), in their focus on domesticity, dedication and brave political stance. This is particularly evident in the case of Mark and Cengay, who at the time of their wedding were not able to have a legal civil union, yet they perform their ceremony as a ritual event. Whilst since this date South Africa has now offered the provision of legalised civil partnership for same-sex couples (since November 2006), Mark and Cengay's transgressive agency reflected emerging possibilities for lesbians and gay men worldwide. Within this dynamic is the context of religion and issues of family identity, revealing same-sex partners as challenging the dominance of heterosexuality.

Figure 7.3   Mark (left) and Cengay (right) in a scene from *Gay on the Cape* (Clifford Bestall for BBC, 2004, UK). Mark and Cengay 'are married' in a personal and public expression of commitment. Image courtesy of Clifford Bestall.

In *Gay on the Cape*, Mark and Cengay participate in a local radio show, offering a positive opportunity to broadcast their engagement. Within this, their priest Father Marlow on hearing a personal attack from the radio audience, affirms:

> We are not talking about two guys who are lusting over each other, who are promiscuous, we are talking about two responsible young men who would like to be in a committed relationship, and who would like to have the right to have that relationship blessed within a religious institution.

This defence locates Mark and Cengay as thoroughly committed partners, who express a strong identification with Christianity in affirming their relationship. Whilst later in *Gay on the Cape* we discover that the couple are denied (by the authorities) their wish to conduct their wedding ceremony in a church, adherence to religion is nonetheless foregrounded. This is primarily evident in the wedding ceremony itself, held by Father Marlow, where Mark and Cengay read their vows to each

Figure 7.4   Esteban Hubner (left) and Leonardo Gorosito (right) depicted at the time of their civil union in Buenos Aires, Argentina, and their contribution to the documentary *Foreign Correspondent: Two to Tango* (Australian Broadcasting Corporation, 2004). Image courtesy of Esteban Hubner and Leonardo Gorosito

other, and their exchange of rings bears religious significance: 'I give you this ring as a sign of my love and commitment to you. As my life partner now and always, and all that I am, and all that I have, honour you.' Mark and Cengay situate themselves in the iconography of the traditional wedding ceremony, signing an unofficial religious document at the close of the event. Whilst this occurs in a civic hall as the Church did not support them, the focus remains on dedication to each other and

. respect for religion. Through these liminal frames, Mark and Cengay perform new expressions of gay partnership, challenging the rejection of the authorities and the Church with personal agency.

Religion also plays a central role in *Two to Tango*, where gay men and lesbians are shown to be involved in positive identification with religious life, yet there is also a criticism of religious authorities. Positive identification may be seen in the number of supporters for popular religious celebrations. As Eric Campbell reports: 'This is how many young people celebrated the [Catholic celebration of the] Day of The Immaculate Conception. More than two thousand [people] squeezed into the Amerika Club, one of Buenos Aires' most gay popular venues.' Revealing support for the Roman Catholic faith, and contextualising this within contemporary forms of celebration, gay men and lesbians are constructing new social worlds, merging old ideas and new possibilities. Although expressing support for and adherence to religion, at the same time they challenge normative traditions, and authoritative voices within them.

In Argentina, a central concern is expressing the need for civil liberties to be free from the influence of the (heterocentric) Church. Furthermore, there is a contention within recent history with regard to the Catholic Church's association with previous oppressive governments. As we are told in *Two to Tango*:

> *Cesar Cigliutti*:   More than 80% of the population belongs to the Catholic Church but it's also true that people believe in separation of Church and State. . . .
> *Eric Campbell*:   The Church has never recovered from the darkest period of Argentina's history, the Dirty War. From 1976 to 1983 a military dictatorship oversaw the execution of thirty thousand dissidents.
>
> *Esteban Hubner*:   The Church lost credibility in Argentina. I remember as a child seeing all the presidents that we have there in the junta with the priests at their side and we know today by the confession, many of the criminals of the military junta that they had priests blessing the bodies before they were thrown in the Rio La Plata River from planes.

Although this presents an emotive and subjective account, prioritising the voices of those who support gay and lesbian lives, the resistance of the Church to recent advances in civil liberties is significant. In Argentina, the support of the Catholic Church for the oppressive military regime in the period of the Dirty War inevitably impacted on expressions of civil liberty, suppressing minority groups.

However, during this period in Argentina there was an effective challenge to patriarchal order, suggesting a move towards emotive display and inclusive responsibility. This was evident in the demonstrations and long-standing work of the Grandmothers of the Plaza de Mayo (see Abuelas, 2008) who as parents and grandparents of missing children staged large-scale protests against the military regime. Through the Grandmothers' activity during the Dirty War, and since this time, they have enabled the recovery of many lost grandchildren who had been forcibly taken by the military from their parents (often just after childbirth). Whilst the parents had 'disappeared' and their children were abducted many of these 'grandchildren' were traced through a gene bank created by the Grandmothers, consequently discovering their lost families. In these extents, and emotively portrayed in Estela Bravo's celebrated documentary *Who am I? The Found Children of Argentina* (2006, Argentina), challenge to gender order and problems with state (and Church) were displayed. This may be seen in the substantial matriarchal display of the Grandmothers of the Plaza de Mayo in challenging oppressive patriarchal order. I argue that such a polarisation may have stimulated a cultural and social environment, encouraging the emergence of a more confident gay and lesbian identity, potentially welcomed by matriarchal influences and new social identifications of intimacy, advocating inclusion. This may also be related in contexts of family and care for children.

As Eric Campbell reports in *Two to Tango* countering the Roman Catholic Church's opposition to gay adoption: 'many children don't have anyone to call a parent [and] Buenos Aires is thought to have at least four thousand street children, most begging or scavenging off garbage to survive'. Through revealing a need for adoption, and the readiness of gay people to become much needed parents, Campbell suggests that the Church prioritises its prejudice against gay people above the humanitarian support of children. Furthermore, Esteban Hubner discussing his suitability to become a parent tells us:

> Well, I'm totally in favour of adoption. I'm a teacher. Leo my partner is a teacher and we are perfectly able and capable to raise children. We are not planning now or in the near future to do that but what is better – to have one child without parents at all, or one child with two mothers or two [fathers]? I think it is much better the second option.

This juxtaposition of enlightened new gay citizens against repressive old world religion elevates the voice of new same-sex civil union partners.

In a reflection which might correlate the current dilemma of unwanted children with the loss of children in the Dirty War, the Church is potentially (historically) aligned with the previous military dictatorship and oppressive order. Resolution and support for family are represented as productively offered by the new socially enfranchised homosexual community. Through these means gay identity is represented as enlightened and responsible, and repressive old orders are revealed to be as interested in self and lacking in humanity.

A shift to humanity and inclusive forms of family is also evident in *Gay on the Cape*, where Cengay (aged 20) discusses details of his family history and his aspirations for the future. He tells us that he is the guardian to his ten-year-old sister, whom he personally removed from his parents' family home to ensure her welfare: 'I am trying my very very best not just for me but my sister as I am trying to create a family that the two of us never really had. . . . [I would like to adopt a child and] I want Mark as well to be the parent of the child.' Through focusing on the idea of the caring and inclusive family, including a desire to care for unwanted children, Cengay expresses the context of the ideal citizen. This focus on family, society and care may be related to Michel Foucault's (2000) [originally 1983]) idea of 'the ethic of care of the self'. Foucault suggested that this may be working on the 'project of the self' for the benefit of others, which engages with the concept of ideal citizenship. He tells us that:

> Care of the self is ethical in itself, but it implies complex relations with others, in the measure where this *ethos* of freedom is also a way of caring for others. . . . *Ethos* implies also a relation with others to the extent that care for self renders one competent to occupy a place in the city, in the community or in interindividual relationships which are proper – whether to exercise a magistracy or to have friendly relationships. (p. 287)

Those who support the care of unwanted children may reveal evidence of the 'ethics of the self', supporting the improvement of society through selfless personal contribution. Cengay's care of his young sister and his desire to adopt reveals his high standard of personal ethics in humanitarian ethos. Similar to Esteban Hubner (discussed above), he foregrounds the need for children to be cared for within an inclusive society, extending beyond contexts of religion which might be resistant to homosexual participation within this.

The partnerships of Esteban Hubner and Leo Gorosito in Argentina, and Mark and Cengay in South Africa, foreground the potential of same-sex coupling as socially aware, expressing traits of ideal citizenship. Whilst in both incidences they contextualise religion, it is significant that they are denied and devalued by the Church. This suggests that dominant theological belief assigns homosexual identity as disharmonious with the concept of ideal citizenship.

Despite this, my final case studies reveal some gay men and lesbians integrating with religious discourse, expressing a need for new levels of understanding and acceptance in theological worlds. At the same time oppression is evident in social worlds largely centred on theological belief, and this impacts on life chances. The context of gay and lesbian identity is discussed below with relation to Islamic belief, and pressures within countries where Islam dictates a disavowed and seemingly impossible life for gay and lesbian people.

Out in Iran and *Jihad for Love:* civil rights, family and belief

When Iranian president Mahmoud Ahmadinejad spoke at Columbia University, New York, in September 2007, the academic audience and the worldwide press were astounded at his denial of the existence of gay men and lesbians in his country.[8] There was a mocking and comedic response to the president's comment that 'he didn't know who had told the audience that there were homosexuals in Iran but it was not true', and this event stimulated new interest in Iran's suppression of diverse sexuality (CNN, 2008). At a similar time Parvez Sharma released his documentary, *A Jihad for Love* (2007, US) (discussed below), which explores the perspective of homosexuals who are devout to the Islamic faith. These diverse events revealed a growing focus on the significance of non-heterosexual identity within Islam. The discussion below considers new storytelling produced by gay men and lesbians within the Islamic world, focusing not only on *A Jihad for Love* and adherence to faith, but also on Farid Haerinejad's documentary for the Canadian Broadcasting Corporation *Out in Iran: Inside Iran's Secret Gay World* (2007), which reveals the emergence of a gay civil rights movement, stimulated by Arsham Parsi and his website Iranian Queer Organisation (IRQO, 2008).[9]

Arsham Parsi (see Figure 7.5) started the revolutionary website Iranian Queer Organisation in 2004, whilst still living in Iran. Although his family warned him about the danger of identifying himself as homosexual, after finding a more positive sense of self through Internet searching (through search engine Google) he became more confident and set up the website hosted in Norway, through contact with an associate

Figure 7.5   Arsham Parsi created the *Iranian Queer Organisation*, a significant web portal supporting gay men and lesbians in Iran, gaining in excess of 5000 members. Image courtesy of Arsham Parsi

(Homan, 2008). The site gained popularity through its ability to disseminate positive messages concerning gay and lesbian identity, and warned of oppression and torture perpetrated against homosexuals in Iran. As Bret Stephens (2008) reports in interviewing Arsham Parsi in the *Wall Street Journal*:

> Arsham Parsi, 27, ... now runs the Iranian Queer Organization (irqo.net) from Toronto. In 2001, he says in a phone interview, 'two of my close friends committed suicide because of the bad situation for queer people.' Their deaths galvanized him to begin a gay and lesbian support group, conducted furtively and electronically, consisting largely of articles on gay-related subjects from English language sources. The enterprise grew to include six separate electronic magazines. 'We used to think we were alone in the world,' Mr. Parsi says. 'With these magazines, we knew we were not.'

Achieving a membership of 5000 Iranian users, the site offered a coalescent sense of identity serving a hidden gay and lesbian community.

However, this stimulation and interaction was considered a threat by the authorities in its formation of an underground movement, and Parsi had to leave the country in fear for his life, later achieving refugee status in Canada.

Farid Haerinejad's documentary *Out in Iran* (Haerinejad for CBC, 2007, Canada) was produced in a covert operation outside of the permission of the Iranian government, revealing a thriving underground gay and lesbian movement inspired by Arsham Parsi's new media connectivity. Haerinejad focuses his story on Mani Zaniar, who continued Arsham Parsi's work leading the Queer Organisation in Iran. Mani tells us:

> The only important thing is that someday I could walk and breathe freely in this country. And get to choose the one I love and live with him freely. To have the same rights as other citizens: to have the right to legal marriage, to have the right to adopt a child. These are very basic things. It's not extraordinary at all.... Right now its hope that's all.

Mani's evocation reveals citizenship expectations echoing gay and lesbian political ideas in the affluent West. At the same time he contextualises the impossible situation of oppression by the authorities in Iran, and the suppression of gay and lesbian life chances. Whilst we discover that Mani, like Arsham Parsi, cannot remain in Iran (CBC, 2008) after his participation in the documentary makes him vulnerable, his optimism for change forms a central narrative thread.

Although Iran is not exclusively oppressive to gay and lesbian lives within the Muslim world – as Brian Whitaker (2006) reveals in his groundbreaking book *Unspeakable Love: Gay and Lesbian Life in the Middle East*, countries such as Jordan and Saudi Arabia are equally problematic – attention has been drawn to Iran partially through its opposition to the United States, and the reporting of high-profile events oppressing homosexuals. One such event which captured international attention was the execution of two young men found guilty of homosexual acts in 2005. Foregrounded in *Out in Iran* as a catalyst for fear and stimulation for agency, the execution of Mahmoud Asgari (17 years old) and Ayaz Marhoni (18 years old) provides an emotive and powerful discursive foundation. Mahmoud and Ayaz were publicly hanged in the Edalat (Justice) Square of the town of Mashhad in north-east Iran. The iconic images of two young men blindfolded, with ropes around their necks just before execution, and then of their bodies swinging from the rope at the end of a crane, reveal substantial action against sexual diversity within oppressive societies. We are told that 'prior to their execution, the teenagers were held in prison for 14 months and severely beaten with 228 lashes' (Gay Orbit, 2006), and later that they were tried under Islamic Sharia law, and subsequently sentenced to death. As an American human rights speaker tells us in *Out in Iran*: 'Most morals cases, sexual offences cases in Iran are tried in closed sessions, information doesn't leak out of the courtroom. Because of stigma and shame families and friends of the accused don't want to talk.' Such isolation and rejection of public support are countered in *Out in Iran* with the display of a coalescent, if fearful, gay and lesbian community. This occurs largely in the representation of individuals willing to reveal their identity, if sometimes partially concealed, within domestic and community social space.

In a pivotal scene in *Out in Iran* Mani Zaniar interviews 'Hooman' and 'Shirin' (whose real names are not revealed). Mani fully represents himself to the camera, and his interviewees' identities are relatively concealed, with Hooman wearing sunglasses, and Shirin's face being only partially viewed by the camera. Hooman identifies as a gay male, and Shirin as a male to female pre-operative transsexual. In the domestic setting of a living room, Hooman reveals that he has been subject to police entrapment involving kidnap, rape and physical abuse, and Shirin advises that although the Iranian state partially supports sex changes, her position as an outsider makes her life untenable.[10] Shirin reveals that even if she had the (state partially funded) sex change, she would be an outcast from society, adding that not only do her parents not want her to have the sex change (because of the social stigma), but also they advise that she should remain in her bedroom until the end of her life. Hooman sums up the untenable position of non-heterosexual people as outside of family and state, yet persecuted and silenced for following their identity ideals: 'They want to abuse and torture us, and we can't say anything about it.'

This tension and pressure against identity is juxtaposed with Mani Zaniar's bravery and 'audacity' in supporting gay visibility. Visiting a local coffee shop, the 'Jam-e-Restaurant', with film-maker Farid Haerinejad recording the scene, he reveals a thriving weekly gathering of gay men and lesbians, who whilst they cannot publicly demonstrate their affection, are still able to find a sense of community and camaraderie. Furthermore, Mani visits a park in Tehran, which although it is associated with prostitution, provides a public place for gay men and lesbians to socialise. Here he distributes pamphlets and CDs promoting the growing activist movement, affirming that the authorities are aware of the extent of gay and lesbian life, but that they 'don't want to have a

Figure 7.6   Documentary maker Parvez Sharma. His documentary *Jihad for Love* challenged perceptions of gay identity within the Islamic faith. Image courtesy of Parvez Sharma

full scale crack down, as that would open up a debate about gay rights'. This reveals the complexity of Foucaultian concepts of power (see Chapter 3) that resistance provides an opportunity for identity progression. It is suggested that the governmental authorities are aware that large-scale attention might stimulate the promotion of gay and lesbian discourse.

Whilst there is resistance by the dominant Islamic social order to acknowledge the existence, or positive nature, of sexual diversity, many gay men and lesbians adhere to the Islamic faith and consider themselves as worthy citizens. Parvez Sharma's documentary *A Jihad for Love* foregrounds this potential, generating resistant discourse through positive theological identification. Consequently, rather than responding to political and social pressures exerted against the self, to demonstrate civil worthiness Parvez Sharma (see Figure 7.6) provides an impetus questioning the contemporary theological constitution of Islam, which might deny acceptance. This form of agency distances the Western-centric drive

. of civil liberty as may be sensed in *Out in Iran*, and foregrounds dominant theological discourse, engaging personal belief.

Filmed over 5½ years in 12 countries and in 9 languages, Parvez Sharma's *A Jihad for Love* was an enduring and large-scale project. Furthermore, Sharma (A Jihad for Love, 2008) tells us that the film 'seeks to reclaim the Islamic concept of a greater Jihad' which whilst it is often associated with war, may be interpreted as 'an inner struggle' or 'to strive in the path of God'. This focus on theological belief and striving for inner meaning is reflected in Sharma's genuine devotion to Islam. He tells us in an interview on CBC's news programme *The Hour*:

> All the subjects [in *A Jihad for Love*] are coming out as Muslims first: their sexual identities are actually secondary, because they are claiming Islam and saying we have the right to be Muslim as much as anybody else – we are Muslims first and our faith is profound and deep. (YouTube, 2008c)

Sharma situates gay men and lesbians as valued believers within the Islamic faith, rather than focusing on their need for civil liberty as a social minority. In claiming that their identities are founded on popular belief, rather than minority social positioning, he challenges dominant interpretations of Islam and its exclusionary practices. Sharma further elucidates:

> A sexual revolution of immense proportion was part of the very birth of Islam. There was a promise of gender equality. There were frank and honest discussion [in] the prophet's time, and in the Qur'an about sexual behaviour and sexual morality, and there was stress on the sexual act just for pleasure beyond reproduction ... somewhere in the history of this 1427 year old religion we lost our way and stopped having these discussions, that we used to have as Muslims. (YouTube, 2008d)

In questioning the historical interpretation of Islam as potentially distanced from its original thinking, Sharma indicates a relationship between gay and lesbian identity and theological reasoning. Despite the contemporary peripheral location of sexual diversity as outside and beyond the Islamic faith, he opens up debates about their contiguity.

However through foregrounding religious belief, we might consider that Parvez Sharma resists westernised democratic ideals which advocate a separation between religious institution and civil liberty. This may appear evident in his statement that religious belief takes primacy over social (sexual) identity. Despite this I argue that Sharma does provide a 'Western like' democratic focus, however he does this through foregrounding family struggles as an arena in which to explore democracy. Democratic (Western) ideals of civil liberty are played out relating the liberty desired for members of family, rather than the freedom (per se) of individuals in society.

Therefore whilst religion is foregrounded in *A Jihad for Love*, a focus on family and relationships provides the emotive and discursive drive. If we consider Brian Whitaker's (2006) work on gay and lesbian life in the Middle East he foregrounds this potential, exploring the family in relation to expectations of conformity and incidences of oppression:

> A point made repeatedly by young gay Arabs in interview was that parental ignorance is a large part of the problem: the lack of public discussion about homosexuality results in a lack of level-headed and scientifically accurate newspaper articles and books and TV programmes that might help relatives to cope better. The stigma attached to homosexuality also makes it difficult for families to seek advice from their friends. Confronted by an unfamiliar situation, and with no idea how to deal with it themselves, the natural inclination of parents from a professional background is to seek help from another professional such as a psychiatrist.... Contrary to the medical opinion prevailing in the rest of the world, the belief that homosexuality is some form of mental illness is widespread in the Middle East, and many of the psychiatrists who treat it do nothing to disabuse their clients. (p. 21)

Whilst adherence to theological belief is foregrounded in *A Jihad for Love*, issues such as family pressures leading to the oppression and torture of gay men and lesbians foregrounds a civil liberties debate which dislocates a purely theological focus.

Evidence of this is seen in a pivotal sequence in *A Jihad for Love* where a father is represented as discussing his homosexual identity with his children. Taking a journey by car as if on a day out with the children, the father asks his children how they would respond if he was punished by the authorities, which in Sharia law could lead to the death penalty. A young daughter (face concealed in post-editing) responds to her father that if he was stoned (publicly executed) she hopes that he would not suffer and that he would 'die one time with the first stone'. Through this honest and unsophisticated response, we are presented with the impossible confrontation of theological oppression with real social lives, where a child raised under a fundamentalist regime cannot easily comprehend the value of diverse humanity (even though this is represented as 'light hearted', with the child laughing after this comment). Furthermore, a focus on relationships and 'normative' domesticity is also evident in *A Jihad for Love,* where Arsham Parsi (discussed above) is filmed by Parvez Sharma, and is in conversation with a male couple who are romantically physically entwined, lying together on a hillside. He asks for details of their 'wedding' involving the purchase of rings and the testament of friends. Through foregrounding a domestic ideal within a romantic setting, this encourages a sensibility of normality and everydayness. In these instances, gay identity is located in family and domestic scenarios, despite its seemingly impossible situation as outside dominant beliefs and customs.

Parvez Sharma foregrounds theological belief, situating gay and lesbian identity as a real segment of Islamic society. He reveals their peripheral but (just) manageable situation of gay and lesbian experience, telling us: 'As long as you are not marching on the street, as long as you are not having a gay pride, as long as you are not waving your rainbow flag, and saying you're gay, I am queer I am Muslim – it's OK' (YouTube, 2008c). At the same time he challenges the authorities from within. Through contextualising the value of gay and lesbian lives within the Islamic faith, and their trial within family and relationships, he offers liminoid potential in reframing ideas (see Chapter 6). Although he appears to reject a civil liberty focus which might connect to social advances in the West, he sensitises audiences to the value and strength of gay and lesbian lives, focusing on their situation within family and the Islamic world.

This, I argue, offers a new focus, reconstructing wider concepts of gay and lesbian community. *Out in Iran* and *A Jihad for Love* reveal hidden stories of a connected, yet dislocated world, foregrounding democratic ideals in the progression towards civil liberties. Whilst it may not yet be possible to reconcile gay and lesbian identity issues within the Islamic world, through the performativity of new storytelling, boundaries are challenged and potentials are revealed. Emerging potential within discursive space may not necessarily be hollow reverberations going nowhere, but ripples gathering momentum and extending towards change.

Conclusion

Through distance from North American and European culture, gay and lesbian identity outside of the affluent West may appear to be disconnected, and 'other'. Despite this, I argue that new storytellers within the 'developing world' are not only 'valid', but also they offer groundbreaking global visions of social action and connectivity. 'Other' storytellers are forging a new frontier, which although it is inspired by social advances in Western civil liberties, provides new contexts for gay and lesbian community. This, I argue, is beneficial in political, social and cultural terms, informing a wider understanding of diverse sexual identity.

The arrest of the Cairo 52 in Egypt (2001), the speech by Iranian president Mahmoud Ahmadinejad in New York (2007), and the barbaric public hanging of two young men in Iran (2005), provided realisation to local and global communities foregrounding the rejection, denial and (continuing) extermination of gay and lesbian lives. Responses to these (I argue) represent a new frontier extending beyond the police oppression of Stonewall and the media demonisation by Anita Bryant, which for the West offered new challenges leading to change, unification and coalescence. 'Other' storytellers are addressing worldwide audiences, reflecting their social and political ideals. Whilst they are enabled by attention drawn from resistant, punishing and generally oppressive regimes, it is evident that new stories are seeping through, and enlightened concepts of humanity are starting to emerge. As evidenced in the work of Reinaldo Arenas, and significantly within *Before Night Falls*, other storytellers offer visions of self-awareness, instinct and political aspiration. These might challenge the subordinated status of the once colonised, in the construction of post-colonial narratives foregrounding intimacy, bravery and revolution.

Dangerous Living: Coming Out in the Developing World and *Out in Iran: Inside Iran's Secret Gay World* reveal a changing landscape where new storytellers are fighting oppression. Whilst in many instances compromises are made, and often we see the most prominent civil rights leaders departing for the West in refuge, new narratives are emerging, and the 'queer diaspora' is finding its form. Through the advent of new media dissemination and social networking, not only are civil rights expectations witnessed and performed, but also positive identifications are taking hold. Through the sharing of stories, cultural and social transactions take place, and new social positions are beginning to emerge. For gay and lesbian identity, new storytellers in the developing world are revealing their strength, determination and dedication, robustly challenging subordination.

Whilst we may view this through the frame of Western media, which maintains the imagined definition of cultural boundaries and social hierarchies, I would argue that the liminal frames are shifting and new storytellers are challenging the dominant world. Therefore the representations of gay partnership and same-sex union seen in *Two to Tango* and *Gay on the Cape* do not just reveal passing moments of possibility, but are constructions offering new landscapes of progression and fulfilment. The focus on the ritual dedication of same-sex partners extends beyond ceremonies and social re-enactments, and progresses towards the construction of new domestic lives. As I have discussed elsewhere (Pullen, 2007a), this may be considered as a move towards domesticity, which for gay and lesbian lives projects a future connected to social production, continuance and durability.

These new landscapes are under construction not only in the traditional and historic West (Pullen, 2007a), but are significantly progressing in the contemporary and shifting post-colonial world. Although we may consider that 'new world' confidence has been gained through witnessing advances in the affluent West, it is significant that 'other' storytellers are embedding new levels of engagement and connectivity. Parvez Sharma's *A Jihad for Love* is a testament to this confidence in addressing new frontiers of unimaginable proportion. Through his dedication to reveal the devotion of gay men and lesbians within the Islamic faith, he philosophises on the potential of a modified future which is all-encompassing. Parvez Sharma for the Islamic faith progresses the earlier work of Sandi Simcha Dubowski for Judaism (in the documentary *Trembling Before G-D* (2004, US) (see Pullen, 2007a)), where gay men and lesbians are not peripheral 'others', but integral components of theistic socially defied worlds. Whilst I would argue that personal identity should not necessarily rely on dominant religion, these levels of belief and engagement reveal complex, challenging and potentially rewarding routes to change.

'Other' storytelling is not peripheral and distanced: through its new levels of engagement it is central, pertinent and striking. Although these new stories are only just emerging, I believe that through their instinctive drive in revealing a deeper potential, they provide new formations in social landscape which will endure.

Conclusion: Cohesion, Fragmentation and 'Becoming'

New storytelling for gay and lesbian identity concerns aspects of cohesion, fragmentation, and 'becoming'. This book has revealed the coalescent nature of narrative, and how stories may be connected through a progression of diverse opportunities within the media, leading to confidences in identity, and new political, community and identity actions. At the same time, individuals (often working in isolation) are not necessarily aware of the wider stories to be told, and their work may be considered as fragmented. Hence there is a tension between the themes of coalescence, isolation and agency. Stories of personal identification are inevitably intimate, however, their strength is not so much in how these 'personal' narratives comfortably fit together, but in how they reveal the diversity of individual experience, which appears to be connected. We are bonded not by the similitude of the stories that we tell, but by our performative potential as enablers of self-storytelling.

Such enablement, however, should not be considered as an agency and a drive towards cohesive subjectivity, evident in the terms gay and lesbian identity, it should be related to the mobility of stories, and the potential of 'becoming', signalling new opportunities of engagement. In this sense following the philosophy of the 'machine', which for Deleuze and Guattari (2010) 'has no subjectivity or organising centre, it is nothing more than the connections and productions it makes, [and] therefore has no home or ground; it is in a constant process of deterritorialisation, or becoming other than itself' (Colebrook, 2010: 55). Hence in the manner that gay and lesbian identity is related to no particular territory, such as may be possessed by a nation or a state, it is the process of movement evident in the 'machine' of new storytelling which is central. The absence of a specific and contained landscape does not confine identification possibility, rather contexts such as the 'imagined gay community' (Pullen, 2007) which is not fixed and stabilised, enables opportunities of 'becoming'. New storytelling concerns mobility, and constant changing landscapes, evident in the diversity of identity, relative to multifarious textual and generic forms.

New storytellers are of varying constitution, from the celebrated writer (such as Gore Vidal) to the anonymous voice (such as the participants in *Male Homosexual* (BBC Radio, 1965, UK) (both discussed in Chapter 1)), revealing a confidence in self-identity which extends beyond the personally reflexive, offering political identification potentials. In this way, whilst this book has focused on the potential of Anthony Giddens' (1992) concept of self-reflexivity, as revealing how contemporary society is informed by personal, and not necessarily authoritative, reflection, a crucial point is the enabling flow of performance and identification. This ultimately relates to a potential of the 'becoming', where gay men and lesbians as both audiences, and potential producers, offer mobile expressions of self-storytelling, in the production of self-reflexive narratives.

A key point of concern for new storytellers is the potential to challenge dominant myths. When new storytellers offer their life stories as examples of identity, new role models are potentially formed, and audiences are likely to be educated as to the diversity of gay and lesbian lives, and there is a potential for mobility.

I have offered a framework of narrative possibility, which has extended from the middle of the twentieth century to the present, revealing the political expression of gay and lesbian identity ideals. The literary and contemporary media oriented case studies reflect an emerging world, where brave storytellers discuss their personal lives, revealing intimacy, sensitivity, awareness and strength. Factual media performers such as Peter Adair, Pedro Zamora (see Chapter 4), Debra Chasnoff (see Chapter 5) and Parvez Sharma (see Chapter 7), foregrounded a political documentary vision, in new expressions of hope. Public figures such as Peter Wildeblood and Quentin Crisp (see Chapter 2), did not necessarily begin with a political strategy, but responded to oppressions, strengthening their vision of identity expression. Celebrities within the popular frame, such as k.d. lang (see Chapter 1), Ellen Degeneres and George Michael (discussed in Chapter 2), did not reject a public gay identity, but offered personal stories of engagement. Furthermore, whilst the personal lives of Dirk Bogarde and Russell Harty (see Chapters 3 and 4) seem partially obscured, they offer much clarity, within political and humanistic expressions. The evocative literary works of Gore Vidal (see Chapter 1), Armistead Maupin, Sarah Waters, Tony Kushner (see Chapter 3) and Alan Bennett (see Chapter 6) might be appreciated as crafted archetypes of genre; however, more substantially their stories are interwoven with expressions extending from their personal lives.

I have argued that storytelling is neither simply linear, nor obviously congruent. It offers diverse political expressions based on personal political narrative potentials, inspiring agency, opportunity and mobility.

Central within this is the emerging context of 'online' new media, and its potential to bring audiences together, providing new connectivities for emerging self-reflexive storytellers. The example of Waymon Hudson (see Chapter 1), and his political expressions of self within 'online' new media, provides a glimpse of an emerging activism through storytelling. The coalescent discourse of the members of the *Ultimate Brokeback Forum* (see Chapter 4) and the courageously candid personal aspirations of contributors to the *Gay Youth Corner* (see Chapter 6); allow new formations to progress, and challenges to be made. Significantly, the context of youth and its progressive identification potentials for gay and lesbian lives (see Chapter 6), reveals stimulations for new storytelling, distinct from those of the past.

Despite this progress, a new frontier remains, which further resonates with issues of fragmentation, cohesion and becoming. Within the developing world, new narratives are forming and gay men and lesbians are gaining confidence in personal identity (see Chapter 7). However, despite improving life chances in some instances, for example: my discussion of civil partnerships in South Africa, and Argentina (with regard to *World Weddings: Gay on the Cape* and *Foreign Correspondent: Two to Tango*), many gay men and lesbians are still leaving home countries in fear of persecution, or even of execution (such as Dilcia Molina (discussed in the introduction and Chapter 7), Ashraf Zanati, Arsham Parsi and Mani Zaniar (discussed in Chapter 7)). In addition the rise of gay youth suicides within the west (see Introduction), reveals a contemporary world where the agency of caring and grieving parents such as Tammy Aaberg (see Introduction), Judy Shepard (see Pullen, 2007) and Mary Griffith (see Aarons, 1996), reveals a pathway to a non-judgemental world. In these conditions Carl Rodgers (1959) notion of 'unconditional positive regard', forms a central strand in developing empathetic communication, to LGBT youth.

Gay and lesbian community reveals a changing landscape of identity potentials. I argue that new storytelling reflects opportunities of progress, revealing the shift from 'being' an outsider subjective identity towards the potential of 'becoming' offering new pathways of mobility. As Tony Kushner (1995) so evocatively attests at the close of *Angels in America* (discussed in Chapter 3): 'We won't die secret deaths anymore. The world only spins forward. We will be citizens. The time has come' (p. 280). Such temporal urgency is pertinent, in striving for new opportunities. Whilst

. many advances have been made, as evident in the progressive narratives discussed within this book, at the same time vulnerable 'queer' youth world wide, and LGBT citizens in non-Western territories, are experiencing, in many instances, increasing oppression from dominant worlds. Whilst we may move forward with the 'turning world', it is important that diversity, and becoming, are central stands of engagement, rather than homogeneity, and arriving.

Notes

Introduction: Placing the Self within the Frame

1. This is performed by the Mammas and the Papas (see Chapter 6).
2. See also Pullen 2010, where I discuss the murder of Lawrence King (aged 15), and online new media responses to the tragedy. Lawrence presented an effeminate and sexually ambiguous identity and was murdered on 12 February, 2008 in cold blood at school by a fellow classmate Brandon McInerney (aged 14), who Lawrence had earlier indicated a desire to be his Valentine.
3. On 9 July, 2010, Justin Aaberg aged 15 killed himself. He had come out when he was 13, but was bullied at school. Cody J. Barker aged 17 took his life and died on 13 September, 2010, he had been working in his school to form a gay alliance, and was active in the community. Also in September 2010, severely bullied at school – Asher Brown aged 13 shot himself in the head, while Seth Walsh aged 13 hanged himself, remaining in a coma for nine days before he eventually died. In that same month, gay identified Raymond Chase aged 19, hanged himself in his dorm, and Billy Lucas aged 15, who was told by fellow students to kill himself, then hanged himself in a barn later that day. In addition in the same month (of September 2010), Tyler Clementi, a freshman student of Rutger's university in the United States, was secretly filmed (with a male sexual partner) on a webcam by his room mate in service of humiliation, and this was streamed on the web. On discovering the news, Tyler allegedly left a note on Facebook that he would end his life. His death appears as a suicide. In addition, in September 2011, Jamey Rodemeyer aged 14 committed suicide, after receiving 'relentless torment on school social networking sites' (ABC News, 2011) for being gay.
4. The significance of Judy Shepard's work in supporting her son, alongside Tammy Aaberg's similar devotion, should also be related to the transformative maternal potential of Mary Griffth. The book *Prayers for Bobby* (Aarons, 1996) and the documentary of the same name (Russell Mulcahy, 2008), reveal an inspiring story of a mother who had rejected her son, Bobby, for his gay identity, yet after reflecting on the trauma of his suicide and her actions in rejecting him for being gay, she became a political icon for PFLAG (Parents, Families and Friends for Lesbians and Gays) and LGBT integration within the Christian community.

1 New Storytelling: Transitions from the Past

1. Howard Auster had changed his name to Howard Austen early in his career, on advice from Gore Vidal to avoid advertising his Jewish identity at a time when it was hard to obtain work as a Jew (Vidal, 1995). In Gore Vidal's memoir, Howard's name is restored to the original spelling; hence I have adopted it here.
2. I use the term 'literature' in the general sense as 'serious writing', esteemed by authority such as academia.

3. I am only discussing the media of radio in this chapter, as a precursor to later developments in television, film and new media through the World Wide Web.

4. It is important to note that in some non-Western countries conversely homosexuality under certain circumstances may be considered to offer positive myths. For example the Fa'afafine (feminised domesticated male homosexuals) of Samoa (briefly discussed in Chapter 7) are considered a blessing to heteronormative households, in their ability to work at home. However, I would argue that whilst this offers some positive context, it is not beneficial, or liberating, to the homosexual individual.

5. Roland Barthes's original quote uses the opposition of lion and Negro, in relation to an analysis of a black soldier giving a French salute. I have made the substitution of imperial power and the dispossessed, partly to reflect the changing use of the term 'Negro', since this work was first published, and partly to clarify the contrast/opposition.

6. The programme was transmitted in two parts. Unfortunately the second episode is no longer available from the archive (Ledgard, 2008).

7. Male homosexuality was legalised for those aged over 21, with certain conditions, in 1967 (see Chapters 2 and 3).

8. Alan Bennett's play *An Englishman Abroad* (BBC, 1983, UK) discusses Guy Burgess's life as an expatriate spy in Russia (see Chapter 6).

9. Here I am citing the revised edition produced in 1963: the original edition of 1948 concluded with a murder and suicide. Gore Vidal was pressured by his publishers to end the original text this way, and desired to change it.

10. See Almond (2012), plus the documentary *Jobriath A.D* (Kieran Turner, 2011).

11. Tom Robinson was famously criticised for marrying a woman, and seeming to neglect a homosexual identity (Knitting Circle, 2008a). Boy George in his initial career suggested that he would rather have a cup of tea than sex with a man or a woman, despite being considered as exclusively homosexual later in his career (Knitting Circle, 2008b).

2 Gay Identity and Self-Reflexivity

1. Christopher Isherwood tells us in *Christopher and His Kind* (1977) that his earlier autobiographical work *Lions and Shadows* (1947 [originally 1938]) was imbued with fictional licence, as he did not want to disclose the more intimate details of his sexuality.

2. 'The Theatres Act of 1968 repealed the Lord Chamberlain's power to censor stage plays before granting a licence for performance' (British Library, 2008), this was informed by the government report on 'Censorship of the Theatre' (HMSO, 1967). John M. Clum tell us of similar restriction in New York: 'Legislators added the Wales Padlock Act to the New York penal code. The Act outlawed plays "depicting or dealing with, the subject of sex degeneracy, or sex perversion." The threatened penalty, if a theatre housed a play that "would tend to the corruption of youth or others", was padlocking for a year and, potentially revoking its operating licence' (Clum, 2000: 74).

3. *The Green Bay Tree* appeared in London and on Broadway in 1933 with Laurence Olivier.

4. An example of early gay literature is considered to be E.M. Forster's *Maurice* written in 1913, published in 1971 (see Forster, 1992).

5. Before the emergence of the homosexual it is important to note that same-sex desire identities had existed (such as The Mollys – see Carl Miller, 1996); however, as this investigation foregrounds homosexual identity in relation to its heterosexual equivalent it is necessary to commence at this point.

6. Mary McIntosh argued that the homosexual should be considered under these terms as a social being before Foucault (see Weeks, 2000 and Pullen, 2007a).

7. Alan Sinfield (1994) tells us 'Oscar Wilde appeared in three trials in 1895. In the first he sued Lord Queensbury for libel, but dropped the case when Queensbury was discovered to have embarrassing evidence about Wilde's activities. In the second Wilde was prosecuted by the state for gross indecency, but this was inconclusive. At the third he was found guilty of gross indecency, with another person' (p. 1). He was sentenced to two years with hard labour, first in Wandsworth prison, London, and then Reading gaol.

8. See also Alan Sinfield (1994), where he notes that there are many scholars who have made this connection (p. 3).

9. Homosexual acts between women have not been recognised as illegal in the United Kingdom. However, 'from 1885 to 1967 all male homosexual acts and male homosexuality in England and Wales as set out in the law were completely illegal. The criminalisation of male homosexuality came with section 11 of the Criminal Law Amendment Act of 1885, which sought to reaffirm moral and social order within an outbreak of concern over national identity in the uproar over Home Rule for Ireland and the decline of the Empire, city lifestyles and contamination, and the overall political perception of sexual depravity' (Edwards, 1994: 17). In 1967 sex was made legal between 'two men over 21 in private' (i.e. no one else in the same house), neither of them in the Armed Forces or the Merchant Navy. [Significantly] this [only] applied only to England and Wales' (Queer Chronology, 2001).

10. It stated that 37 per cent of American men had experience of at least one homosexual activity to the point of orgasm since adolescence (Kinsey et al., 1948: 626).

11. In England and Wales during 1954 (the year of the second Montagu trial) there were 6357 alleged homosexual offences known to the police, of which 2442 persons were subject to legal proceedings (subject to trial) (HMSO, 1957).

12. Wildeblood (1955) tends to focus on obtaining acceptance (more than equality); however, I am arguing that his impact laid a pathway towards equality.

13. At the time of writing Ellen DeGeneres is a highly successful talk show host in *The Ellen DeGeneres Show* (Warner Bros., 2003–, US).

14. On 25 April 1998 Ellen's coming-out episode formed the centrepiece of a 'coming out' season on Channel 4 in the United Kingdom.

15. At the time of writing George Michael remains an international popular musician of great success.

16. *Queer as Folk* is discussed later (Chapter 5) in relation to the impact of creator Russell T Davies.

17. Obviously the incident of George Michael did involve an actual legislative trial, but it was more concerned with trial by media.

18. The episode was entitled the 'Puppy Episode' in an allusion to a comment from a TV executive that the answer to Ellen's dilemma as a lesbian may be to own a puppy, rather than have a same-sex partner (*Real Ellen Story*).

19. *Time Magazine*, 14 April 1997. Ellen is depicted filling the front cover of the magazine.

20. Anne Heche reports this in the documentary the *Real Ellen Story* (Channel 4, 1998, UK).

21. Although a new series of *Ellen* was commissioned immediately after this commercial success, Ellen DeGeneres later claimed that the series was not supported enough by the ABC network and subsequently the ratings fell, leading to the cancellation of the series in July 1998.

22. BBC News online, website, 9 December 1998.

23. 'The Human Rights Campaign offered free "Ellen Coming-Out House Party" kits. Supporters held get-togethers to watch the episode and collect money for HRC.... They expected to mail out three hundred kits.... They ultimately sent three thousand kits' (Capsuto, 2000: 393).

3   Community, History and Transformation

1. 'The world's first legally recognized same sex marriages were performed on 14 January 2001 in Toronto. They were deemed to be legal, as of that date, by order of the Court of Appeal for Ontario on 10 June 2003, setting off court victories across Canada [leading to national legislation offering gay marriage in July 2005]. The Netherlands became the first country to legalize same sex marriage, on 1 April 2001' (Equal Marriage, 2008), with a few other European countries later offering this (see Equal Marriage, 2010). In the United States, the state of Massachusetts adopted gay marriage in May 2004, while a number of other states have followed suit. At the time of writing Connecticut, District of Columbia, Iowa, New Hampshire, New York and Vermont, also offer same sex marriage. While California also did offer this, it was rescinded under Proposition 8. Despite this there have been attempts to over turn this to restore same sex marriage there (see Ballotpedia 2010). Civil partnerships for same sex couples commenced in the UK in December 2005, offering similar rights as married couples.

2. I have used the term 'pluralism' instead of 'liberation' in opposition to 'assimilation' (Seidman, 2004: 183), as pluralism suggests a fairer distribution of power (Rimmerman: 2002: 4), and liberation, even though it is commonly used in terms relating sexual freedom, connotes freedom per se. Hence liberation is subjective, and potentially also applies to assimilation (in the imagined liberties offered).

3. Dirk Bogarde is further discussed in Chapter 4 with regards to his appearance with Russell Harty.

4. *Victim* was refused a seal of approval in the United States of America in 1962, and 'also received a hostile reception from critics' (Bourne, 1996: 160), therefore prohibiting its cinematic release.

5. *Victim* was first transmitted in the United Kingdom on the independent television stations of Rediffusion on 31 May 1968 at 10.30 p.m., and later Thames

on 24 April 1974 at 10.30 p.m. (Burrows, 2001). Rediffusion and Thames were regional commercial television broadcasting companies, who consecutively transmitted programming to the London area in the United Kingdom. The 1968 transmission is likely to have been the first in the United Kingdom. These transmission dates and times were also verified by the ITC (Bell, 2001).

6. The police officers in *Victim* also advise us that statistically at that time 90 per cent of the cases of blackmail were of a homosexual nature.

7. Regarding the books: *Tales of the City* (1978) was followed by *More Tales of the City* (1980) and *Further Tales of the City* (1982), all of which were adapted for television. Further sequels (not yet adapted) include: *Babycakes* (1984), *Significant Others* (1987), *Sure of You* (1989) and *Michael Tolliver Lives* (2007).

8. At the time of writing, all Sarah Waters' novels (including *Affinity* (1999) and *The Night Watch* (2007)) offer progressive visions of same-sex desire. Also *Affinity* was adapted as a television drama by ITV in 2008.

4 Factual Media Space: Intimacy, Participation and Therapy

1. Oprah Winfrey first appeared as a talk show host on television in 1984, in *AM Chicago* (WLS-TV). This was later adapted and retitled as *The Oprah Winfrey Show*, entering national syndication in 1986 (Oprah, 2008).

2. *The Jenny Jones Show* was recorded on 6 March 1995. Three days later Scott Amedure murdered Jon Schmitz, shooting him twice in the chest.

3. Harty appeared in *Russell Harty Plus* on ITV between 1973 and 1981, and then appeared in a variety of television programming until the time of his illness. Notably his television series *Mr Harty's Grand Tour* for the BBC (1988) was a high-profile event (see Harty, 1988).

4. Whilst we may not truthfully assess that at the time of the interviews the guests could all be read in this way, at the time of writing: Frankie Howerd, Tennessee Williams, Gore Vidal, Elton John, Barry Humphries and April Ashley (discussed above) may be considered in these terms.

5. *Some of Your Best Friends* (Ken Robinson, 1971, US) predates *Word is Out* (see Pullen, 2007a); however, it was produced for independent audiences. Also the performance of Lance Loud in *An American Family* (PBS, 1973) may be considered as an early representation of gay men in documentary. However it is not included here, as the focus of the text was not sexual diversity (although it was apparent in reading the ambivalent representation, and later was fully evident in the press – see Pullen, 2007a).

6. The moment of discovering Pedro's condition may have been a surprise to roommates. And although Mary Ellis Bunim (co-producer) tells us that potential participants were not informed they would be living with a person who has AIDS 'during the interview process [they] were asked about views on AIDS and people who test positive for HIV' (cited in Grubbs, 2002: 19).

7. The story of *Brokeback Mountain* was first published in *The New Yorker* on 13 October 1997. It later formed part of a collection of short stories by Proulx focusing on Wyoming (Proulx, 2003 [originally 1999]).

8. From this point, within citations, I am adopting the abbreviation of MUBF for 'Members of the Ultimate Brokeback Forum'.

5   Commodity and Family

1. *One Wedding and a Revolution* captures the frantic days leading up to the bold political decision of San Francisco mayor Gavin Newsom to start issuing marriage licences to gay and lesbian couples (Newday, 2007). Long-time lesbian activists Phyllis Lyon (79) and Del Martin (83) were the first to be married, and the ceremony is recorded by Chasnoff. Unfortunately the licences were later revoked in May 2005 as unconstitutional (see Chapter 3, note 1).

2. *Suddenly Last Summer* was adapted from a play by Tennessee Williams, first performed on Broadway in 1958. *The Children's Hour* was adapted from a stage play written by Lillian Hellman in 1934. It was first adapted into a film entitled *These Three* in 1936 also directed by William Wyler, but because of the Hayes production code the lesbian storyline was exchanged for a heterosexual love triangle. The later film adaptation discussed here restores not only the title, but also the lesbian storyline.

3. For example Harvey Fierstein in the documentary *Celluloid Closet* (Rob Epstein and Jeffrey Friedman, 1995, US) (based on Vito Russo's (1987) book) states this, in relation to the positive potential of the sissy.

4. A notable exception may be *American Beauty* (Sam Mendes, 1999, US) written by openly gay Alan Ball; however, the domestic gay male couple represented are peripheral characters.

5. *The Last of England* (1987), *Derek Jarman: Today and Tomorrow* (1991), *Modern Nature: Journals of Derek Jarman* (1992), *At Your Own Risk: a Saint's Testament* (1993), *Smiling in Slow Motion: Diaries, 1991–94* (2001).

6. Evidence may be seen in the teen soap opera *As If* (Channel 4, 2001–4, UK) depicting a young openly gay man in search of romance and sexual fulfilment with equality to peers in a friendship network, and *Bad Girls* (ITV, 1999–2006, UK) which despite the setting of a women's prison, did foreground lesbian partnerships as more fulfilling than heterosexual equivalents (particularly series three which closed with a romantic pastiche of the lesbian lead protagonists) (see Pullen, 2007b).

7. I would like to reference the work of Mark Harold (2005) for stimulating this discussion.

8. The book *The Last of England* (1987) was republished as *Kicking the Pricks* in 1997.

9. Derek Jarman (1987) actually advises that he took them from his father in order to preserve them.

10. I would argue that *Angels in America* references this scene within the film adaptation (discussed in Chapter 3), where the character of Prior returns to Earth from Heaven and is similarly depicted.

11. Debra Chasnoff presents this finding in *It's Elementary; Talking about Gay Issues in School*, where children reveal that they get their ideas about gay identity from television.

12. For example in series three of Russell T Davies' reinvented *Doctor Who*, in an episode titled 'Gridlock' (series 3, episode 3) where an elder lesbian couple are represented as normative, but this is only a fleeting characterisation.

13. As part of this John Barrowman was featured on the cover of *OUT* magazine, October 2007.

6   Teenage Identity and Ritual

1. *Coronation Street* did not include any sexually diverse characters until the addition to the cast of a transsexual character (Hayley) in 1998, and then a gay man (Todd) who would be represented stereotypically as an outsider and the cause of a family break-up (see Pullen cited in Daniel, 2004; Pullen, 2007b). Jonathan Harvey's participation on the writing team has seen a development in the representation of sexually diverse characters, foregrounding the character of Sean Tully (at the time of writing).
2. 'Dream a Little Dream of Me' by The Mamas and Papas is also used in *Beautiful Thing*, and is discussed briefly in the introduction to this book (with reference to the film).
3. See the essay 'A Common Assault' in *Untold Stories* (Bennett, 2004). This not only reveals details of the assault perpetrated against Bennett and his partner (in Italy, May 1992), but also may be considered as his first open admission of his (homo)sexual identity.
4. Many of Alan Bennett's characters express camp sensibilities (see Complete Review, 2008).
5. Lucas Hilderbrand also identifies the Alain Berliner Film *Ma Vie en Rose* (1997, France) within this analogy, where a young child explores his gender identity.
6. The characters in *Velvet Goldmine* are fictional; however, they may be related to historical characters within the pop industry of the 1970s. For example, the character of Brian Slade may be viewed as David Bowie, Mandy Slade as Angie Bowie, Curt Wilde as Iggy Pop and Jack Fairy as Brian Eno.
7. It is not surprising that Jack Fairy, who represents Brian Eno, is seen to possess the green emerald first within the pop music movement, as he is regarded as an original prime source of inspiration.
8. It was performed for more than one year not only within the UK, but also Australia, Hong Kong and the US.
9. This sense of teamwork is highly evident in the documentary accompanying the DVD of *The History Boys*.
10. Dakin could be read as bisexual, as he offers his body to Irwin in sexual gratitude for successful tutoring in gaining access to Oxford.
11. Learning Programmes is the title of Channel 4's daytime educational content.
12. Transsexual identity has been discussed in a number of Channel 4 documentaries, including at a similar time of broadcast to this series the programme *Lucy the Teenage Transsexual*, which was positively received, but was broadcast in the evening slot inferring an address to an adult audience rather than school education.
13. LGB Teens reports that the age of consent in Northern Ireland remains 17.
14. User BAJ 103 is cited on his profile as male gay, aged 17 and living in the US.
15. It is interesting to note that 'BAJ 103' does not appear to foreground his gay identity within MySpace, although there are more personalised new media provisions there.

7   Other Storytelling and the New Frontier

1. I am using the term 'developing world' to relate to a diverse range of countries where Western gay identity is not considered as prominent. I have

.   avoided the term 'non-Western countries', as West/East oppositions are problematic, and not truly representational. Hence the term '(developed) world'
or 'affluent West' is applied where 'Western' gay identity is discussed.

2.   This is not to say that exclusively Western modes of history or performance
are enabling, but that in terms of mass media these provide a dominant and
useable language.

3.   The context of diaspora is also related to the construction of the (imagined)
gay community in Chapter 3.

4.   This is represented in *Dangerous Living: Coming Out in the Developing World*.

5.   This may also be considered in relation to Arsham Parsi and Mani Zaniar in
Out in Iran (discussed below).

6.   In a dramatic invention, the film depicts Gómez Carriles as covering
Reinaldo's face with a plastic bag to assist in his suicide.

7.   This also occurs in the affluent West.

8.   President Mahmoud Ahmadinejad also denied the existence of the Holocaust.

9.   The site was originally entitled the Persian Queer Organisation.

10.   The documentary *Transsexual in Iran* (Tanaz Eshagian for the BBC, 2008, UK)
reveals the tribulations of transsexuals in Iran, many of whom appear to
be homosexuals caught in a life where they must appear to (legally) progress
towards a sex change in order to avoid further persecution. The documentary
also foregrounds the persecution of transsexuals post-operative, revealing one
case where an individual is rejected by her family and society, and must resort
to prostitution in order to find a living. Also I am indebted to Sahar Bluick,
who as a graduate student at Bournemouth University wrote her dissertation
on this subject area (see Bluck, 2007).

References

Works cited

Aaron, M., ed. 2004. *New Queer Cinema: a Critical Reader*. New York: Rutgers.

Aarons, L. 1996. *Prayers for Bobby: A Mother's Coming to Terms with the Suicide of her Son*. New York: HarperOne.

Adorno, T. and Horkenheimer, M. 1977. 'The Culture Industry: Enlightenment as Mass Deception' in J. Curran, M. Gurevitch and J. Woollacott, eds, *Mass Communication and Society*. London: Edward Arnold.

Akass, K. and McCabe, J., eds. 2006. *Reading the L Word*. London: I.B. Tauris.

Almond, M. 2012. 'The Man Who Fell to Earth,' *The Guardian*, 28 March.

Althusser, L. 1971. 'Ideology and Ideological State Apparatuses' in *Lenin and Philosophy and Other Essays*. New York and London: Monthly Review Press, pp. 127–86.

Anderson, B. 1983. *Imagined Communities: Reflections on the Origin and Spread of Nationalism*. London: Verso.

Annan Committee. 1977. *Home Office Report of the Committee on the Future of Broadcasting*. London: HMSO.

Arenas, R. 1993. *Before Night Falls*. New York: Viking/Penguin.

Arthurs, J. 2004. *Television and Sexuality*. London: Open University Press.

Atwell, L. 1988. 'Word is Out and Gay USA', in A. Rosenthal, ed., *New Challenges for Documentary*. Los Angeles: University of California Press, pp. 571–80.

Bakhtin, M. 1965. *Rabelais and his World*, trans. H. Iswolsky. Cambridge, Mass.: MIT Press.

Bakhtin, M. 1994. 'Selected Writings', in P. Morris, ed., *The Bakhtin Reader: Selected Writings of Bakhtin, Medvedev, Voloshinov*. London: Edward Arnold.

Barthes, R. 1993. *Mythologies*, repr. London: Vintage.

Baudrillard, J. 1981. *For a Critique of the Political Economy of the Sign*, trans. Charles Levin. St Louis: Telos Press.

Baudrillard, J. 1994. *Simulacra and Simulation*, trans. Sheila Faria Glaser. Ann Arbor: University of Michigan Press.

Bauman, Z. 1992. *Intimations of Postmodernity*. London: Routledge.

Bawden, A. 2008. 'Sad to be Gay', *The Guardian*, 29 January.

Bawer, B. 1993. *A Place at the Table. The Gay Individual in American Society*. New York: Poseidon Press.

Beck, U. 1992. *Risk Society: Towards a New Modernity*. London: Sage.

Beemyn, B., ed. 1997. *Creating a Place for Ourselves: Lesbian, Gay and Bisexual Community Histories*. New York: Routledge.

Bell, D. and Binnie, J. 2000. *The Sexual Citizen: Queer Politics and Beyond*. Cambridge: Polity.

Bell, M. 2001. Personal communication with Mark Bell of the ITC, April 2001.

Bell, V. 1999. *Performativity and Belonging*. London: Sage.

Bennett, A. 1994. *Writing Home*. London: Faber and Faber.

Bennett, A. 2004. *Untold Stories*. London: Faber and Faber.

Bennett, A. 2006. *The History Boys: the Film*. London: Faber and Faber.

Bennett, T., Boyd-Bowman, S., Mercer, C. and Wollacott, J., eds. 1985. *Popular Television and Film*. London: Open University.

Bennett, T. and Cook, P. 2003. *The Complete Beyond the Fringe*, new edn. London: Methuen Drama.

Benshoff, H. and Griffin, S., eds. 2004. *Queer Cinema: the Film Reader*. New York: Routledge.

Bergling, T. 2001. *Sissyphobia: Gay Men and Effeminate Behavior*. New York: Harrington Park Press.

Berry, C., Martin, F. and Yue, A., eds. 2003. *Mobile Cultures: New Media in Queer Asia*. Durham: Duke University Press.

Berube, A. 1990. *Coming Out under Fire: the History of Gay Men and Women in World War Two*. New York: Free Press.

Bhabha, H. 2004. *The Location of Culture*. London: Routledge.

Bluck, Sahar. 2007. 'Transsexuals in Iran'. Unpublished BA Television Studies dissertation. Bournemouth University, United Kingdom.

Bogarde, D. 1978. *Snakes and Ladders*. London: Phoenix.

Bogarde, D. 1986. *Backcloth*. London: Viking/Penguin.

Bourne, S. 1996. *Brief Encounters: Lesbians and Gays in British Cinema 1930–1971*. London: Cassell.

Brandt, G. 1993. 'The Jewel in the Crown (Paul Scott – Ken Taylor): the Literary Serial or the Art of Adaptation' in G. Brandt, ed., *British Television Drama in the 1980s*. Cambridge: Cambridge University Press, pp. 196–213.

Brito, M. 2007. Personal communication, October 2007.

Broverman, N. 2008. 'Mixed Messages' in *The Advocate*, 8 April, issue 1005, pp. 28–33.

Brownworth, V. A. 1992. 'America's Worst Kept Secret: AIDS is Devastating the Nation's Teenagers, and Gay Kids are Dying by the Thousands', in *The Advocate*, 24 March, pp. 38–46.

Brunsdon, C. 1997. *Screen Tastes: Soap Opera to Satellite Dishes*. London: Routledge.

Bucknell, K. 2000. 'Who is Christopher Isherwood?' in J. J. Berg and C. Freeman, eds, *The Isherwood Century: Essays on the Life and Works of Christopher Isherwood*. Madison: University of Wisconsin Press, pp. 13–29.

Burrows, E. 2001. Personal communication with Elaine Burrows of the British Film Institute, April 2001.

Butler, J. 1999. *Gender Trouble*, repr. London: Routledge.

Caitlin, R. and Futterman, D. 1998. *Lesbian and Gay Youth: Care and Counseling*. New York: Columbia University Press.

Campbell, J. 1988. *The Hero with a Thousand Faces*. London: Paladin.

Capsuto, S. 2000. *Alternate Channels: the Uncensored Story of Gay and Lesbian Images on Radio and Television*. New York: Ballantine Books.

Carlson, M. 1996. *Performance: a Critical Introduction*. London: Routledge.

Carringtom, C. 1999. *No Place like Home: Relationships and Family Life among Lesbians and Gay Men*. Chicago: University of Chicago Press.

Carroll, N. 1996. 'Toward a Theory of Film Suspense', in *Theorizing the Moving Image*. Cambridge: Cambridge University Press, pp. 94–117.

Chasin, A. 2000. *Selling Out: the Gay and Lesbian Movement Goes to Market*. New York: St Martin's Press.

Chatman, S. 1978. *Story and Discourse: Narrative Structure in Fiction*. London: Cornell University Press.

Christian, A. J. 2011. Book review: 'Gay Identity, New Storytelling, and the Media' in *Communication, Culture and Critique* 4, pp. 118–20.

Clendinen, D. and Nagourney, A. 1999. *Out for Good*. New York: Simon and Schuster.

Clinton, B. 1994. White House press release, 11 November.

Colebrook, C. 2010. *Gilles Deleuze*, repr. London: Routledge.

Clum, J. M. 2000. *Still Acting Gay*, rev. edn. New York: St Martin's Griffin.

CNN 1998. Transcript, 13 April.

Coldstream, J. 2004. *Dirk Bogarde: the Authorized Biography*. London: Weidenfeld and Nicolson.

Cole, J. 2007. Personal communication, 1 October.

Collins, W. 1994a. *The Moonstone*. London: Penguin.

Collins, W. 1994b. *The Woman in White*. London: Penguin.

Collis, R. 1999. *k.d. lang*. Bath: Absolute Press.

Corner, J. 1991. 'Meaning, Genre and Context: the Problematics of "Public Knowledge" in New Audience Studies' in J. Curran and M. Gurevitch, eds, *Mass Media and Society*. London: Methuen.

Crisp, Q. 1981. *How to Become a Virgin*. London: Gerald Duckworth and Co.

Crisp, Q. 1984. *The Wit and Wisdom of Quentin Crisp*, edited and compiled by G. Kettelhack. New York: Alyson Publications.

Crisp, Q. 1997. *Resident Alien: the New York Diaries*, rev. edn. London: Flamingo.

Crisp, Q. 2007. *The Naked Civil Servant*, rev. edn. London: Harper Perennial.

Crisp, Q. 2008. *How to Go to the Movies*. New York: St Martin's Press.

Danaher, G., Schirato, T. and Webb, J., eds. 2000. *Understanding Foucault*. London: Sage.

Dave, P. 2006. *Visions of England: Class and Culture in Contemporary Cinema*. London: Berg.

Davis, N. 2007. ' "The Invention of a People": Velvet Goldmine and the Unburying of Queer Desire' in J. Morrison, ed., *The Cinema of Todd Haynes: All that Heaven Allows*. London: Wallflower Press.

D'Emilio, J. 1983. *Sexual Politics, Sexual Communities: the Making of a Homosexual Minority in the United States 1940–1970*. Chicago: The University of Chicago Press.

D'Emilio, J. 1990. 'Gay Politics and Community in San Francisco since World War II' in M. Duberman, M. Vicinus and G. Chauncey, eds, *Hidden from History: Reclaiming Gay and Lesbian Past*. New York: Meridian, pp. 456–73.

Deitcher, D., ed. 1995. *The Question of Equality: Lesbian and Gay Politics in America since Stonewall*. New York: Scribner.

Deleuze, G. 1994. *Difference and Repetition*, trans. P. Patton, New York: Columbia University Press.

Deleuze, G. and Guattari, F. 2010. *A Thousand Plateaus*, repr. London: Continuum.

Doane, M. A. 2004. 'Pathos and Pathology: the Cinema of Todd Haynes' in *Camera Obscura: Feminism, Culture and Media Studies*, no. 57. Durham: Duke University Press, pp. 1–21.

Dominguez, J. I. 1978. *Cuba, Order and Revolution*. Cambridge: Harvard University Press.

Doty, A. 1993. *Making Things Perfectly Queer: Interpreting Mass Culture*. Minneapolis: University of Minnesota Press.

Drake, R. 1998. *The Gay Canon: Great Books that Every Gay Man should Read*. New York: Anchor Books.

Du Gay, P. 1997. 'Introduction' in *Production of Culture/Cultures of Production*. London: Sage, pp. 1–10.

Dyer, R. 1986. *Heavenly Bodies: Film Stars and Society*. London: British Film Institute.

Dyer, R. 2000. *The Matter of Images*, 2nd repr. London: Routledge.

Dyer, R. 2001. *Stars*, repr. London: British Film Institute.

Dyer, R. 2007. *Pastiche*. London: Routledge.

Edwards, T. 1994. *Erotics and Politics: Gay Male Sexuality, Masculinity and Feminism*. London: Routledge.

Ellen, B. 1999. 'Careless Whispers', *Guardian Unlimited*, 19 September.

Elliott, A. 1996. *Subject to Ourselves: Social Theory, Psychoanalysis and Postmodernity*. Cambridge: Polity Press.

Ellis, J. 1999. 'Queer Period: Derek Jarman's Renaissance' in E. Hanson, ed., *Out Takes: Essays on Queer Theory and Film*. Durham: Duke University Press, pp. 288–315.

Ellis, J. 2008. *The Uses of the Past: Derek Jarman's Histories of Sexuality*. Minneapolis, University of Minnesota Press (forthcoming).

Farmer, B. 2000. *Spectacular Passions: Cinema, Fantasy, Gay Male Spectatorships*. Durham: Duke University Press.

Fellows, W., ed. 1998. *Farm Boys: Lives of Gay Men from the Rural Midwest*. Madison: University of Wisconsin.

Finnegan, R. 1997. 'Storying the Self: Personal Narratives and Identity' in H. Mackay, ed., *Consumption and Everyday Life*. London: Sage, pp. 65–112.

Fisher, J., ed. 2006. *Tony Kushner: New Essays on the Art and Politics of the Plays*. Jefferson: McFarland.

Fiske, J. 1994. *Television Culture*, repr. London: Routledge.

Forster, E, M. 1992. *Maurice*, repr. London: Penguin.

Foucault, M. 1989. *The Archaeology of Knowledge*. London: Routledge.

Foucault, M. 1998. *The History of Sexuality*, Vol. 1, trans. Robert Hurley, repr. London: Penguin.

Foucault, M. 2000. *Ethics: Essential Works of Foucault 1954–1984*, Vol. 1. London: Penguin.

Fraser, J. 2004. *Close Up: an Actor Telling Tales*. London: Oberon Books.

Fraser, N. 1989. *Unruly Practices: Power, Discourse and Gender in Contemporary Social Theory*. Minneapolis: University of Minnesota Press.

Fraser, N. 1997. *Justice Interruptus: Critical Reflections on the 'Postsocialist' Condition*. New York: Routledge.

Fricke, A. 1981. *Reflections of a Rock Lobster*. Boston: Aly Cat Books.

Fuss, D. 1995. *Identification Papers*. London: Routledge.

Gale, P. 1999. *Armistead Maupin*. Bath: Absolute Press.

Gamson, J. 2005. *The Fabulous Sylvester*. New York: Henry Holt and Company.

Gamson, J. 1998. *Freaks Talk Back: Tabloid Talk Shows and Sexual Nonconformity*. Chicago: Chicago University Press.

Gauntlett, D. 1995. *Moving Experiences: Understanding Television's Influences and Effects*. London: John Libbey.

Gauntlett, D. 2002. *Media, Gender and Identity: an Introduction*. London: Routledge.

Gauntlett, D. and Horsley, R., eds. 2004. *Web Studies*, 2nd edn. London: Edward Arnold.

Geis, D. R. and Kruger, S. F., eds. 1997. *Approaching the Millennium: Essays on Angels in America*. Ann Arbor: University of Michigan Press.

Geraghty, C. 2005. *My Beautiful Launderette*. London: IB Tauris.

Giddens, A. 1992. *Modernity and Self Identity: Self and Society in the Late Modern Age*, repr. Cambridge: Polity Press.

Giddens, A. 1995. *The Transformation of Intimacy: Sexuality, Love and Eroticism in Modern Societies*, repr. Cambridge: Polity Press.

Gilbert, H. and Tompkins, J. 1996. *Post Colonial Drama: Theory Practice and Politics*. London: Routledge.

Gillespie, P., ed. and Kaeser, G., photo. 1999. *Love Makes a Family: Portraits of Lesbian, Gay, Bisexual, and Transgender Parents and their Families*. Amherst: University of Massachusetts Press.

Gilroy, P. 1997. 'Diaspora and Detours of Identity' in K. Woodward, ed., *Identity and Difference*. London: Sage, pp. 7–61.

Gluckman, A. and Reed, B., eds. 1997. *Homoeconomics: Capitalism, Community and Gay Life*. London: Routledge.

Goffman, E. 1987. *The Presentation of Self in Everyday Life*. London: Pelican.

Gray, N. 2007. Personal communication, September.

Gross, L. 2001. *Up from Visibility: Lesbians, Gay Men, and the Media in America*. New York: Columbia University Press.

Groundspark. 2007. *Respect for All project*, press release.

Grubbs, J. 2002. 'New Channels: the *Real World* as Social Movement Communication'. Unpublished dissertation, University of Illinois, Springfield.

Habermas, J. 1962. *The Structural Transformation of the Public Sphere: an Inquiry into a Category of Bourgeois Society*, trans. T. Burger and F. Lawrence. Cambridge: Polity Press.

Haerinejad, F. 2008. Personal communication, February.

Hall, S. 1980. 'Encoding/decoding', in Centre for Contemporary Cultural Studies, ed., *Culture, Media, Language: Working Papers in Cultural Studies, 1972–79*. London: Hutchinson, pp. 128–38.

Hall, S. 1997. 'The Spectacle of the "Other"' in S. Hall, ed., *Representation: Cultural Representations and Signifying Practices*. London: Sage, pp. 223–79.

Hanson, E., ed. 1999. *Out Takes: Essays on Queer Theory and Film*. Durham: Duke University Press.

Harold, M. 2005. 'Russell T Davies and *Doctor Who*: Resistance and Transgression of Gender Identity'. Unpublished graduate dissertation, University of Bournemouth.

Hart, K. R. 2000. *The AIDS Movie: Representing a Pandemic in Film and Television*. New York: The Haworth Press.

Harty, R. 1974. *Russell Harty Plus*. London: Purnell Book Services.

Harty, R. 1988. *Mr Harty's Grand Tour*. London: Century.

Harvey, S. 2000. 'Channel Four Television: From Annan to Grade' in E. Buscombe, ed., *British Television: a Reader*. Oxford: Oxford University Press, pp. 92–117.

Herdt, G. 1997. *Same Sex, Different Cultures*. Boulder: Westview Press.

Hilderbrand, L. 2007. 'Mediating beyond Queer Boyhood: *Dottie Gets Spanked*' in J. Morrison, ed., *The Cinema of Todd Haynes: All that Heaven Allows*. London: Wallflower Press.

Hill, J. 1986. *Sex, Class and Realism: British Cinema 1956–1963*. London: British Film Institute.

History Project. 1998. *Improper Bostonians: Lesbian and Gay History from the Puritans to the Playground*. Boston: Beacon Press.

HMSO. 1957. *Report on Homosexual Offences and Prostitution*. Sir John Wolfenden (Chairman). London: Her Majesty's Stationery Office.

HMSO. 1967. *Joint Committee on Censorship of the Theatre*. London: Her Majesty's Stationery Office.

Hobson, D. 2008. *Channel 4: the Early Years and the Jeremy Isaacs Legacy*. London: IB Tauris.

Howe, D. J. and Walker, S. J. 2003. *The Television Companion: the Unofficial and Unauthorised Guide to 'Doctor Who'*. London: Telos.

Howes, K. 1993. *Broadcasting It: an Encyclopaedia of Homosexuality on Film, Radio and TV in the UK 1923–1993*. London: Cassell.

Hudson, W. 2008. Personal communication, 20 June.

Hughes-Freeland, F. and Crain, M. M. 1998. *Recasting Ritual: Performance, Media, Identity*. London: Routledge.

Isherwood, C. 1947. *Lions and Shadows: an Education in the Twenties*. Norfolk, Conn.: New Directions.

Isherwood, C. 1977. *Christopher and His Kind*. London: Methuen.

Isherwood, C. 1978. *Goodbye to Berlin*. St Albans: Triad/Panther.

Ishii-Gonzales, S. 2007. 'To Appear, to Disappear: Jean Genet and Poison' in J. Morrison, ed., *The Cinema of Todd Haynes: All that Heaven Allows*. London: Wallflower Press.

Jameson, F. 1991. *Postmodernism or the Cultural Logic of Late Capitalism*. London: Verso.

Jarman, D. 1987. *The Last of England*. London: Constable.

Jarman, D. 1991. *Derek Jarman: Today and Tomorrow*. London: Salmon.

Jarman, D. 1992. *Modern Nature: Journals of Derek Jarman*. London: Vintage.

Jarman, D. 1993. *At Your Own Risk: a Saint's Testament*. London: Vintage.

Jarman, D. 2001. *Smiling in Slow Motion: Diaries, 1991–94*. London: Vintage.

Jivani, A. 1997. *It's Not Unusual: a History of Lesbian and Gay Britain in the Twentieth Century*. London: Michael O'Mara Books.

Joyner Priest, P. 1995. *Public Intimacies: Talk Show Participants and Television Tell-All TV*. New Jersey: Hampton Press.

Kaplan, E. A. 1989. *Rocking around the Clock: Musictelevision, Postmodernism and Consumer Culture*, 2nd repr. London: Routledge.

Katz, J. N. 1995. *The Invention of Heterosexuality*. New York: Dutton.

Kinsey, A. C., Pomeroy, W. B. and Martin, C. E. 1948. *Sexual Behavior in the Human Male*. Philadelphia: Saunders.

Kiska, T. 1997. 'TV Ratings: "Ellen" Moves ABC out in Front' in *The Detroit News*, 7 May.

Kramer, L. 1999. 'The Sadness of Gore Vidal' in D. Weise, ed., *Gore Vidal: Sexually Speaking*. San Francisco: Cleis Press, pp. 252–71.

Krochmal, S. N. 2007. 'On-Screen John Barrowman Plays a Sex Mad Alien Investigator. In Real Life he's from Glasgow' in *OUT*, no. 167, October, pp. 101–5.

Kushner, T. 1995. *Angels in America*. New York: Theatre Communications Group.

Lechte, J. 2000. *Fifty Key Contemporary Thinkers: From Structuralism to Postmodernity*. London: Routledge.

Ledgard, C. 2008. Personal correspondence by email, 5 February.

Leiner, M. 1994. *Sexual Politics in Cuba: Machismo, Homosexuality and AIDS.* Boulder: Westview Press.

Leith, D. and Myerson, G. 1989. *The Power of Address: Explorations in Rhetoric.* London: Routledge.

LeVay, S. and Nonas, E. 1995. *City of Friends: a Portrait of Gay and Lesbian Community in America.* Cambridge: MIT Press.

Lévi-Strauss, C. 1972. *Structural Anthropology*, repr. London: Peregrine.

Lévi-Strauss, C. 1978. *Structural Anthropology*, Vol. 2, repr. London: Peregrine.

Livingstone, S. and Lunt, P. 1994. *Talk on Television: Audience Participation and Public Debate.* London: Routledge.

MacCabe, C. 2007. 'The Angelic Conversation', DVD booklet. London: BFI.

McChesney, R. 1997. *Corporate Media and the Threat to Democracy.* New York: Seven Stories Press.

McIntosh, M. 1996. 'The Homosexual Role', in S. Seidman, ed., *Queer Theory/ Sociology.* Oxford: Blackwell Press, pp. 33–63.

McLeod, J. 1997. *Narrative and Psychotherapy.* London: Sage.

Martin, D. 2004. 'Street Crimes: What is Going Down on Coronation Street?', *Gay Times* 311, August, 24–7.

Martinac, P. 1997. *k.d. lang.* Philadelphia: Chelsea House Publishers.

Marx, K. 1977. *A Contribution to the Critique of Political Economy.* Moscow: Progress Publishers.

Medhurst, A. 1997. 'Camp' in A. Medhurst and S. Munt, eds, *Lesbian and Gay Studies: a Critical Introduction.* New York: Cassell, pp. 274–93.

Members of the Ultimate Brokeback Forum. 2007. Brokeback Mountain: *the Impact of the Film.* Livermore: Wingspan Press.

Miller, C. 1996. *Stages of Desire: Gay Theatre's Hidden History.* London: Cassell.

Miller, J. 1997. 'Heavenquake: Queer Analogies in Kusher's America', in D. R. Geis and S. F. Kruger, eds, *Approaching the Millennium: Essays on Angels in America.* Ann Arbor: University of Michigan Press.

Montaigne, M. De. 1991. *Michel De Montaigne: the Complete Essays*, trans. and ed. M. A. Screech. London: Penguin.

Morgenthaler, E. 1991. 'Pedro's Story: Teen with AIDS Virus Tries to Teach Youths Some Lessons for Life', *The Wall Street Journal* 4 September, pp. A1, A4.

Morris, P., ed. 1994. *The Bakhtin Reader: Selected Writings of Bakhtin, Medvedev, Voloshinov.* London: Edward Arnold.

Morrison, J., ed. 2007. *The Cinema of Todd Haynes: All that Heaven Allows.* London: Wallflower Press.

Mouffe, C. 1988. 'Hegemony and New Political Subjects: Towards a New Concept of Democracy', in C. Nelson and L. Grossberg, eds, *Marxism and the Interpretation of Culture.* Basingstoke: Macmillan Education.

Munoz, J. E. 1998. 'Pedro Zamora's Real World of Counterpublicity: Performing an Ethics of the Self' in S. Molly and R. McKee Irwin, eds, *Hispanisms and Homosexualities.* Durham: Duke University Press, pp. 175–93.

Munoz, J. 1999. *Disidentifications: Queers of Color and the Performance of Politics.* Minneapolis: University of Minnesota Press.

Munt, S. 2000. 'Shame/Pride Dichotomies in *Queer as Folk*', *Textual Practice* 14(3): 531–46.

Murphy, R. 1992. *Sixties British Cinema.* London: British Film Institute.

. Negt, O. and Kluge, A. 1993. *Public Sphere and Experience: Towards an Analysis of the Bourgeois and Proletarian Public Sphere*, repr. Minneapolis: University of Minnesota Press.

Nichols, B. 2001. *Introduction to Documentary*. Bloomington: Indiana University Press.

Nietzsche, F. 1995. *The Birth of Tragedy*, repr. London: Dover.

Nixon, S. 1997. 'Circulating Culture' in *Production of Culture/Cultures of Production*. London: Sage, pp. 221–34.

Patton, C. and Sánchez Eppler, B., eds. 2000. *Queer Diasporas*. Durham: Duke University Press.

Pickering, M. 2001. *Stereotyping: the Politics of Representation*. Basingstoke: Palgrave Macmillan.

Plummer, K. 1997. *Telling Sexual Stories: Power, Change and Social Worlds*, repr. London: Routledge.

Plummer, K. 2001. *Documents of Life: an Invitation to a Critical Humanism*. London: Sage.

Plummer, K. 2003. *Intimate Citizenship: Private Decisions and Public Dialogues*. Washington: University of Washington Press.

Propp, V. 1968. *Morphology of the Folktale*, trans. Laurence Scott, 2nd edn. Austin: University of Texas Press.

Proulx, A. 2003. 'Brokeback Mountain', in *Close Range: Wyoming Stories*. New York: Scribner, pp. 251–85.

Pullen, C. 2004. 'The Household, the Basement and *The Real World*', in S. Holmes and D. Jermyn, eds, *Understanding Reality Television*. London: Routledge, pp. 211–32.

Pullen, C. 2005. 'Gay Performativity and Reality Television: Alliances, Competition and Discourse', in J. Keller and L. Strayner, eds, *The New Queer Aesthetic on Television: Essays on Recent Programming*. Jefferson: McFarland.

Pullen, C. 2007a. *Documenting Gay Men: Identity and Performance in Reality Television and Documentary Film*. Jefferson: McFarland.

Pullen, C. 2007b. 'Non-Heterosexual Characters in Post-War Television Drama: From Covert Identity and Stereotyping, towards Reflexivity and Social Change', in D. Godiwala, ed., *Alternatives within the Mainstream II: Queer Theatre in Postwar Britain*. Cambridge: Cambridge Scholars Press.

Pullen, C. 2008. '*Brokeback Mountain* as Progressive Narrative and Cinematic Vision: Landscape, Emotion and the Denial of Domesticity' in A. Hunt., ed., *Annie Proulx and the Geographical Imagination*. New York: Lexington Books.

Pullen, C. 2010a. '"I Like Your Coat": Bisexuality, the Female Gaze and the Romance of Sexual Politics', in A. Ireland, ed., *Illuminating 'Torchwood': Essays on Narrative, Character and Sexuality in the BBC Series*. Jeffersno: McFarland, pp. 135–52.

Pullen, C. 2010b. 'The Murder of Lawrence King: Online Stimulations of Narrative Copresence' in C. Pullen and M. Cooper (eds), *LGBT Identity and Online New Media*. New York: Routledge, pp. 17–36.

Pullen, C. ed. 2012. *LGBT Transnational Identity and the Media*. Basingstoke: Palgrave Macmillan.

Punch, K. F. 1998. *Introduction to Social Research: Quantitative and Qualitative Approaches*. London: Sage.

Pykett, L. 2005. *Authors in Context: Wilkie Collins*. Oxford: Oxford University Press.

Riggs, M. 1991.'Tongues Untied' in E. Hemphill, ed., *Brother to Brother: New Writings by Black Gay Men*. Conceived by Joseph Beam. Boston: Alyson Publications.

Rimmerman, C. A. 2002. *From Identity to Politics: the Lesbian and Gay Movements in the United States*. Philadelphia: Temple University Press.

Riviera, S. 1995. 'In their Own Words' in *The Question of Equality: Lesbian and Gay Politics in America since Stonewall*. New York: Scribner.

Robertson, W. 1993. *k.d. lang: Carrying the Torch*, repr. Toronto: ECW Press.

Rogers, C. 1959. 'A Theory of Therapy, Personality and Interpersonal Relationships, as Developed in the Client-centered Framework', in S. Koch, ed., *Psychology: A study of Science, Vol. III. Formations of the Person in the Social Context*. New York: McGraw Hill.

Rogers, C. 1971. *On Becoming a Person: a Therapist's View of Psychotherapy*. London: Constable.

Rogers, C. 1983. *The Freedom to Learn for the 80's*. Columbus: Charles E. Merrill Publishing Company.

Rogers, C. 2005. 'Education' in H. Kirschenbaum and V. Land Henderson, eds, *The Carl Rogers Reader*. London: Constable, pp. 297–334.

Román, D. 1998. *Acts of Intervention: Performance, Gay Culture, and AIDS*. Bloomington: Indiana University Press.

Rubenstein, H. 1994. 'Pedro Leaves us Breathless' in *POZ*, Vol. I, no. 3, August/September, pp. 38–41, 79–81.

Ruditis, P. 2003. *Queer as Folk: the Book*. New York: Pocket Books.

Ruffolo, D. V. 2009. *Post-Queer Politics*. Farnham: Ashgate.

Russell, G. 2006. *Doctor Who: the Inside Story*. London: BBC Books.

Russo, V. 1987. *The Celluloid Closet*, rev. edn. New York: Harper & Row.

Savin-Williams, R. C. 1998. *And Then I Became Gay: Young Men's Stories*. London: Routledge.

Schechner, R. 2002. *Performance Studies: an Introduction*. London: Routledge.

Schofield, M. 1960. *A Minority: a Report on the Life of the Male Homosexual* (released under the pseudonym of Gordon Westwood). London: Longmans.

Seidman, S. 1996. 'Introduction' in S. Seidman, ed., *Queer Theory/Sociology*. Oxford: Blackwell, pp. 1–29.

Seidman, S. 2004. *Beyond the Closet: the Transformation of Gay and Lesbian Life*. New York: Routledge.

Sender, Katherine. 2004. *Business, Not Politics: the Making of the Gay Market*. New York: Columbia.

Shairp, M. 1933. *The Green Bay Tree: a Play in Three Acts*. London: George Allen and Unwin.

Shattuc, J. 1997. *The Talking Cure: TV Talk Shows and Women*. New York: Routledge.

Sinfield, A. 1994. *The Wilde Century: Effeminacy, Oscar Wilde and the Queer Movement*. New York: Columbia University Press.

Sinfield, A. 1998. *Gay and After*. London: Serpent's Tail.

Sontag, S. 1989. *Aids and its Metaphors*. New York: Farrar, Strauss and Giroux.

Stallybrass, P. and White, A. 1995. *The Politics and Poetics of Transgression*, repr. New York: Cornell University Press.

Starr, V. 1994. *k.d. lang: All You Get is Me*. London: HarperCollins.

Streitmatter, R. 1995. *Unspeakable: the Rise of the Gay and Lesbian Press*. Boston: Faber and Faber.

Sullivan, A. 1995. *Virtually Normal: an Argument about Homosexuality*. London: Picador.

Summers, C., ed. 2002. *Gay and Lesbian Literary Heritage*. New York: Henry Holt.

Thoms, P. 1992. *The Windings of the Labyrinth*. Athens: Ohio University Press.

Todorov, T. 1981. 'Introduction to Poetics', trans. R. Howard. Minneapolis: University of Minnesota Press.

Tracy, K. 1999. *The Real Story of Ellen*. Toronto: Birch Lane Press.

Tudor, A. 1974. *Image and Influence*. London: Allen and Unwin.

Turkle, S. 1995. *Life on the Screen: Identity in the Age of the Internet*. New York: Simon and Schuster.

Turner, V. 1982. *From Ritual to Theatre: the Seriousness of Human Play*. New York: Performing Arts Journal Publications.

Unks, G., ed. 1995. *The Gay Teen: Educational Practice and Theory for Lesbian, Gay, and Bisexual Adolescents*. New York: Routledge.

Van Druten, J. 1958. 'I am a Camera', in J. Gassner, ed., *Best American Plays Fourth Series. 1951–1957*. New York: Crown Publishers.

Van Zoonen, L. 2001. 'Desire and Resistance: Big Brother and the Recognition of Everyday Life', in *Media Culture and Society* Vol. 23, pp. 669–77.

Vidal, G. 1975. *Myron*. London: William Heinemann.

Vidal, G. 1986. *Myra Breckinridge*, repr. London: Grafton Books.

Vidal, G. 1995. *Palimpsest: a Memoir*. London: André Deutsch.

Vidal, G. 1997. *The City and the Pillar*, revised. London: Little, Brown and Company.

Vidal, G. 2000. 'Montaigne' in F. Kaplin, ed., *The Essential Gore Vidal*. London: Little, Brown and Company, pp. 894–904.

Vidal, G. 2006. *Point to Point Navigation*. New York: Doubleday.

Vorlicky, R., ed. 1998. *Tony Kushner in Conversation*. Ann Arbor: University of Michigan Press.

Wallace, L. 2003. *Sexual Encounters: Pacific Texts, Modern Sexualities*. New York: Cornell University Press.

Warner, M. 1993. 'Introduction', in M. Warner, ed., *Fear of a Queer Planet*. Minneapolis: University of Minnesota Press, pp. vii–xxxi.

Waters, S. 1998. *Tipping the Velvet*. London: Virago.

Waters, S. 1999. *Affinity*. London: Virago.

Waters, S. 2002. *Fingersmith*. London: Virago.

Waters, S. 2007. *The Night Watch*. London: Virago.

Watney, S. 2000. *Imagine Hope: AIDS and Gay Identity*. London: Routledge.

Webb, C. L. 1998. Associated Press, 8 April.

Weeks, J. 1990. *Coming Out: Homosexual Politics in Britain from the Nineteenth Century to Present*, rev. edn. London: Quartet Books.

Weeks, J. 1996. 'The Construction of Homosexuality' in S. Seidman, ed., *Queer Theory Sociology*. Oxford: Blackwell, pp. 41–63.

Weeks, J. 2000. *Making Sexual History*. Cambridge: Polity Press.

Weeks, J. and Porter, K., eds. 1998. *Between the Acts: the Lives of Homosexual Men 1885–1967*, 2nd edn. London: Rivers Oram Press.

Weeks, J., Heaphy, B. and Donovan, C., eds, 2001. *Same Sex Intimacies, Families of Choice and Other Life Experiments*. London: Routledge.

Weston, K. 1991. *Families We Choose: Lesbians, Gays, Kinship*. New York: Columbia University Press.

Whitaker, B. 2006. *Unspeakable Love: Gay and Lesbian Life in the Middle East.* London: Saqi.

White, H. 1990. *The Content of the Form: Narrative Discourse and Historical Representation*, repr. Baltimore: Johns Hopkins University Press.

White, M. 1992. *Tele-Advising*. Chapel Hill: University of North Carolina Press.

Wilde, O. 1891. *The Picture of Dorian Gray*. London: Ward Lock and Company.

Wildeblood, P. 1955. *Against the Law: the Classic Account of a Homosexual in 1950s Britain*. London: Weidenfeld and Nicolson.

Willett, J. 1964. *Brecht on Theatre*. London: Eyre Methuen.

Wilson, S. 2003. *Oprah, Celebrity and Formations of Self*. London: Palgrave Macmillan.

Woods, G. 1998. *A History of Gay Literature: the Male Tradition*. New Haven: Yale University Press.

Woods, T. 1999. *Beginning Postmodernism*. Manchester: Manchester University Press.

Woodward, K., ed., 1997. *Identity and Difference*. London: Sage.

Wollen, R. 1996. *Derek Jarman: a Portrait*. London: Thames and Hudson.

Internet sources

ABC News 2011. http://abcnews.go.com/Health/jamey-rodemeyer-suicide-ny-police-open-criminal-investigation/story?id=14580832#.TstaEmcxs00. Accessed 19 November 2011.

Abuelas. 2008. http://www.abuelas.org.ar/english/history.htm. Accessed 31 January 2008.

Ballotpedia. 2010. California: Proposition 8 (2008) http://ballotpedia.org/wiki/index.php/California_Proposition_8_(2008). Accessed 4 August 2010.

BBC. 2008a. 'BBC Writer's Room'. http://www.bbc.co.uk/writersroom/opportunity/wolff.shtml. Accessed 24 June 2008.

BBC News 24. 2008. 3 January 2008. http://news.bbc.co. uk/media/avdb/news/world/video/142000/bb/142409_16x9_bb.asx?ad=1&ct=50. Accessed 29 January 2008.

British Library. 2008. http://www.bl.uk/projects/theatrearchive/method.html. Accessed 24 July 2008.

Bryne, C. 2007. 'Russell T Davies: the Savior of Saturday Night Drama'. *The Independent*. http://www.independent.co.uk/news/media/russell-t-davies-the-saviour-of-saturday-night-drama-473512.html. Accessed 20 September 2007.

CBC. 2008. 'Inside Iran's Secret Gay World'. http://www.cbc.ca/sunday/2007/03/030407_1.html. Accessed 25 July 2008.

Channel 4 Learning. 2008. 'Coming Out to Class'. http://www.channel4learning.com/support/programmenotes/micro/comingout/index.html. Accessed 22 May 2008.

CNN 2008. 'Ahmadinejad Speaks; Outrage and Controversy Follow'. http://edition.cnn.com/2007/US/09/24/us.iran/index.html. Accessed 8 July 2008.

CNN. 2011. http://edition.cnn.com/video/#/us/2010/10/04/lkls.on.bullied.to.death.cnn?iref=allsearch. Accessed 19 November 2011.

Commercial Closet. 2003. '"Language of Love" Do You Speak MTV?' http://www2.commercialcloset.org/cgi-bin/iowa/portrayals.html?record=474. Accessed 15 March 2003.

Commercial Closet. 2008. http://www.commercialcloset.org/common/news/ reports/detail.cfm?Classification=report&QID=4587&ClientID=11064&TopicID =0& subnav=about&subsection=about. Accessed 25 July 2008.

Complete Review. 2008. http://www.complete-review.com/reviews/bennetta/ unreader.htm. Accessed 22 July 2008.

Department of Health. 2008. *Stand up for us: Challenging Homophobia in Schools*. Originally published 2004. http://www.wiredforhealth.gov.uk/PDF/ stand_up_for_us_04.pdf. Accessed 19 December 2008.

Duerden, N. 2007. 'Sitting Pretty'. *The Observer*. http://observer.guardian.co.uk/ review/story/0,6903,1345132,00.html. Accessed 14 November 2007.

Equal Marriage. 2008. http://www.samesexmarriage.ca/equality/world.html# netherlands. Accessed 22 November 2008.

Fight OUT Loud. 2008a. http://www.fightoutloud.org/. Accessed 24 July 2008.

Fight OUT Loud. 2008b. http://www.fightoutloud.org/ourstory.html. Accessed 24 July 2008.

Gay Orbit. 2006. 'Iranian Gay Youths Hanged' Posted by: Michael, 21 July 2005. http://gayorbit.net/?p=2459. Accessed 11 October 2006.

Gay Youth Corner. 2008a. http://www.thegyc.com/. Accessed 20 January 2008.

Gay Youth Corner. 2008b. http://www.thegyc.com/content/blogcategory/108/ 145/. Accessed 20 January 2008.

Gay Youth Corner. 2008c. http://www.thegyc.com/content/blogcategory/107/ 171/. Accessed 20 January 2008.

Gay Youth Corner. 2008d. http://www.thegyc.com/comprofiler/task,userProfile/ user,33276/Itemid, 172/. Accessed 20 January 2008.

Gay Youth Corner. 2008e. http://www.thegyc.com/comprofiler/task,userProfile/ user,22731/Itemid,171/. Accessed 20 January 2008.

Gay Youth Corner. 2008f. http://www.thegyc.com/comprofiler/task,userProfile/ user,38694/Itemid,193/. Accessed 20 January 2008.

Gay Youth Corner. 2008g. http://www.thegyc.com/comprofiler/task,userProfile/ user,38422/Itemid,171/. Accessed 20 January 2008.

GLTBQ. 2008. Reinaldo Arenas (1943–1990). http://www.glbtq.com/literature/ arenas_r.html. Accessed 28 January 2008.

Homan, 2008. 'Fighting for Tomorrow', an interview with Arsham Parsi, by Afdhere Jama. http://www.homanla.org/New/Arsham_oct06.htm. Accessed 20 July 2008.

Homo Politico. 2008a. http://homopolitico.tumblr.com/. Accessed 24 July 2008.

Homo Politico. 2008b. http://homopolitico.tumblr.com/page/5. Accessed 24 July 2008.

Homo Politico. 2008c. http://homopolitico.tumblr.com/page/6. Accessed 24 July 2008.

Huffington Post. 2011 'Hate Crimes Bill Signed Into Law 11 Years After Matthew Shephard's Death'. http://www.huffingtonpost.com/2009/10/88/hate-crimes-bill-to-be-si_n_336883.html. Accessed 19 November 2011.

IRQO. 2008. http://www.irqo.net/. Accessed 8 July 2008.

Jihad for Love. 2008. Parvez Sharma Interviewed on CNN International Live. http://www.ajihadforlove.com/video.html. Accessed 19 December 2008.

Kettelhack, G. 2007. 'Who is Quentin Crisp?' http://www.crisperanto.org/bio/ index.html. Accessed 20 July 2007.

Knitting Circle. 2008a. 'Tom Robinson'. http://www.knittingcircle.org.uk/ tom-robinson.ashx Accessed 21 June 2008.

Knitting Circle. 2008b. 'Boy George'. http://www.knittingcircle.org.uk/boygeorge. ashx. Accessed 21 June 2008.

LGB Teens. 2008a. http://www.channel4.com/health/microsites/L/lgb_teens/ index.html. Accessed 20 January 2008.

LGB Teens. 2008b. http://www.channel4.com/health/microsites/L/lgb_teens/ girls/10-years-later.html. Accessed 20 January 2008.

LGB Teens. 2008c. http://www.channel4.com/health/microsites/L/lgb_teens/ boys/10-years-later.html. Accessed 20 January 2008.

LGB Teens. 2008d. http://www.channel4.com/health/microsites/L/lgb_teens/ boys/relationships-and-sex.html. Accessed 20 January 2008.

Manrique, J. 2008. 'After Night Falls: the Revival of Reinaldo Arenas'. http:// www.villagevoice.com/news/0049,manrique,20375,1.html. Accessed 28 January 2008.

Morales, E. 2008. 'Dreaming in Cuban: a Gay Rebel Writer Attains Celluloid Immortality, Tuesday, December 5th 2000'. http://www.villagevoice.com/2000-12-05/news/dreaming-in-cuban/. Accessed 25 January 2008.

Newday. 2007. 'Debra Chasnoff'. http://www.newday.com/filmmakers/Debra_Chasnoff.html. Accessed 12 November 2007.

Oprah. 2008. http://www.oprah.com/about/press/about_press_bio.jhtml. Accessed 2 May 2008.

PFLAG. 2012. 'Parents, Families and Friends of Lesbians and Gays'. www.pflag.org/. Accessed 12 April 2012.

Progressive Grass Roots Politics. 2008. http://progressivegrassrootspolitics. blogspot.com/. Accessed 20 January 2008.

Queer Chronology. 2001. http://equality-alliance.diversity.org.uk/Chronology. html. Accessed 15 July 2001.

Stephens, B. 2008. 'The Queerest Denial: Ahmadinejad Says there are no Gays in Iran, Tuesday, October 2, 2007'. http://opinionjournal.com/columnists/ bstephens/?id=110010679. Accessed 15 February 2008.

YouTube. 2008a. http://www.youtube.com/watch?v=1wy4EAigSBw. Accessed 24 July 2008.

YouTube. 2008b. http://www.youtube.com/watch?v=TTeHr9upaWk. Accessed 24 July 2008.

YouTube. 2008c. 'The Hour'. http://www.youtube.com/watch?v=ipYpzWMnXi4& NR=1. Accessed 14 February 2008.

YouTube. 2008d. 'OUT at TIFF'. http://www.youtube.com/watch?v= 5pZC3ZwjMXU&NR=1. Accessed 14 February 2008.

YouTube. 2011. http://www.youtube.com/user/itgetsbetterproject. Accessed 28 May 2011.

Select Filmography

Absolutely Positive (1990), documentary film, 87 minutes. Director: Peter Adair. Producer: Janet Cole. Frameline Distribution, US.

The AIDS Show (1989), documentary film, 58 minutes. Directors and Producers: Peter Adair and Rob Epstein. Docurama, US.

Angelic Conversation (1985), film drama, 78 minutes. Director: Derek Jarman. Producer: James Mackay. Original Sonnets: William Shakespeare, read by Judi Dench. BFI, UK.

Angels in America (2003), television drama, 352 minutes. Director: Mike Nichols. Producer Celia Costas. Screenplay: Tony Kushner. HBO, US.

Arena: the Private Dirk Bogarde (2001), television documentary, 120 minutes. Director: Adam Lowe. Associate Producer: Nicholas Shakespeare. Assistant Producer: Jane Bywaters. BBC, UK.

Beautiful Thing (1996), film drama, 85 minutes. Director: Hettie MacDonald. Screenplay: Jonathan Harvey. Producers: Tony Garnett and Bill Shapter. Film Four, UK.

Before Night Falls (2001), film drama documentary, 133 minutes. Director Julian Schnabel. Producer: John Kilik. Screenplay: Cunningham O'Keefe, Lazaro Gomez and Julian Schnabel, based on the autobiography of Reinaldo Arenas. Twentieth Century Fox, US.

Brokeback Mountain (2005), film drama, 134 minutes. Director: Ang Lee. Producers: Diana Ossana, James Schamus. Screenplay: Larry McMurtry and Diana Ossana, based on the short story by Annie Proulx. Focus Features, US.

Coming Out to Class (2007), television documentary, 48 minutes. Director and Producer: Bernie Kay. Executive producers: Mandy Chang and Mira King. Narrator: Marcos 'Q Boy' Brito. Channel 4, UK.

Dangerous Living: Coming Out in the Developing World (2003), documentary film, 60 minutes. Director and Writer: John Scagliotti. Producers: Dan Hunt and Janet Baus. Executive Producer: Red Williams. After Stonewall, First Run Features, UK.

Dirk Bogarde: Above the Title: a Conversation with Russell Harty (1986), television documentary, 50 minutes. Director and Producer: Nick Gray. Yorkshire Television, UK.

Doctor Who: The Idiot's Lantern (2006), television drama episode, 45 minutes. Director: Euros Lyn. Producer: Phil Collinson. Executive Producers: Russell T Davies and Julie Gardner. Screenplay: Mark Gattis. BBC, UK/Wales.

Dottie Gets Spanked (1993), film drama, 30 minutes. Director and Writer: Todd Haynes. Red Carnelian Productions, US.

The Education of Gore Vidal (2003), television documentary, 84 minutes. Director and Writer: Deborah Dickinson. Producer: Matt Kapp. Associate Producer: Erike Frankel. Executive Producer: Susan Lacy. PBS, US.

Ellen: the Puppy Episode (1997), television situation comedy (double) episode, 60 mins. Created by Neal Marlens, Carol Black and David S. Rosenthal. Director: Gil Junger. Associate Producer: Christine Stentz. Coordinating Producer:

Ken Ornstein. Co-producers: David Flebotte, Alex Herschlag and Mark Wilding. Screenplay: Mark Driscoll, Tracy Newman, Dava Saval and Jonathan Stark, based on the narrative of Ellen DeGeneres. ABC, US.

Fingersmith (2005), television drama, 180 minutes. Director: Aisling Walsh. Producer: Georgina Lowe. Executive Producer: Sally Head. Screenplay: Peter Ransley, based on the novel by Sarah Waters. A Sally Head production, UK.

Foreign Correspondent: Two to Tango (2005), television documentary, 15 minutes. Reporter: Eric Campbell. ABC, Australia.

Further Tales of the City (2001), television drama, 180 minutes. Director: Pierre Gang. Producers: Suzanne Girard and Josee Lacelle. Executive Producers: Alan Poul, Tim Bevan and Luc Chatelain. Screenplay: Armistead Maupin and James Lecesne, based on the novel by Armistead Maupin. Showtime, US.

The Garden (1990), film drama, 86 minutes. Director: Derek Jarman. Producer James Mackay. Channel 4 and British Screen in association with ZDF and Uplink present a Basilisk production, UK.

The History Boys (2006), film drama, 107 minutes. Director: Nicholas Hytner. Producers: Kevin Loader, Nicholas Hytner and Damian Jones. Screenplay: Alan Bennett. BBC Films, UK.

In Our Own Words: Teens and AIDS (1995), documentary film, 30 minutes. Producer and Writer: Jennie Blake. Family Health Productions Inc., US.

It's Elementary – Talking about Gay Issues in School (1996), documentary film, 78 minutes. Director: Debra Chasnoff. Producers: Helen S. Cohen and Debra Chasnoff. A production of Women's Educational Media, New Day Films, VHS, US.

A Jihad for Love (2007), documentary film, 81 minutes. Director: Parvez Sharma. Producers: Parvez Sharma and Sandi Simcha Dubowski. Halal Films, US/UK/France/Germany/Australia.

Jobriath A.D. (2011), documentary film, 102 minutes. Director, Writer and Producer: Kieran Turner. Editor: Danny Bresnik. Cinematographers: Michael Canzoniero, Pj Gaynard. Sound: Rachel Chancey. Music: Ian Moore, Jason Staczek. Eight Track Tape Productions, US.

The Last of England (1987), film drama, 87 minutes. Director: Derek Jarman. Producers: James Mackay and John Boyd. Anglo International Films, UK.

More Tales of the City (1998), television drama, 295 minutes. Director: Pierre Gang. Producer Kevin Tierney. Executive Producers: Alan Poul, Suzanne Girard and Tim Bevan. Screenplay: Nicholas Wright, based on the novel by Armistead Maupin. Channel 4, UK/US.

The Naked Civil Servant (1975), television drama documentary, 85 minutes. Director: Jack Gold. Producer: Barry Hanson. Screenplay: Philip Mackie, based on the autobiography of Quentin Crisp. Thames Television, UK.

Out in Iran: Inside Iran's Secret Gay World (2007), television documentary, 22 minutes. Director and Producer: Farid Haerinejad. Writer: Evan Solomon. CBC, Canada.

Parkinson: Interview with George Michael (1998), television talk show, 45 minutes. Director: Stuart MacDonald. Producer Danny Dignan. Executive Producer: Beatrice Ballard. BBC, UK.

Prayers for Bobby (2009), television drama, 85 minutes. Director: Russell Mulcahy. Producer: Damien Ganczewski. Teleplay: Kate Ford. Lifetime TV, US.

. *Queer as Folk* (1999), television drama, 255 minutes. Directors: Charles McDougall and Sarah Harding. Producers: Russell T Davies and Nicola Shindler. Screenplay: Russell T Davies. Channel 4, UK.

Queer as Folk (2000–5), television drama series, 5 seasons (83 episodes × 48 minutes approx.). Directors: Michael DeCarlo, Kelly Makin, Kevin Inch, Alex Chapple, David Wellington, Bruce McDonald, Russell Mulcahy, Jeremy Podeswa, John Greyson, Kari Skogland, Thom Best, John Fawcett, Chris Grismer and Laurie Lynd. Screenwriters: Ron Cowen, Daniel Lipman, Russell T Davies, Michael MacLennan, Efrem Seeger, Brad Fraser, Del Shores, Shawn Postoff, Jason Schafer, Jonathan Tolins, Michael Berns, Matt Pyken, Richard Kramer, Garth Wingfield, Karen Walton and Doug Guinan. Showtime, US.

Queer as Folk 2 (2000), television drama, 87 minutes. Director: Menhaj Huda. Producers: Russell T Davies and Nicola Shindler. Screenplay: Russell T Davies. Channel 4, UK.

The Real Ellen Story (1998), television documentary, 52 minutes. Directors: Fenton Bailey and Randy Barbato. Producer: Lesli Klainberg. Series Producers: Frances Berwick and Laura Pierce. Associate Producer: Tiffany Flynn. Channel 4, UK.

The Real World: San Francisco (1994), television documentary series, 20 × 30 minute episodes. Directors: George Verschoor and Robert Fisher. Producer: George Verschoor. Co-Producer: Clay Newbill. Bunim Murray for MTV, US.

Sarah Waters: Sex and the Victorian City (2004), television documentary, 30 minutes. Director: Claire Hobday. Production Coordinator: Christian Watt. Production Manager: Sue Davies. Executive Producer: David Okuefuna. Narrator: Dilly Barlow. BBC, UK.

Sebastiane (1976), film drama, 90 minutes. Director: Derek Jarman. Producers: Howard Maslin and James Whaley. Disctac Ltd, UK.

Tales of the City (1993), television drama, 302 minutes. Director: Alistair Reid. Producer: Alan Poul. Executive Producers: Richard Kramer, Armistead Maupin, Sigurjon Sighvatsson and Tim Bevan. Screenplay: Richard Kramer, based on the novel by Armistead Maupin. Channel 4, UK/US.

A Taste of Honey (1961), film drama, 100 minutes. Director and Producer: Tony Richardson. Screenwriters: Shelagh Delaney and Tony Richardson, based on the play by Shelagh Delaney. British Lion Films, UK.

That's a Family! (2000), documentary film, 35 minutes. Directors: Debra Chasnoff and Fawn Yacker. Producers: Debra Chasnoff, Ariella J. Ben-Dov and Fawn Yacker. Associate Producers: Kate Stilley and Emily Swaab. Executive Producer: Helen S. Choen. Women's Educational Media, VHS, US.

Tipping the Velvet (2002), television drama, 178 minutes. Director: Geoffrey Sax. Producer: Georgina Lowe. Executive Producer: Sally Head. Screenplay: Andrew Davies, based on the novel by Sarah Waters. A Sally Head production, UK.

Tongues Untied (1989), documentary film, 55 minutes. Producer and Director: Marlon T. Riggs. Associate Producer: Brian Freeman. Strand Home Video, and Frameline Distribution, VHS, US.

Torchwood: Captain Jack Harkness (2006), television drama episode, 50 minutes. Director: Ashley Way. Producers: Richard Stokes and Chris Chibnall. Executive Producers: Russell T Davies and Julie Gardner. Screenplay: Catherinie Tregenna. BBC, UK/Wales.

Velvet Goldmine (1998), film drama, 124 minutes. Director: Todd Haynes. Producer: Christine Vachon. Screenwriter: James Lyons and Todd Haynes. Miramax, US.

Victim (1961), film drama, 95 minutes. Director: Basil Dearden. Producer: Michael Relph. Screenplay: Janet Green and John McCormick. Allied Films/Rank, UK.

Word is Out: Stories of Some of our Lives (1977), documentary film, 130 minutes. Produced by the Mariposa Film Group: Peter Adair, Nancy Adair, Veronica Brown, Robert Epstein and Lucy Massie Phenix. New Yorker Films, VHS, US.

World Weddings: Gay on the Cape (2004), television documentary, 30 minutes. Director and Producer: Clifford Bestall. Series Producer: Sam Bagnall. Executive Producer: Karen O'Connor. BBC, UK/South Africa.

Wrestling with Angels (2006), documentary film, 98 minutes. Director, Producer and Writer: Freida Lee Mock. A Sanders & Mock/American Film Foundation Production, US.

Index

4 Learning (Channel 4)   185
Aaberg, Justin   4, 5
Aaberg, Tammy   4, 5, 10, 231
Absolutely Positive   108, 120–3, 254
acceptance   19, 33, 61, 124, 133, 172,
    199, 218, 222, 235
Adair, Peter   108, 119–24, 130,
    134–6, 230, 254, 257
Advocate   31, 45, 62, 67–8, 90, 143
affirmation   20, 87, 95–6, 122–3, 157,
    169, 188, 190–1
*Against the Law: the Classic Account of
    a Homosexual in 1950s Britain*
    23, 59
age of sexual consent   189
Ahmadinejad, Mahmoud (President
    of Iran)   218
AIDS   32, 73, 101–4, 108, 119, 129,
    134–5, 149–50, 155, 160, 201,
    203, 211, 237, 254, 256
AIDS Show, The   103, 108, 119, 254
Althusser, Louis   21
Amedure, Scott (murder of)   110, 237
American Beauty   238
American Public Broadcasting Service
    119
An American Family   237
An Englishman Abroad   179, 234
*And then I became Gay: Young Men's
    Stories*   168
Angelic Conversation   152–3, 155–6,
    254
Angels in America   73, 100–2, 104–5,
    231, 238, 254
Anglocentric   10
antistructure   171, 174, 195
Apollonian and Dionysian   102–4
archetypes   47
Arena   88, 254
Arenas, Reinaldo   200, 207, 208–11,
    254
Argentina   199, 212–13, 215–16, 218,
    231

As If   237
Asgari, Mahmoud   221
Ashley, April   115, 237
assimilation   27, 78–9, 83, 104, 236
Atwell, Lee   121
Auster, Howard   14, 28–9, 40, 233
autobiographical   42, 44–6, 71, 117,
    149, 152, 178–80, 200, 234

Babycakes   237
Backcloth   117
Bad Girls   238
BAFTA   118
Bakhtin, Mikhail   172
Bale, Christian   180
Barnett, Samuel   182–3
Barker, Cody J.   4, 233
Barrowman, John   161–2, 238
Barthes, Roland   17, 18, 234
Batty Boy   186
Baudrillard, Jean   144–6
Bawer, Bruce   78
BBC   22–5, 40, 68, 75, 88–90, 96–7,
    139, 150, 157, 174, 179, 199, 230,
    234, 237, 240
BBC News 24   212–13
BBC News Online   234
Beautiful Thing   1, 2, 4, 167, 174–8,
    195, 239, 254
Becoming a Person   124, 130
'being' and 'becoming'   xii, xiv, 4, 9,
    11, 229–31
Beemyn, Brett   76
Before Night Falls   200, 207–12, 254
Bell, Vikki   81
Bennett, Alan   113–14, 118, 167,
    174, 178–81, 184–5, 195, 230,
    234, 239, 255
Berliner, Alain   239
Berry, Chris   202
Berry, Glen   2, 176
Berube, Allan   16, 81, 141
Bethesda Fountain, New York   103–4

*Between the Acts: Lives of Homosexual
Men* 16
Beyond the Fringe 179
Bhabha, Homi 206–7
Biblioteca Nacional José Martí 209
bisexuality 32, 36, 89, 93, 94, 95,
139, 150, 161, 162, 170, 181, 186,
188, 189, 239
black civil rights 65
blackmail (and homosexuality) 42,
83, 86–7, 159, 177, 237
Blake, Jeanne 108, 120, 128
Bluck, Sahar 240
Blue 149–50
Bogarde, Dirk 2, 8, 11, 29, 83–9,
104–5, 108, 113, 115–18, 135,
230, 236, 254
Bourne, Stephen 87
Bowie, Angie 238
Bowie, David 32, 180, 239
Boy George 32, 234
Brazil 212
Brechtian distantiation 67
Brief Encounter 162–3
Brito, Marcos (also known as Q Boy)
166–8, 185–8, 254
Brokeback Mountain 107, 108, 130–2,
134, 136, 237, 254
Brown, Asher 4, 232
Bryant, Anita 200, 226
Burgess, Guy 24, 60, 179, 234
Butler, Judith 115

Cabaret 24, 45
Cairo 52, 198, 200–1, 226
Caitlin, Ryan 169, 171
Cambridge Friends School 148
camp 113, 119, 142, 179, 239
Campbell, Eric 213, 216, 254
Canada 33, 76, 197, 199, 220, 236,
255–6
Capitol Hill 120
Carlson, Marvin 54, 173
carnivalesque 67, 93–5, 172
Carriles, Gómez 211, 240
Carroll, Noel 94–5
Cassin, Gregg 122, 124
Catholic Church 211, 254

CBC 199, 220, 223, 255
Celluloid Closet, The 238
Channel 4 2, 19, 64, 75, 89, 139,
166–7, 175–6, 185–6, 188, 236,
238, 239, 254, 255, 256
Chase, Raymond 4, 232
Chasnoff, Debra 138–41, 146–7, 149,
163–4, 169, 230, 237, 255, 256
Chatman, Seymour 6, 92
childhood 46, 51, 208, 210
Children's Hour, The 142, 238
Choosing Children 140
Christianity 63, 101, 134, 156,
200, 214
Christopher and his Kind 46, 234
citizenship 5–6, 9, 10, 14, 16, 35, 39,
40–1, 44, 47, 57, 67, 70, 72, 76,
78, 80, 104, 111–12, 139, 180,
199, 209, 218, 220
and enfranchisement 76, 184
City and the Pillar, The 12–15, 27, 29,
40, 170, 180
civil liberty 216, 222–4, 226
civil partnership 32, 76, 78, 189–90,
212–13, 231, 236
classics, Roman and Greek 15
Clementi, Tyler 4, 233
Clinton, Bill 66, 67, 120, 129
Clum, John M. 47–9, 107, 141, 234
CNN 69
coalescence 1, 9, 10, 19, 25,
50, 78–9, 136, 171, 195, 226, 229
coalition 76, 103–4, 141
Cohen, Roy 102
Colebrook, Claire 9
Collins, Wilkie 90–1, 97
colonial 10, 80, 198, 203, 205, 206,
209, 227
Columbia University, New York 218
coming out 35, 43, 63–4, 67–8, 79,
85, 167–8, 170–1, 179, 187, 189,
191, 235
Coming Out to Class 166–8, 185–6,
190, 193, 195, 254
*Coming Out under Fire: the History of
Gay Men and Women in World War
Two* 16
Commercial Closet 143, 202

commodity   6, 35, 48, 67, 110, 135–45, 146, 150, 156–8, 160, 163, 164, 178, 192, 238
Congress   120
connectedness   xiii
Connecticut   236
'Consort, The'   35
Coronation Street   174, 239
Cowen, Ron   160, 256
Coz I Love You   181
Crain, Mary M.   173
Criminal Law Amendment Act of 1885   234
Crisp, Quentin   42–3, 54–8, 71–2, 230, 255
Cuba   120, 200, 207–12
Cullen, Dave   130–2
cult television   161
culture of consumption   144

D'Emilio, John   414
Daily Mail   59, 60
Danaher, Geoff   7, 81
Dangerous Living: Coming Out in the Developing World   1, 197–8, 200, 203–7, 227, 240, 254
'Danny Boy'   35
Dave, Paul   153
Davies, Russell T   19, 138–9, 150–1, 156–65, 235, 238, 254–6
Davis, Nick   180
Dearden, Basil   74, 83–4, 87, 177, 255
DeGeneres, Ellen   32, 43, 59, 62–7, 69–72, 85, 230, 235, 255
Deleuze, Gilles   3, 9, 229
democracy   10, 47, 107, 109, 112, 132–3, 146, 173, 197, 224
Dench, Judi   155
Derek Jarman: a Portrait   137
Dern, Laura   64
developing world   xiii, 11, 197–201, 203–8, 212–13, 226–7, 231, 239, 257
deviancy   18, 31, 35, 52–3, 142, 169
  labelling of   17, 142
diaspora   76, 199, 202–3, 227, 240
Dickens, Charles   90–1, 97
difference and repetition   3

Dirk Bogarde: Above the Title – a Conversation with Russell Harty   88–9, 115–16, 118, 236, 254
Dirty War (in Argentina)   216
discourse   2–8, 17–18, 21–2, 24, 44, 51–2, 59, 65–6, 68–70, 75, 76, 92, 103, 108, 113–15, 118, 129, 151–2, 163, 175, 177, 188, 192, 193, 195, 200–1, 206, 218, 222, 231
  cohesive   7
  homosexual   8, 59, 68, 114
disenfranchised   76, 91, 93, 100, 109, 117, 124, 135, 172
displaced abjection   94
dissidence   58, 64
Doane, Mary Ann   179
Doctor Who   139, 150, 157–8, 161–4, 238, 254
domesticity   18, 20, 113, 117, 134–5, 149–51, 155–6, 158, 164, 212–13, 225, 227
dominant history   74
Donahue   110
Donahue, Phil   109–10
Donovan, Catherine   47
Dottie Gets Spanked   179–80, 254
Drake, Robert   15
Dream a Little Dream of Me   1, 239
Drummer Hodge   183–4
Du Gay, Paul   143
Dubé, Eric   170

economy of narratives   144, 164
Education of Gore Vidal, The   12, 28, 254
effeminacy   55–7, 61, 179, 209, 210
Egypt   197, 200, 226
El Morro Castle   209, 211
Electra Records   32
Ellen   62–5
Ellen DeGeneres Show   235
Elliot, Cass (also known as Mama Cass)   175
Elliott, Anthony   82
Ellis Bunim, Mary   237
Ellis, Jim   152

emotion 21, 29, 34, 37, 48, 65, 86, 98, 108, 111, 112–13, 117–18, 120, 122, 147, 155, 168–9, 176, 208
Eno, Brian 180, 239
Epstein, Rob 119, 236, 253, 256
equality 17, 23, 26, 61, 78, 103, 111, 121, 133, 143, 146, 148, 170–1, 180, 198–9, 201, 224, 235, 238
Etheridge, Melissa 35
exchangeability of narratives 137, 144–5, 147, 164

Fa'afafine 232
factual media space 107–9, 111, 118, 135–6
Falwell, Jerry 63
families of choice 86, 123
family values 139
Far From Heaven 179–80
Farm Boys: Lives of Gay Men from the Rural Midwest 16
Farmer, Brett 142
Fellows, Will 16
fictional and factual contexts of narrative and media 2, 3, 9–10, 11, 16, 18, 41–2, 71, 73, 140
Fight OUT Loud 14, 32, 36, 37, 38
film studies xiii
Fingersmith 75, 89, 91, 96–8, 105, 254
Finnegan, Ruth 146
Fiske, John 21
Foreign Correspondent: Two to Tango 199, 212–13, 215, 227, 231, 255
Forster, E. M. 235
Forwood, Tony 8, 29, 84–6, 88–9, 104, 115–18
Foucault, Michel 7, 19, 51, 57–8, 70, 76–7, 80–1, 160, 201, 217, 222, 235
fragmentation and cohesion 80, 229
frames of action 9, 77
Fraser, John 88
Fraser, Nancy 7, 77, 112
Free Cinema 177
Fricke, Aaron 170–1
Friedman, Jeffrey 236

Furnish, David 32
Further Tales of the City 237, 255
Fuss, Diana 8, 10
Futterman, Diane 169, 171

Gamson, Joshua 108–11, 135
Garden, The 137, 152, 155–6, 255
Garnett, Tony 175, 254
Gauntlett, David 51, 132, 145
gay and lesbian community 9, 10, 26–7, 33, 35, 40, 45, 75–6, 78–81, 83, 87, 104–5, 119, 133, 135, 136, 149, 160, 196, 200, 202, 203, 220, 221, 226, 231
Gay and Lesbian Literary Heritage 15
gay and lesbian non-Western identity 10, 83, 197–228, 232
gay and lesbian political activists movement 3
gay and lesbian youth 6, 35, 39, 120, 128, 154, 161, 165, 166–95, 231
Gay Canon: Great Books That Every Gay Man Should Read 15
gay marriage 18, 236
'Gay Messiah' 35
Gay to Zed 186
Gay Youth Corner 167–8, 173, 185, 190–5, 231
gay youth narratives 4, 6, 9, 11, 171, 178
Genet, Jean 179
Gibson, Tom 134
Giddens, Anthony 6, 10, 38, 46–7, 77–8, 99, 107, 112, 121, 126, 152, 202, 210, 230
Gilbert, Helen 206
Gillespie, Peggy 16
Gilroy, Paul 76
Gimmie, Gimme, Gimmie 174
Goffman, Erving 8
Goodbye to Berlin 44–5
Gorosito, Leonardo 213, 218
Grandmothers of the Plaza de Mayo 216
Gray, Nick 88, 115, 118, 254
Green Bay Tree 42, 47–9, 234
Greene Salwak, Betty 131, 134
Griffith, Bobby 232

Griffith, Mary 231, 232
Griffiths, Richard 182–3
GroundSpark (formally known as
    Women's Educational Media)
    140–1
Guattari, Pierre-Félix 229

Habermas, Jürgen 112
Haerinejad, Farid 199, 219–20, 222,
    255
Hall, Radclyffe 53
Hall, Stuart 22, 50, 142
Hardy, Thomas 183–4
Harold, Mark 238
Hart, Kylo-Patrick R. 144
Harty, Russell 88, 89, 108, 113–18,
    135–6, 230, 235–6, 253
Harvey, Jean 56
Harvey, Jonathan 1, 10, 167, 174–6,
    178, 195
Hawes, Keeley 96
Haynes, Todd 167, 174, 178–80, 184,
    195, 254, 257
Hayton, Bill 212
Heaphy, Brian 47
Heche, Anne 66, 236
Hellman, Lillian 238
Hensher, Phillip 84
Herdt, Gilbert 198
Hilderbrand, Lucas 180, 239
Hill, John 87, 178
Hirschfield, Scott 147
historical drama 90, 92
History Boys 167, 179–84, 255
*History of Gay Literature: the Male
    Tradition* 15
History Project 16
Hollywood 26, 31, 48–9, 130, 141–3
holograms 145
home movies 137, 151–2, 155, 164
Homo Politico 14, 32, 36, 37, 39
homophobia 36, 130, 164, 153, 188,
    206–9
homophyly 144–5
Honduras 1, 3, 203–4
Hour, The 223
Howes, Keith 54
Hubner, Esteban 213, 216–18

Hudson, Waymon 14, 31, 33, 35–9,
    41, 231
Hughes-Freeland, Felicia 173
Human Rights Campaign 236
humanist education 146, 164
humanity 101, 103–4, 113, 117–18,
    120, 123, 135–6, 149, 212, 217,
    225, 227
Hurt, John 42
hybridity 34, 94–5, 201, 206–7
hyperreal 145

I Am a Camera 44–5
I'm Not There 178
identification 8, 10
    audience 14, 31, 33, 35–9, 41, 230
    intended 83
    therapeutic 9
identities-in-difference 79
identity, archetypal 19
    sexual 26–7, 32, 34–5, 40, 47, 79,
        113–14, 126, 147, 149, 157, 178,
        185, 187–8, 195, 206, 209, 224,
        226, 239
    signposted 113–14, 135
    Western centred 9, 143, 196–203,
        205–7, 222, 224, 226
imagined gay community 26, 35, 76,
    78, 83, 105, 133, 136, 202–3, 240
*Improper Bostonians: Lesbian and Gay
    History from the Puritans to the
    Playground* 16
In Our Own Words: Teens and AIDS
    120, 128
Ingénue 14, 31, 34–5
institutional reflexivity 77, 82, 121
Internet/World Wide Web 9, 41,
    166–7, 201–2, 219, 234
interpellation 21, 22
intimacy 6, 9, 10, 23, 35, 38, 47, 71,
    107–9, 111–13, 118, 122–3, 152,
    156, 164, 191, 200, 210, 216, 230
intimate citizenship 6, 39, 42, 47,
    70, 72, 111–12, 139
Iran 199, 218, 219–22, 226–7, 240
Iranian Queer Organisation 199,
    219, 220
Isherwood, Christopher 3, 15–16,
    42, 44–7, 71, 90, 234

Islam/Islamic   199, 218–19, 221–7
*It's Elementary; Talking about Gay Issues
    in School*   140, 146–7, 149, 237,
    254
It Get's Better Project   4

Jardine, Lisa   97
Jarman, Derek   137–9, 149–55,
    163–5, 238, 254–5
The Jenny Jones Show   110, 235
Jerry Springer   110
Jewish/Judaism   101, 232
Jihad for Love   199, 218–19, 222–7,
    255
Jobriath (born Bruce Wayne
    Campbell)   32
Jobriath, A.D.   254
John Whiting Award   174
John, Elton   32, 227, 237
Joyner Priest, Patricia   109
Jubilee   137

Kaeser, Gigi   16
Kamens, David   128
King, Lawrence   233
King, Lawrence (murder of)   14, 32,
    36–9
Kinsey, Alfred   59, 72, 235
Kluge, Alexander   4, 112
KQED (public broadcasting)   121
Kramer, Larry   27
Kushner, Tony   15, 73–5, 100–1,
    103–5, 230, 231, 254

L Word, The   160
Ladies and Gentlemen   69
lang, k. d.   14, 31–5, 39, 41, 230
Larry King Live   5
Last of England   137, 151–3, 155, 238,
    255
Lauper, Cyndi   37
legalisation and illegality of
    homosexual acts   17, 23, 25,
    50, 54, 59–60, 68–70, 72, 83,
    100, 177, 213, 220, 234, 235, 236
Leiner, Marvin   208–10
Leith, Dick   6
Let's Get Real   140

LeVay, Simon   76
Lévi-Strauss, Claude   17, 19–20
LGB Teens   167, 185–6, 188–90, 192,
    239
LGBT   2, 10, 36–67, 39, 143, 188
liberty   12, 18, 23, 27, 37–8, 78, 133,
    199, 201, 205–7, 211, 216, 222–4,
    226
life story   6–7, 155, 230
liminal   105, 113, 121, 168, 171–4,
    181, 184–5, 194–5, 206–7, 213,
    215, 227
liminoid   171–3, 181, 185, 195,
    206–7, 226
Lions and Shadows   45, 233
Lipman, Daniel   160
literature   2, 9, 10, 13–16, 25, 30, 49,
    185, 208–9, 233, 235
Livingstone, Sonia   111
Look Back in Anger   177
Lord Chamberlain's Office   47, 50,
    141
Lord Montagu   23, 59, 60
Lord Queensbury   235
*Love Makes a Family: Portraits of
    Lesbian, Gay, Bisexual, and
    Transgender Parents and their
    Families*   16
Lucas, Billy   4, 233
Lucy the Teenage Transsexual   239
Lunt, Peter   111
Luther Burbank Middle School   148
Lyon, Phyllis   238

Ma Vie en Rose   239
MacDonald, Hettie   175–6, 254
Make Your Own Kind of Music   177
Male Homosexual   3, 12, 14, 22–5,
    40–1, 230
Mamas and the Papas   175, 177, 232
Manchester   76, 150
Manhattan County School   147
Marhoni, Ayaz   221
marriage, gay/same-sex   235
Martin, Del   238
Martin, Fran   202
Martinac, Paul   35
Marxist base and superstructure   7
Mashhad, Iran   221

Massachusetts 235
Maupin, Armistead 15, 75,
   89–92, 94–7, 100, 105, 230,
   255, 256
Maurice 235
McCarthy era 102
McChesney, Robert W. 133
McIntosh, Mary 51, 235
McLeod, John 132
McInerney, Brandon 233
McNally, Edward 60
Mexico 212
Michael Tolliver Lives 96, 237
Michael, George 43, 59, 62–4,
   67–72, 230, 235, 256
Mirror, The 69
modern history 80–1
Modesty Blaise 88
Molina, Dilcia 1, 3, 4, 10, 203–5, 231
Mollys, The 51, 235
Montagu trials 59, 68, 71–2, 235
Montaigne, Michel de 29, 30–1, 44
Mora, Ana 212–13
Morales, Ed 211
More Tales of the City 94, 237, 255
Mormon 101, 102
Morrison, James 178
Mouffe, Chantal 112
Mr Harty's Grand Tour 236
MTV 120, 201–2, 257
Munoz, José 79
Munt, Sally 159
Murphy, Robert 177
My Beautiful Launderette 175
My Big Gay Prom 186
My Lover Sea 211
Myerson, George 6
Myra Breckinridge 14, 26–8, 31, 40
Myron 14, 26, 27, 40
myth and mythologies 6, 12–14,
   16–20, 25, 31, 40–1, 49, 159, 162,
   170, 205, 230, 234

Naked Civil Servant, The 42–3, 54–8,
   254
narrative theory, traditional 7
narrative, archetype 200
National Film Theatre 177

National Union of Cuban Writers and
   Artists 209
Neal, Scott 2, 176
Negt, Oskar 112
neo-liberal 153
Netherlands 235
new frontier 197, 203, 207, 226–7,
   231
new queer cinema 50, 151
new technologies xiii, 161, 194,
   201–2
New York 76, 101, 103, 147, 218,
   226, 234
New York Times 28
New Yorker 237
News of the World 118
Newsom, Gavin 238
Nietzsche, Frederick 102
Nixon, Sean 144
Nonas, Elizabeth 76
non-heterosexual 16, 27, 42, 44, 51,
   107, 109, 119, 121, 123, 137, 139,
   143, 146, 151, 158, 163, 168, 171,
   195, 199, 219, 222
non-Western xiv, 10, 83, 198,
   234, 240
nostalgia/nostalgic 89–90, 100, 105

Observer 157
Olivier, Laurence 233
online new media 1, 4, 9, 32, 107,
   109, 110, 135–6, 190, 192, 194–5,
   231
oppositional (or proletarian) public
   sphere 95, 108, 111–13, 118,
   122–4, 135, 142
otherness 6, 18, 31, 35, 53, 66, 200,
   205
*Out in Iran: Inside Iran's Secret Gay
   World* 199, 218–22, 226–7, 240,
   255
Outside 67–9
Oxford University 179, 182, 184

Pacific Sun 89
Parkinson 68–70, 254
Parks, Rosa 65
Parsi, Arsham 219–20, 225, 231,
   240

pastiche 57, 162–3, 179, 238
Patton, Cindy 203
Penn State University 170
performative space 108
performativity 3, 71, 78, 135, 152, 168, 202, 226
PETA (People for the Ethical Treatment of Animals) 33–4
Peters, Jermaine 107, 133
PFLAG (Parents, Families and Friends for) Lesbians and Gays 233
Phil Donahue Show, The 110
PHSE (personal health and school education) 188
Pickering, Michael 205
Picture of Dorian Gray, The 181
pink dollar (or pink pound) 143
Pitt-Rivers, Michael 59–60
placing the self within the frame 1, 5, 10–11
play of signs 144
Plummer, Ken 7, 8, 42, 44, 47, 51, 70, 72, 112, 139
pluralism 104, 236
Point to Point Navigation 14, 29, 40
Poison 179
political frame 35
Pop, Iggy 180, 239
post gay 16, 165
post-colonial 206, 227
postmodern 3, 8, 37, 73, 75, 80–3, 105, 110, 122, 179
power
    and confession 70
    and discourse 76–7, 118, 173
    modern (or Foucaultian) 7, 77
    and resistance 19, 25, 58
POZ Magazine 124–5
Prayers for Bobby 233, 255
Priest, Hamish 190
Private Dirk Bogarde, The 88, 89, 254
Proposition 8 36, 236
public figures 2, 20–1, 230
public space 1, 4, 99, 178
public sphere 4, 9, 99, 108, 111–13, 118, 123–4, 133, 135
Puppy Episode (*Ellen*) 63–6, 236, 254
Pykett, Lynn 97–8

Queer as Folk 19, 63, 139, 150–1, 157–61, 163–4, 235, 255
queer diaspora 199, 203, 227
Queer Eye for the Straight Guy 49
queer identity 2, 3, 15, 43, 48, 50–2, 78, 141, 164
queer theory xiii, 95, 104, 164
queering of identity 156

Reagan, Ronald 73
Real Ellen Story 64, 236, 256
Real World 108, 120, 126–7, 129, 202, 256
realism 67, 83, 87, 155, 167, 174–8, 192–3, 195
Recasting Ritual: Performance, Media, Identity 173
Rediffusion 236
Reflections of a Rock Lobster 170
reflexive project of the self 6, 45
relay of narratives 20, 22, 40, 229
Renati, Jacqueline 212–13
Resident Alien: the New York Diaries 55
Respect for All project 141
Reynolds, John 60
Ricki 110
Riggs, Marlon 79, 255
ritual 6, 70, 127, 166–74, 178–9, 182, 199–200, 212–13, 227, 239
Robinson, Tom 32, 234
Rodemeyer, Jamie 4, 233
Rogers, Carl 108, 124, 130, 149
role models 9, 31, 32, 169, 191–2, 194, 210, 230
romance 1, 29, 35, 90, 93–4, 99, 105, 111, 126, 130, 152, 162, 166–8, 170–4, 184, 193, 195, 202, 238
Room at the Top 177
Ruffolo, David V. 3, 11
Russell Harty Plus 114–15, 237
Russia 24, 60, 179, 235
Russo, Vito 48, 50, 107, 142, 238

sad young man 48
Safe 178
Saint Sebastiane 150
Samoa 199, 232

San Francisco   76, 79, 89, 93, 100, 103, 120, 126, 128, 140, 148, 238, 256

San Francisco Chronicle   89

Sánchez Eppler, Beningo   203

Sasser, Sean   120, 126

Savin-Williams, Ritch   168–71

Scagliotti, John   1, 3, 198, 200–1, 204, 254

Schechner, Richard   172

Schirato, Tony   7

Schnabel, Julian   200, 207, 211, 254

Schofield, Michael (pseudonym Gordon Westwood)   22, 24–5

school   33, 38–9, 97, 140–1, 146–9, 159, 164, 169–70, 176, 181–2, 186–9, 193, 210, 238, 239

Seaton, Jean   24

Sebastiane   150

Second World War   56, 117, 162

Seidman, Steven   78, 95, 235

self-reflexive/reflexivity   2, 6, 9, 13, 20, 28, 33, 37, 39–47, 50, 52, 71–4, 78, 82, 84, 88, 92, 104, 106, 110, 120–1, 123–4, 129–30, 132, 136–7, 139, 145, 149, 155, 163, 180, 185, 194–5, 199, 212, 230, 234

Serial, The   89

Servant, The   88

Sex and the City   192

Sexual Behaviour in the Human Male   59

Shairp, Mordaunt   42, 49–50

shame   13, 14, 22, 31, 35, 43, 61, 67–8, 70, 72, 122, 139, 150, 159–60, 164, 221

Shapter, Bill   175, 254

shared experience   39, 77, 144–6, 164

Sharma, Parvez   218, 222–5, 227, 230, 255

Shattuc, Jane   109

Shepard, Judy   4, 233

Shepard, Matthew   4

sign value   144, 163

Significant Others   237

simulation   145

Sinfield, Alan   52, 55, 58, 141, 235

Smith, Senator Robert   146

Snakes and Ladders   86–7

social agency   6, 70, 73–4, 109, 111, 118, 123, 129, 132, 135, 191

social construction   xii, 8, 16, 49, 50, 75, 113, 156, 203

social networking   xiii, 33, 35, 166–7, 173–4, 190–1, 195, 199, 201–2, 227

Sodomite, the   51

Some of Your Best Friends   237

Spain   76, 78, 235

Spanish Gardener   88

Stallybrass, Peter   93–4

stars   20, 22, 32, 33, 142

Stephens, Bret   220

stereotypes   19, 47, 61, 70, 158–9

stigma   13, 22, 169, 221, 222, 224

Stirling, Rachel   96

Stonewall   16, 55, 57, 200–1, 226

subversion   3, 58, 62, 64, 67, 69, 72, 82, 114

Suddenly Last Summer   142, 236

suicide   4, 71, 84, 142, 211, 220, 233, 234, 240

Sullivan, Andrew   78

Summers, Claude   15

Sun, The   64, 69

Sure of You   235

Swinton, Tilda   153

Sydney   76

Sydney Morning Telegraph, The   59

Sylvester (born as Sylvester James)   32

symbolic exchange   144

Syms, Sylvia   85–6

Tales of the City   75, 89–90, 92–3, 95–6, 105, 237, 256

Talk on Television: Audience Participation and Public Debate   111

talk show   65, 68, 107–14, 135–6, 237

Taste of Honey, A   177, 256

telling sexual stories   6, 44, 139

textual analysis   2, 6, 42

Thames Television   237

That's a Family 140, 147, 255
Thatcher, Margaret 153
theatre 28, 47–8, 99, 199, 141, 171, 181–2, 234
Theatres Act of 1968 234
thematic framework 9
therapeutic discourse 65, 69–70, 129
therapy 46, 62, 65, 70, 107, 121, 124, 130, 132
and agency 130
and subversion 62
These Three 236
Thomas, Colin 22–3
Thompson, Emma 103
Thoms, Peter 91–2
Time Magazine 64, 234
Tipping the Velvet 75, 89, 91, 96–9, 105, 256
Tompkins, Joanne 206
Tongues Untied 79, 256
Torchwood 139, 150, 161–4, 254
Toronto 76, 220
transformation 20–1, 27, 51, 67, 69, 73, 82–3, 100, 104, 107, 122–3, 129, 137, 149, 155, 163, 203, 206
of intimacy 10
transformative 83, 99
transgender 36–7, 89, 93, 200
transitions in storytelling 13
transsexual 26, 94–5, 115, 118, 210, 221, 239
Transsexual in Iran 240
Trembling Before G-D 227
trial by media 58, 62–3, 236
Tribute to Pedro Zamora 129
Tudor, Andrew 21
Turner, Victor 168, 171–2, 174

Ultimate Brokeback Forum 4, 107, 130–6, 231, 237
unified subject (history as a) 80–2, 105
Unks, Gerald 168, 171
Untold Stories 239
Uruguay 212–13
use and exchange 136, 141, 144, 149, 156, 163
utterances 6

Velvet Goldmine 237
vernacular narrative/storytelling 14–16, 22, 25, 31, 33, 35, 40
Victim 74, 83–4, 86, 88, 104–5, 177, 236, 256
Vidal, Gore 2, 12–16, 26–31, 40–1, 170, 180, 230, 233, 234, 237, 254
vulnerability 4, 5, 6, 9, 57, 108, 110, 117–18, 128, 149, 155, 156

Wainwright, Rufus 35
Wake Me Up Before You Go Go 64, 67
Wales Padlock Act (New York) 141
Wall Street Journal 120, 220
Wallace, Lee 198
Walsh, Seth 4, 233
Warner, Michael 78
Waters, Sarah 75, 89–92, 96–8, 100, 105, 230, 255, 256
Watney, Simon 201
Webb, Jen 7
Wedding and a Revolution 238
Weeks, Jeffrey 16, 47, 52, 61, 75, 149
Well of Loneliness 53
Wells Sledge, Lydia 131–2
Western democratic ideals 198
Weston, Kath 123
Whitaker, Brian 221, 224
White, Allon 93–4
White, Hayden 18
White, Mimi 64, 69–70, 129
Who am I? The Found Children of Argentina 216
whole person (learning/identity) 108, 119, 125, 127, 129–30, 135, 149
Wilde, Oscar 43, 51–3, 58, 141, 181, 233
Wildeblood, Peter 23, 43, 58–63, 72, 230
Will Rogers Park 63, 70
Williams, Tennessee 8, 237, 238
Windings of the Labyrinth 91
Winfrey, Oprah 65, 109–10, 237
Wit and Wisdom of Quentin Crisp 55
Wolfenden Report 23, 59, 83

Wollen, Roger   137
Woman in White, The   91
Woods, Gregory   15
Word is Out: Stories of Our Lives   108, 119–22, 237, 258
World Weddings: Gay on the Cape   199, 212–14, 217, 227, 257
Wrestling with Angels   73, 258

YouTube   4, 25
York, Michael   45
Yue, Audrey   202

Zamora, Pedro   108, 119–21, 124–6, 128–30, 134–6, 208, 230
Zanati, Ashraf   197–8, 204–5
Zaniar, Mani   220–2, 231, 240

.